TACKLING MILITANT RACISM

WARNING: THIS BOOK COULD CONTAIN RACIALLY
OFFENSIVE MATERIAL – 'SAY NO TO RACISM'

Tackling Militant Racism

PETER JEPSON

ASHGATE

Published by
Ashgate Publishing Limited
Gower House
Croft Road
Aldershot
Hants GU11 3HR
England

Ashgate Publishing Company
Suite 420
101 Cherry Street
Burlington, VT 05401-4405
USA

Ashgate website: http://www.ashgate.com

British Library Cataloguing in Publication Data
Jepson, Peter
    Tackling militant racism
    1.Racism - Law and legislation - Great Britain 2.Hate
    crimes - Great Britain 3.Racism - Great Britain -
    Prevention 4.Racism - Government policy - Great Britain
    I. Title
    345.4'1'025

Library of Congress Cataloging-in-Publication Data
Jepson, Peter, 1950-
    Tackling militant racism / Peter Jepson.
        p. cm.
    Includes bibliographical references and index.
    ISBN 0-7546-2163-4
    1. Hate crimes--Great Britain. 2. Hate speech--Great Britain--Criminal provisions. 3.
Race discrimination--Law and legislation--Great Britain--Criminal provisions. 4.
Minorities--Legal status, laws, etc.--Great Britain. 5. Hate crimes--England--Prevention.
I. Title.

KD8035 .J48 2002
345.41'025--dc21   2001053600

ISBN 0 7546 2163 4

Printed and bound by Athenaeum Press, Ltd.,
Gateshead, Tyne & Wear.

Contents

List of Figures and Tables

1 Introduction – Tackling Militant Racism

Crimes that are motivated by racial hatred have a special and compelling call on our conscience.

Professor Lawrence, in his book *Punishing Hate*[1] justifies these words by referring to the approach that the media takes to racist crime. He suggests that newspaper coverage of crime reflects the concerns of society and he demonstrates how numerous assaults occur every day and yet these receive little, and then only local, attention. Similarly, Lawrence argues, that the general public ordinarily cares little whether any particular assault leads to a prosecution of the perpetrators and, if it does, whether any particular prosecution results in a conviction. He argues, this pattern of indifference contrasts sharply with the reaction to crimes that implicate race relations, going on to justify the introduction of enhanced sentencing for crimes motivated by race.

Professor Lawrence's comments clearly relate to the United States and this book is not directly concerned with problems that occur in that country. However, it is important to recognise that in the United Kingdom race crime is also of major concern. Indeed, a glance through newspapers over the past five years may suggest that one crime has been dominant – that is the murder of Stephen Lawrence.[2] The typical response to such heightened awareness is to introduce enhanced sentencing for racist crime. Professor Lawrence took this approach, and likewise so did the British Government when it established the racial aggravation offences in the Crime and Disorder Act 1998.[3] In this book I do not disagree with such an approach, but I take the view – once espoused by the British Prime Minister Tony Blair – that 'we should tackle not just crime – but the causes of crime'. In this book I attempt to tackle not just the crime, but the causes of racist crime.

To undertake this task I start, in this introductory chapter, by defining just what militant racism is. I then seek to give an example of militant racism – displaying any crimes that may be involved and then providing a general profile that depicts the perpetrators of such acts. I produce evidence of 'authoritative' claims of a link between an increase in racist crime and the distribution of racist literature, then giving a brief preview of the way that I intend, in this book, to tackle the problem of militant racism.

What is Militant Racism?

Militant racism, on the basis of the *Concise Oxford Dictionary*,[4] can be defined as:

> *militant 1* combative, aggressively active especially in support of a cause. *2* engaged in warfare – *n.* a militant person, esp. a political activist.

> *racism 1 a*: a belief in the superiority of a particular race; prejudice based on this *b*: antagonism towards other races, esp as a result of this. *2* the theory that human abilities etc. are determined by race.

Thus, the term 'militant racism' can be determined as 'combative and aggressive action, or activity, in support of a cause which signifies and promotes antagonism/hostility[5] towards people of other races'.

By its very definition militant racism is concerned with antagonism and hostility associated with racist activity, which is clearly narrower than the wide terminology of racism which is all encompassing and includes prejudice and beliefs based upon the superiority of a particular race. Therefore, the concern associated with militant racism is that of concern for racist antagonism or hostility rather than any racist beliefs, with it being accepted that a person's 'beliefs' in the form of 'thoughts' are almost impossible to police effectively.[6]

Militant racism is also different from racial discrimination, which can be determined, as per section 1 of the Race Relations Act 1976, as treating a person less favourably on racial grounds, with a civil breach being possible either directly or indirectly by the actions of an employee[7] and organisation.

Within society the expression of militant racism can often be seen through material that may stir up racial hatred and/or discrimination. It can also be seen on the streets, in terms of the criminality of racial harassment and violence. Indeed, it is quite frequently alleged[8] that racist criminality is orchestrated or stirred up by militant gangs and organisations, these gangs, or organisations often being political in nature, in the sense that they may work within and promote views consistent with the nationalist ideas of certain political parties. However, this does not mean that such militant gangs and political groups conduct all acts of racial harassment or violence directly, or even indirectly. Rather, it is argued that the street activity[9] of such groups serves to raise racial tensions within communities and thereby stir up racial discrimination and hatred. Some evidence of this can be found from research data compiled in Hounslow, where it was found that a doubling of racist incidents in the west of the Borough had a sinister connection with the activity of extremist racist groups and the distribution of their offensive literature. Despite such an argument, it is important to recognise that there is no irrevocable proof that racist literature and materials are directly responsible for racist crime. Though there does exist some anecdotal evidence that shows that in areas where there is a high incidence of racist material being distributed, racial crime is often on the increase.

An Example of Militant Racism and the Variety of Laws that can be Applicable

In subsequent chapters of this book I will produce examples of militant racist activity and material. However, in this introductory section I provide an illustration of militant racist activity by considering, and legally analysing, a news story from the *Daily Telegraph* written by the journalist Hugh Muir.[10]

THESE RACIST THUGS WILL NEVER STOP ME TEACHING

The thing Alison Moore remembers most vividly before losing consciousness is the final insult. As a group of four teenagers kicked and punched her senseless, amid fits of cackling, they screamed at her 'Black bitch'.

She cannot guess how long the attack lasted, but when she woke up she realised her attackers had left her under a hedge.

The first sensation she felt was excruciating pain. Most of the blows had come from behind her as she hunched forward to try and protect her face. She then realised that she could not move her legs. Although dazed, she managed to use her mobile phone to raise the alarm.

Miss Moore, 30, suffered cracked ribs, internal bleeding and severe bruising. She spent six days in hospital and even now walks with a limp.

The teacher, who has a six-year old daughter, at first thought the attack at Sandhurst Junior School, in Catford, south-east London, was just a matter of bad luck.

But 10 days later she was forced to revise her thinking. 'I was on my own at home one evening and I heard the letterbox open. I thought it was a circular. When I went to look at it I realised it was a death threat, telling me not to go back to school. It really frightened me.

I didn't know if the attackers knew I was the only black teacher in the school and had been waiting for me. It was also possible that someone had read about the attack in the local newspaper and was making mischief.'

The police did what they could to make her flat secure. Locks were installed, and a panic alarm was fitted and linked directly to the local police station.

But on March 13th her tormentors struck again. 'I had difficulty getting to sleep and went upstairs to take some medication. As I opened my kitchen door, I saw a man wearing a balaclava and gloves who had forced open my kitchen window and was trying to come in. The thing that frightened me was that he must have heard me entering the kitchen but he just stood there to make sure that I saw him. He was trying to instil fear in me.' The police arrived quickly and searched the area with tracker dogs. They failed to catch the intruder or his accomplice but they did find their handiwork – a collection of swastikas and National Front logos which had been daubed on the door.

After each incident, Miss Moore had denounced her abusers and had voiced her determination to stay, but a further incident last week proved too much.

'A local reporter told me he had just received a telephone call from someone who said they were going to "do me in" that night. That evening the police came to the flat and stayed with me until I had left.'

Miss Moore hopes her abusers will be unable to trace her new home but nevertheless intends to return to school as soon as she is physically able. Her mother, Olga, and her great-aunts were teachers and she says it is a family tradition she intends to maintain.

'I'll be scared to go back to school. The thought of whatever else might happen petrifies me, but I love my job. I would be unhappy elsewhere. I feel like I'm running away from my home but I couldn't live if I ran away from my job as well.'

Doctors have told her she may make a full recovery but Miss Moore says it is unlikely that she will ever be the same. 'I was an outgoing person but these days I get very tearful. I'm very nervous, even when the telephone rings. I find it hard to deal with it all.'

'I realise that the people responsible for all this are a minority. My friends are all nationalities. I don't look at colour. I look at who people are and I think others should do the same.'

These harrowing words give an example of militant racism in the last decades of the twentieth century.[11] This form of militant racism may not be regarded as fully typical, because the threat of murder and the need for police protection suggests the nature of the racism is more extreme than the average incident of racial harassment or violence. However, it does display characteristics that are synonymous – with militant racists often using graffiti, violence, and terror to intimidate and harass victims. What is also consistent is that those committing racist attacks, harassment and violence, often evade detection – essentially because they act in a clandestine fashion with the anticipation of avoiding identification.[12]

Obviously, there are existing criminal laws that can deal with many forms of militant racism – especially when it takes its form in harassment or violence. If we examine this story concerning Alison Moore, a few obvious basic criminal offences spring to mind.

1   The attack by four teenagers on Alison Moore can be classified as a common assault and battery. This can result in up to six months' imprisonment and/ or a fine[13] – i.e. assuming that the necessary *actus reus*[14] and *mens rea*[15] is established.

2   It is also possible that, as per section 47 of the Offences Against the Person Act 1861, charges could be brought for an assault occasioning actual bodily harm[16] – with an outcome of up to five years imprisonment should guilt be established.

3   The daubing of swastikas and National Front logos on the door of Alison Moore constitutes an offence under section 1 of the Criminal Damage Act 1971. This carries a sentence maximum of imprisonment of up to 10 years, but in practice usually involves a fine for such limited damage to property.[17]

4   There is also some evidence of intentional harassment, which could establish grounds for an offence under Section 4a of the Public Order Act 1986. This carries a period of 6 months imprisonment and/or a fine.[18]

5   The threat to the life of Alison Moore could (if the evidence justified which it does not seem to) result in charges being brought in relation to the offence of threatening to kill – resulting in up to 10 years imprisonment.[19]

While these basic offences may reflect established criminal charges, there is also a possibility that under the new Crime and Disorder Act 1998 additional/ alternative[20] charges could be brought for racially aggravated common assault,[21] racially aggravated actual bodily harm,[22] racially aggravated intentional harassment,[23] and/or racist criminal damage.[24] Indeed, these secondary offences could be associated with and brought alongside the basic offence and, if proved, would result in enhanced sentencing for racist crime.[25]

Who are the Perpetrators of Acts of Militant Racism?

Sadly, the perpetrators of the racist crime against Alison Moore have not been identified. As such, it is impossible to give an accurate description of those who were the perpetrators of this particular act. What is more, even if the police could track down the perpetrators, it can be seen that there exists a variety of applicable laws which inevitably begs a question for this book – Do we need any more laws to tackle racist crime? What would be the value of another string to the bow?

Research conducted by the Home Office[26] into the perpetrators[27] of racial harassment and violence, concludes that those who commit racial harassment and violence are of all ages, including young children,[28] youths, adults[29] and older people, even pensioners,[30] with the majority of incidents committed by those between the ages of 11 and 25.[31] Perpetrators may be both male and female and often act together as groups of friends or as families. To this extent, the perpetrators often consider that the views they hold towards ethnic minorities are shared by the communities to which they belong. This belief is reinforced by the wider community failure to condemn the perpetrators, which thereby indirectly reinforces the racist behaviour.

The Home Office research provides a profile of the *15–18-year-old perpetrator of racist crime*. This suggests that his parents and grandparents may have expressed racist views and that on leaving school, he may have hung around with older racist youths – being dispirited by having nothing to do, and in a continual search for some kind of role or identity. He may enjoy going to football matches and the sense of belonging to a large powerful group that such matches engender. He finds it easy to latch on to far-right ideals especially where far-right parties are active locally.[32] These ideals provide scapegoats for the insecurity he faces, while giving a sense of belonging to a particular group. *Likewise, an 11–14-year-old perpetrator of such racist activity* has grown up in an area where racist views are prevalent and regularly expressed. Having little educational input from his parents, he has low self-esteem and bullies children he perceives as weak, in order to gain prestige among his peers whom he is unable to impress in other ways. Together with his peers, and especially older youths, he may engage in continual harassment of neighbouring families and particular individuals at school. He is also at times abusive and threatening to people he passes on the street.

While this Home Office research could conceivably be criticised for the limitations of the depth of analytical research,[33] its findings are generally consistent with other data. For example, a survey carried out by Preston

Borough Council in 1992 summarised the perpetrators of racial harassment and violence as being white, male, young (15–25), in a group and unknown to the victim.[34] Likewise, the British Crime Survey[35] found that for Afro-Caribbean victims of perceived racially motivated violence or threats, 82 per cent of the perpetrators were described as white, 75 per cent as male and 36 per cent as between the ages of 16 and 25. For Asian victims the figures were again 82 per cent white perpetrators, with 87 per cent being male and 53 per cent between the ages of 16–25.

In Germany, in research carried out at the University of Trier,[36] analysis of 1,398 records of 'violence against aliens' identified four categories of perpetrators:

- *sympathisers*: those who are usually employed and not particularly political or xenophobic but become involved in violence as part of a group, being influenced by peer pressure;

- *criminal adolescents (thugs)*: low achievers, who have grown up in dysfunctional families. They have a long history of offending and they use violence as a way of settling daily conflicts;

- *xenophobic/ethnocentrics*: they are generally poor and unemployed and see their own deprivation as a result of having to compete with others – aliens – for apparently scarce resources. They are likely to join groups of skinheads with their violence less legitimised by political right wing ideology (but they can be influenced by it) so much as by personal feelings of disadvantage and being treated unequally as a German as compared to an alien or asylum seeker;

- *politically motivated extreme right-wingers*: these are well educated and well resourced and engage in systematic, organised violence against aliens, legitimised by their xenophobia. They are prepared to use and organise violence and have many contacts with other organisations.

Balancing on a Tightrope of Libertarian Acceptability

From this profile it is self evident that in pursuing my task of tackling militant racism I will stray into politics since a great deal of militant racism stems from the far-right of politics in the United Kingdom. However, in this book I do not seek to challenge the political agenda or ideas of any political party. Indeed, my starting point is that, although I may as the writer of this book disagree with their political agenda, I do respect the right of such political groups and parties to pursue their political dreams. Obviously as I recognise in this book, any such pursuit needs to be consistent with existing laws and any proposed changes to our laws should not be taken without due consideration of the impact this may have on an individual's right to freedom of thought and expression.[37]

A central feature of discussing reforms associated with race law is that it involves almost continually 'balancing on a tightrope of libertarian acceptability'.[38] This metaphor, which is consistent with that used by Sandra Coliver in her work *Striking a Balance*, reflects the inherent conflict between the rights of individuals who wish freedom to express racist views and the perceived desire of society to treat people equally – i.e. irrespective of their race and gender. Alongside this latter societal goal, is also the right of the individual who wishes to be treated equally and not have his/her rights undermined by another person's racist expressions.

While I will be walking this libertarian tightrope, I have no intention of repeating the *Enforcement of Morals* debate promoted by Lord Devlin in the 1960s.[39] Indeed, I will not be pursuing this line because I believe that society has moved on since the 1960s – with laws tackling racial discrimination now established and generally accepted by society. Accordingly, I will be proceeding on the premise that in the United Kingdom, we already have established laws – such as the Race Relations Acts of 1976 and Part III of the Public Order Act 1986[40] – that are tackling racial discrimination and the stirring up of racial hatred. My main concern is the evident inconsistency of outcome from the application of these laws.

By way of illustration, civil race discrimination cases occur on an almost daily basis in Employment Tribunals[41] – with employers being found liable for either direct or indirect racial discrimination.[42] By comparison, there have been on average fewer than two criminal convictions per year for stirring up racial hatred – since the Public Order Act 1986 came into force – with only 23 cases resulting in convictions.[43] The civil case of *Burton and Rhule v DeVere Hotels* [1996] IRLR 596 is a classic example of the evident legal inconsistency in this area. In *De Vere*, the hotel was found liable for racial discrimination, and in breach of the Race Relations Act 1976, because they subjected their employee(s) to the detriment of harassment.[44] This finding applied even in the circumstances of the harasser being a third party speaker who had subjected two black waitresses at the hotel to racial remarks.

Quite apart from the questionable issues surrounding the liability of an organisation for a third party's racist activity,[45] the irony of the case is that racist 'jokes', although often 'racially offensive', do not normally provide grounds for legal action against the expresser of such jokes. This applies because the criminal law does not penalise 'racial offence', and legislation generally requires any words used to be 'threatening, abusive and/or insulting'[46] – with an intent/likelihood for fear of violence[47]/harassment[48] or racial hatred[49] – for a prosecution to succeed. What is more, the two black waitresses from the De Vere case are unlikely to have a civil means of redress against the speaker personally – i.e. unless the words used amounted to a defamation of character[50] – because the Race Relations Act 1976 makes no provision for an individual victim of racial abuse to seek compensation from any person other than an employer or the provider of goods, facilities, premises and services to the public.

In a limited and indirect way, this problem was recognised by the government in 1976, when in a White Paper[51] it was acknowledged that:

> Relatively few prosecutions have been brought under Section 6 of the 1965 Act and none has been brought under s.6 of the Theatres Act [i.e. for stirring up racial hatred]. However, during the past decade, probably largely as a result of Section 6, there has been a decided change in the style of racialist propaganda. It tends to be less blatantly bigoted, to disclaim any intention of stirring up racial hatred, and to purport to make a contribution to public education and debate. Whilst this shift away from crudely racialist propaganda and abuse is welcome, it is not an unmixed benefit. The more apparently rational and moderate is the message, the greater is its probable impact on public opinion. But it is not justifiable in a democratic society to interfere with freedom of expression except where it is necessary to do so for the protection of disorder or for the protection of other basic freedoms.[52]
>
> The present law does not, however, penalise the dissemination of ideas based on the assumption of racial superiority or inferiority of facts (whether true or false) which may encourage racial prejudice or discrimination. It is arguable that false and evil publications of this kind may well be more effectively defeated by public education and debate than by prosecution and that in practice the criminal law would be ineffective to deal with such material. Due regard must also, of course, be paid to allowing the free expression of opinion. *The Government is not therefore at this stage putting forward proposals to extend the criminal law to deal with the dissemination of racialist propaganda in the likelihood that group hatred will be stirred up by it. It recognises, however, that strong views are held on this important question and will carefully consider any further representations that may be made to it* (my emphasis).[53]

While the government in 1976 sought to avoid taking legislative steps that limit freedom of expression, it did provide for a counter expression approach by giving responsibilities to the Commission for Racial Equality (CRE) to 'take action to educate and persuade public opinion'.[54] Indeed, in the 22 years since this statement there have been some excellent educational anti-racist programmes from the Commission for Racial Equality (CRE).[55] However, a notable weakness of such anti-racist programmes is that the audience that sees these programmes may not be the same one that sees, and may be influenced by, racist material.

In this book I seek to remedy this weakness. One apparent remedy is for the government to introduce laws that prohibit the publication/distribution of 'racially offensive' material[56] that may stir up racial hatred and/or discrimination on the basis that such materials often increase tensions within communities and can lead to racial harassment and violence.[57] While this may seem an obvious solution, to take such steps could be seen as seriously undermining the freedom of the author to express his/her views and for these reasons the approach could be criticised as being incompatible with human rights.[58]

Under the terms of Section 19 of the Human Rights Act 1998, a government minister is required to issue a written statement of compatibility with the 'Convention on Human Rights' in relation to any Bill which he introduces to parliament, or to explain why the Bill fails to comply and why the government nevertheless wishes to proceed with the Bill. To this extent, incompatibility with the 'Convention on Human Rights' should be avoided if at all possible.[59] *While the aim of this research is to examine existing laws which tackle militant racism,[60] the challenge of this book is to propose legislative steps that will make it more difficult for militant racists to stir up racial hatred and/or discrimination through the use of 'racially offensive' materials – without undermining freedom of expression.[61]*

Saying 'No' to the Proscription of Racist Organisations

I do not intend in this book to argue that racist organisations should be proscribed. Accordingly, I will not therefore be considering this issue in detail within the main body of this book.

I take this approach, because it is clear that in the UK proscription is generally considered to be a solution that applies only to organisations that are involved in acts of terrorism. In my judgement this does not in general apply to militant racist organisations. Certainly the London nail-bombings of

April 1999[62] seemed to open up the possibility that certain militant racist groups had moved into terrorist activity, thereby opening up a debate about such a ban.[63] However, under Section 1(2) of the Prevention of Terrorism Act 1989, it is not possible to add domestic terrorist groups to the schedule of proscribed organisations unless they 'Are concerned in, or in promoting or encouraging, terrorism occurring in the United Kingdom and connected with the affairs of Northern Ireland'. Since the London nail-bombings appeared to be associated with domestic affairs, and not Northern Ireland, there were no powers to proscribe domestic groups.[64]

Obviously the law could be changed so that domestic terrorist groups could be proscribed and the government paper – Legislating Against Terrorism[65] – is seeking consultation on such change. The proposals in this consultation paper open the door to the possibility that militant racist groups could be proscribed. This applies, because the proposed definition of terrorism refers to:

> The use of serious violence against persons or property, or threaten serious violence, against persons or property to intimidate or coerce a government, the public or any section of the public for political, religious or ideological ends.

These proposals suggests that any groups found responsible for threats[66] associated with terrorism could be proscribed, notwithstanding that they may not have actually lit the fuse.

Should such proposals become law, it is probably unlikely that such groups would be proscribed, since there is seemingly no direct evidence that they were actually responsible for terrorist activity or the claims associated with the activity. Indeed, it must be possible that the claims of responsibility were hoax calls, in an attempt to blame a particular group for the terrorism.

Obviously should any groups be found to be involved with terrorist activities it may be appropriate to consider proscription of them. However, it is worth noting that not all groups involved in serious violence or terror activities are proscribed. For example, the IRA and INLA have been proscribed, but not the loyalist paramilitaries. This applies despite the fact that there are loyalist groups that have also been involved in serious violence.

The approach of the UK government towards proscription has been one of arguing that it is an effective means of tackling extreme terrorist groups, while displaying a reluctance to proscribe all groups involved in serious violence, preferring instead to respect the right of freedom of association.[67] This displays consistency with Article 11 of the European Convention on Human Rights, which provides a right to freedom of association, subject to limitations as are necessary in a democratic society – i.e. in the interests of national security or crime, for the prevention of crime and disorder etc.[68]

Article 4(b) of the United Nation's CERD Convention[69] calls upon nations to declare as illegal, and to prohibit organisations, that promote and incite racial discrimination – making participation in such organisations an offence punishable by law. However, when the UK government ratified this Treaty in 1969 they did so, 'with due regard to freedom of expression and association'. In chapter 5 of this book, I will discuss the scant protection that the ECHR provides for racist expression. For present discussion purposes, it is important to note that proportionality is often an essential element associated with the ECHR. While it seems likely that the European Court of Human Rights would accept a state's proscription of a racist organisation involved in terrorism, it must be exceedingly unlikely that proscription could be applicable for ALL racial groups – i.e. whether or not they are involved in racial violence.[70] This must especially apply to political parties which display racial discrimination amongst a variety of political policies. Any proscription of such political parties could be seen as undermining the principles that form the basis of a democratic society.[71]

Concluding on the issue of proscription, it is important to recognise that should any group become involved in domestic terrorist activities, then it could become necessary for the government to proscribe them. However, in keeping with the political climate in the United Kingdom, such proscription should apply because the groups pursue terrorist activities and not because they are racist.[72]

As I will show in this book, militant racist activity takes various forms and ranges from the distribution of racially offensive material to individual acts of serious violence. While it may be appropriate to consider proscribing extreme racist organisations that are involved in domestic terrorism, it clearly could not be morally and politically acceptable to proscribe all militant racist groups. This especially applies to groups that are essentially political in nature and may be simply involved in the distribution of material that is racially offensive.

A Preview of the Approach I Shall Take within this Book

The traditional approach to examining a conflict associated with freedom of expression is to make detailed reference to the United States and the case law associated with the First Amendment of the US Constitution. A whole host of cases are applicable, such as *Chaplinski v New Hampshire*,[73] *US v O'Brien*,[74] *Texas v Johnson* and *US v Eichmann*,[75] *Ginsberg v New York*[76] and *Collin v Smith*[77] and most have been examined by a variety of UK academics and authors (the most notable of which have been Street, Howe and Bindman,[78] Barendt,[79] and Coliver[80]). While I am not seeking to undermine the excellent work of such renowned academics, I am conscious that we do not have a written constitution in the United Kingdom that displays the equivalent of the First Amendment. Hence, since such laws do not govern us, I question the direct relevance of the First Amendment to the issue of freedom of expression in the UK[81] and consider that more pertinent issues[82] are raised through examining the matter by taking into account UK/British[83] laws along with any obligations that may exist via European and International Treaties.

Preview

However I start, in chapter 2, by first considering the obligations of local authorities to tackle racism. I do this by exploring the legal responsibilities of a local authority to promote equality of opportunity and by looking at what steps can be taken – considering the civil and criminal legal options available.

To pursue the theme of tackling militant racism further, in chapter 3 I provide an analysis of racist speech and literature. This involves analysing certain racist materials to see if they could possibly provide grounds for criminal prosecution under British criminal laws.

This emphasis on racist literature and material derives from a perception that such material can be potentially damaging in a multicultural society, since it can help raise racial tensions between citizens, though it is important to recognise that there is no irrevocable proof that racist literature and materials are directly responsible for racist crime. As I discussed earlier when referring to material from Hounslow, and with regards to *Searchlight* material,[84] there does exist some anecdotal evidence that shows that in areas where there is a high incidence of racist material being distributed – racial crime is often on the increase.

Chapters 4 and 5 are key chapters within my book. In chapter 4 I outline two key proposals for legislative change, considering the practicalities and problems associated with making it an offence to stir up racial discrimination and/or hatred through the use of 'racially offensive' words. In chapter 5 I develop this further, by refining the proposals and giving consideration to determining if, as amended, they are compatible with the (European) Convention on Human Rights.[85]

Having established my arguments for legislative change, I continue with chapter 6 in which I look for a philosophical basis for the changes I propose – with consideration given to jurisprudential elements deriving from the works of John Stuart Mill, Jean-Jacques Rousseau and John Rawls.

In chapter 7, I look at the Crime and Disorder Act 1998 and a new approach to tackling racist crime which enables courts to pursue a harsher sentencing policy where it is determined that there exists evidence of racial motivation or hostility.

Chapter 8 provides my concluding comment upon this research.

Notes

1   Lawrence, Frederick M., *Punishing Hate – Bias Crimes Under American Law*, Harvard University Press, 1999, p.1.
2   Stephen Lawrence was murdered in a 'racist attack' in April 1993.
3   This will be discussed in chapter 7. See also Jepson, Peter, 'The definition of a racial incident', *NLJ* [1998] 1838 for an outline of the racial offences and how the operate.
4   *The Concise Oxford Dictionary*, 8th edn, ed. R.E. Allen, Clarendon Press, Oxford, 1990. A variety of dictionaries were examined to establish a suitable interpretation. However, with little to choose between the *New Shorter Oxford English Dictionary on Historical Principles* (ed. Lesley Brown, 1993) and *The Concise Oxford Dictionary* definition, I eventually decided that the more concise version was more applicable.
5   Antagonism is defined in *The Concise Oxford Dictionary* as 'active opposition or hostility'. The word 'hostility' is important since it is utilised in the Crime and Disorder Act 1998 in relation to racist crime. See chapter 7, 'Racial Motivation and Hostility'.
6   Article 9 of the European Convention on Human Rights stresses that everyone has the right to freedom of thought, conscience and religion. In the case of *Kikkinakis v Greece* (A 260–A para 31 [1993]), the Court said that the values of Article 9 were at the foundation of a democratic society, though this Article has been interpreted cautiously by the Commission, with the vast majority of cases involving religion. Van Dijk and Van Hoof (*Theory and Practice of the European Convention on Human Rights*, 2nd edn, 1990, p. 397) advocate that there is no line between philosophy and a political programme, saying 'in our opinion, Article 9 actually concerns any ideas and views ...'. The European Human Rights Commission, in the case of *Arrowsmith v UK*, No 7050/75, 19 DR 5 [1978] Com. Rep., paras 69–72, accepted that pacifism fell 'within the ambit' to the right to freedom of thought and conscience because it was a philosophy. However, in disagreeing with Van Dijk and Van Hoof, the authors Harris, Boyle and Warbrick have remarked that the enquiry the Commission made in the *Arrowsmith case* makes it dubious as to whether their 'generous view' will prevail (see *Law of the European Convention on Human Rights*, Butterworths, 1995, pp. 356–7). See also chapter 5 – the section 'Compatibility with the Convention on Human Rights' – where I argue that rights under the ECHR are subject to the provisions in Article 14 of the ECHR. This states that the enjoyment of rights set forth in the Convention shall be secured without discrimination on grounds of sex, race, colour, language, religion, political or other opinion, national or social origin, association with a national minority,

property, birth or other status. To this extent, I concur with Harris et al. by arguing that an individual should not be able to rely upon Article 9 with regards to any racist beliefs.

7   As per Section 32 of the Race Relations Act 1976, an employer is vicariously liable for all acts of his employees or agents.

8   For example, 'Growing up in London's Deep South', *Searchlight*, September 1998, tells the story of Matthew Collins who turned to fascism and then later became an informant for Searchlight helping to provide information exposing C18 activity in vicious racist attacks in Tower Hamlets for a *World in Action* TV programme.

9   Activity here is given a wide interpretation. It primarily includes the distribution of racist materials, but can also include the use of posters, stickers, graffiti and verbal and physical harassment and/or attacks upon ethnic people.

10 *Daily Telegraph*, 23 March 1998. The story of Alison Moore was highlighted on *London Today*, 9 February 1999. This TV programme also displayed some of the racist material sent to her.

11 It is claimed by Professor Bhikhu Parekh, in the All-Party Parliamentary Group on Race and Community (Houses of Parliament Session 1993/4) report entitled *Racial Violence: A Separate Offence?*, that almost a third of the ethnic minority population will suffer, in some form or another, the experience of racial crime/incidents each year. This projected figure is based upon family connections linked to the British Crime Survey (which signified 130,000 [1991], 102,000 [1993], and 143,000 [1995] racial incidents in the respective year (source: 'Ethnicity and Victimisation: Findings from the 1996 British Crime Survey', *Home Office Statistical Bulletin*, Issue 6/98), with the claim that it is not just the victim who suffers but also his/her immediate family.

12 Quite often they will use a facemask. There have also been reports of the use of white hoods by the British Ku Klux Klan – *Sunday Mirror*, 21 September 1997 and *Searchlight*, November 1997. (Note: the wearing of Klan robes has been regarded as an offence under Section 1 of the Public Order Act 1936 which prohibits the wearing of uniforms in connection with political objects – see *The Times*, 8 October 1965.)

13 The penalty for these two common law offences can now be found in section 39 of the Criminal Justice Act 1988.

14 For a discussion on how assault can be established from the use of words that make the victim apprehend immediate force see Clarkson and Keating, *Criminal Law: Text and Materials*, Sweet & Maxwell, 1990, pp. 542–5. So far as battery is concerned, the case of *Wilson v Pringle* [1986] 2 All. E.R. 440 CA, Civil Division, held that in a battery there must be intentional touching or contact in one form or another of the plaintiff by the defendant. That touching must be proved to be a hostile touching.

15 The case of *R v Venna* [1976] Q.B. 421 CA, Criminal Division, establishes that the element of *mens rea* in the offence of assault and/or battery is satisfied by proof that the defendant intentionally or recklessly applied force to the person of another ('reckless' here is given a subjective meaning (whether the defendant foresaw the possibility of the consequences occurring and whether it was unjustifiable or unreasonable for him to take that risk) as per *R v Spratt – The Times*, 14 May 1990).

16 As per *R v Miller* [1954] 2. Q.B. 282 actual bodily harm includes any hurt or injury calculated to interfere with the health or comfort of the victim. The *mens rea* requirement is the same as that required for common assault.

17 The issue of Criminal Damage will be considered in more detail in the chapter 'Racist Speech and Literature'.

18 Harassment under Section 4A of the Public Order Act will be discussed in more detail in chapter 3, 'Racist Speech and Literature'. Issues associated with the Protection from Harassment Act 1997 (which requires conduct on at least two occasions) will also be discussed in that chapter.

19 Section 16 of the Offences Against the Persons Act 1861.

20 They are additional and alternative in the sense that if the evidence so justifies a person can be charged with the basic offence plus the racial equivalent. It then becomes the duty of the jury to determine if the defendant is guilty of the basic offence and, if so, if he is also guilty of the racial equivalent. Assuming the jury determines guilt to both charges, the judge is then legally bound to apply a sentencing policy consistent with the higher 'racial' tariff and must declare such in open court.

21 Up to two years imprisonment instead of six months for the basic offence.

22 Up to seven years imprisonment instead of five years for the basic offence.

23 Up to two years imprisonment instead of six months for the basic offence.

24 Section 82(2) of the Crime and Disorder Act 1998 requires a court, in considering the seriousness of any offence, to treat racial aggravation as an aggravating factor that increases the seriousness of the offence.

25 For a fuller account of this area of law see chapter 7, 'Racial Motivation and Hostility'.

26 Rae Sibbitt, *The Perpetrators of Racial Harassment and Racial Violence*, Home Office Research Study 176. This research was conducted by the Research and Statistics Directorate within the Home Office at the request of the Racial Attacks Group (RAG) which was set up by the government in 1987 in response to concern about racist attacks in Britain.

27 Perpetrators here are given a natural meaning – i.e. those who commit such acts.

28 Some children between the ages of 5–10 were identified as racist perpetrators by housing officials.

29 These are described as adults who have little respect for local authorities, which they see as remote 'politically correct' institutions. They may engage in verbal abuse of their neighbours, especially where their neighbours appear to have obtained resources, which they would have liked: e.g. larger accommodation. They may be physically violent and join forces with other families on an estate in abusing or intimidating individual families. The adult male, in particular, may already be involved in other criminal activity, where violence (or the threat of it) towards others is a normal part of his lifestyle. His views are such that he may not go out of his way to engage in racist attacks (though he may have done so in his youth). However, if he is drunk and finds an excuse to attack a black person – e.g. if one has hurt his friend or where someone has accidentally reversed into his car – he will do so (source: Home Office Research Study 176).

30 These are elderly people who see black people as suitable scapegoats for all their problems, and see these views reinforced by politicians and central government which maintains that immigration controls are necessary to protect jobs and housing (source: Home Office Research Study 176).

31 See Table 3.1, p. 64 of the Home Office Research Study 176.

32 Interestingly the linkage to far-right political parties is not highlighted in the Home Office Research summary despite the fact that there exists strong linkage by a variety of quoted sources throughout the research.

33 It was conducted principally in a small locality of just two London Boroughs.

34 *Hidden from View: A Study of Racial Harassment in Preston*, Preston Borough Council, 1992. This report also refers to a survey of 'visible minorities' in Newcastle, with data that

shows that 95 per cent of racist attacks were conducted by white people, with nearly half saying that the perpetrators were aged between 16 and 24 years old.

35 Aye, Maung N., and Mirlees-Black, C. (1994), *Racially Motivated Crime: A British Crime Survey analysis*, Home Office Research and Planning Paper 82.

36 Wllems, H. (1995), 'Right-wing Extremism, Racism or Youth Violence? Explaining Violence against Foreigners in Germany', *New Community* 21(4), pp. 501–23.

37 Indeed, Articles 9 (thought) and 10 (expression) of the European Convention on Human Rights provide some limited guarantee of protection. This issue of freedom for racist expression will be discussed later in this book. See in particular the discussion on ECHR case 6741/74, *X v Italy* within chapter 5 in the section 'Compatibility with the Convention on Human Rights'.

38 The term 'libertarian acceptability' is applied in the sense of being pleasing to those who advocate free will (see *The Concise Oxford Dictionary* (1990)). This definition of 'libertarian' being synonymous with that provided by Roger Scruton in *A Dictionary of Political Thought*, Pan Books, 1982. Sandra Coliver notably adopted a similar balancing metaphor when she produced her book, *Striking a Balance: Hate Speech, Freedom of Expression and Non-discrimination*, published in 1992 by Article 19 of the Human Rights (Centre of the University of Essex).

39 Devlin, Patrick, *The Enforcement of Morals*, Oxford University Press, 1965.

40 This legislation is similar to that produced by Section 6 of the Race Relations Act 1965. The Race Relations Act 1976 resulted in a slightly revised offence being inserted into Section 5A of the Public Order Act 1936 – thereby reaffirming the traditional view that the problem of racist speech is primarily one of public order.

41 By way of example, in 1995-6 there were 1,737 racial discrimination applications to the Industrial Tribunals of which 676 went to a tribunal hearing – with 405 being settled though ACAS. Of the 676 that went to a hearing 109 were successful – the remainder being either dismissed (375) or disposed of otherwise (114) (source: 'Industrial Tribunals' as published in *Labour Market Trends*, April 1997).

42 See Section 1(1)(a) (direct) and 1(1)(b) (indirect) of the Race Relations Act 1976 for a statutory definition of direct and indirect racial discrimination.

43 Figures provided by the Attorney General (3 August 1998) show that there have been 53 cases submitted to the Attorney General for consent to prosecute. One application was withdrawn and seven were refused. Of the 45 cases in which consent was granted one defendant died before proceedings, no evidence was given in two cases and two cases were stayed by grant of *nolle prosequi* by the Attorney General. The CPS discontinued one case and one defendant was acquitted. Of the remaining 39 cases, 13 were before the courts (which suggests an increase in requests for prosecution during 1998) and three defendants could not be located. Of the 23 cases in which convictions were sustained, 12 resulted in imprisonment and the remainder varied from a conditional discharge to a fine or suspended sentence.

44 A report from the Industrial Tribunal – 'Round Table Dinner "like an NF meeting" ', *Searchlight*, November 1995.

45 For a discussion of this area see Jepson, Peter, 'An Organisation's Liability for Racial Harassment', http://www.peterjepson.com.

46 See Sections 4, 4A and 5 of the Public Order Act 1986. The same prerequisite of '*threat, abuse and/or insult*', together with the 'intent/likelihood of stirring up racial hatred', is also required under Part III of the same Act. This issue will be discussed in various parts of this book but a detailed consideration is given in chapter 3, 'Racist Speech and Literature'.

47 See Section 4 of the Public Order Act 1986 for specific details.

48 See Sections 4A and 5 of the Public Order Act 1986.

49 See Part III of the Public Order Act 1986.

50 They may have a case for defamation. However with no legal aid, the legal costs involved mean that few people – other than those who are reasonably wealthy – can afford to pursue a court action (though a 'no win no fee' policy could conceivably change this).

51 *Racial Discrimination*, Cmnd 6234, HMSO, 1976.

52 Ibid., para 126.

53 Ibid., para 127.

54 Ibid., para 50.

55 One example is the work done with football clubs to 'Kick Racism out of Football'. This, and others, will be referred to in various parts of this book.

56 The establishment of this definition is discussed in detail in chapters 4 and 5, 'Say No to Racism'. However, for current discussion purposes 'racial offence' can be determined as 'a wounding of feelings as a result of expression directed towards a group of persons in Britain defined by reference to colour, race, nationality (including citizenship) or ethnic or national origins'. This is based upon the statutory interpretation of 'racial hatred' (with adaptation) found in Section 17 of the Public Order Act 1986 and *The Concise Oxford Dictionary* definition of 'offence'. This approach establishes consistency with statute and the arguments presented in *Brutus v Cozens* [1972] 2 All ER 1297 (which relates to the words 'threat, abuse and insult') with the issue determined as a matter of fact.

57 See correspondence sent by Cllr Jagdish Sharma, Deputy Leader of Hounslow Council, to the Attorney General dated 19 July 1993 for anecdotal evidence of increased racial tensions and violence, following the distribution of racist literature.

58 That is freedom of expression under Article 10 of the 'European Convention on Human Rights' and the Human Rights Act 1998 (see chapter 5 and the section 'Compatibility with the Convention on Human Rights').

59 This area will be discussed in chapter 5.

60 Existing laws could also be challenged as being incompatible with the Convention on Human Rights. Should an appropriate Court issue a 'statement of incompatibility' an obligation falls upon a minister to review the offending legislation, leaving it to Parliament, should it choose to do so, to pass amending legislation (see Bindman, Geoffrey, 'Protection from Discrimination', [1998] *NLJ* 1617).

61 To this extent, I will need to give an opinion as to whether my proposals for legislative change are compatible with the Convention on Human Rights.

62 'Race Bombers strike again', *The Mail on Sunday*, 25 April 1999.

63 'Neo-Nazi group admits bombing', *The Times*, 20 April 1999.

64 See the comments of Jack Straw MP, the Home Secretary, 'We won't let them pull our society apart', *The Mail on Sunday*, 2 May 1999.

65 Command Paper 3178, available from HMSO and published December 1998.

66 It is not clear from the proposals whether a claim of responsibility would amount to a threat in relation to future activity. Given that a serious of incidents may occur, this must be a possibility.

67 This approach is typified by the comments found in the report *Legislating Against Terrorism*.

68 Harris, Boyle and Warbrick claim that there is no right to freedom of association for purposes that are illegal in national law – noting the powers of the Prevention of Terrorism (Temporary Provisions) Act 1989. See *Law of the European Convention on Human Rights*, Butterworths, 1995, p. 422.

69 The International Convention of the Elimination of All Forms of Racial Discrimination.

70 In the ECHR case of *X v Federal Republic of Germany* (case no 9235/81) the Human Rights court upheld the banning of an exhibition of brochures that alleged that 'the death of Jews under the Third Reich was a Zionist trickery'. Note however, that the case did not involve a ban on the racist organisation. See chapter 5 for a discussion on this and other cases.

71 Thus, a challenge under Articles 10 and 11 of the Convention on Human Rights.

72 For a discussion on banning racist organisations see Lowes, Nick and Silver, Steve, 'To ban or not to ban?', *Searchlight*, June 1999. Note that the general tone of this *Searchlight* article is to reject proscribing racist organisations on the basis that it will force them underground, with the evidence from Germany (where proscriptions applies to some extreme right wing racist groups) showing that it does not prevent racial violence.

73 315 US 568 (1942): the 'fighting words principle'.

74 391 US 367 (1968), which articulated a test to be laid down courts in determining the constitutionality of a government regulation that has the effect of suppressing some form of expression.

75 491 US 397, 403 (1989); 496 US 310 (1990). Both of the cases involved the politically charged issue of flag burning.

76 390 US 629, 633 (1968) which concerns the limits of protection under the First Amendment due to radio transmission. This case is briefly referred to in chapter 5 of this book, 'Say No to Racism'.

77 578 F. 2nd 1197 (7th Circ. 1978). This case concerned a group of Nazis who wished to march through the town of Skokie, Illinois, where a significant number of Jewish survivors of the holocaust lived. The town had passed an ordinance that proscribed demonstrations by people wearing certain military style uniforms or clothing. The ordinance was invalidated by the Federal Court on the grounds that the trauma caused to holocaust survivors on seeing Nazis marching in their community could not justify the suppression of the symbolic expression.

78 Street, H., Howe, G. and Bindman, G., *Street Report*, 1967, which influenced the 1968 legislation on race discrimination.

79 Barendt, Eric, *Freedom of Speech*, Clarendon Press, 1985. In particular, see the chapters 'The Character and Scope of Freedom of Speech' and 'Political Speech'.

80 *Striking a Balance: Hate Speech, Freedom of Expression and Non-discrimination*, Article 19, 1992. In particular, the contributions by Schnieder, R.G., 'Hate Speech in the United States: Recent Legal Developments'; Delgado, R., 'Campus Antiracism Rules: Constitutional Narratives in Collision'; Strossen, N., 'Balancing the Rights to Freedom of Expression and Equality: A Civil Liberties Approach to Hate Speech on Campus'; Coliver, S., 'Hate Speech Laws: Do they Work?'.

81 This does not mean that US case law is irrelevant to this book. On the contrary, it will be used in comparative terms when dealing with racial motivation and hostility (see chapter 7). It will also be applicable when consideration is given to the thorny problem of controlling race hate material that is circulated worldwide via the internet (see chapter 5).

82 For a critical look at United States hate crime legislation see Jacobs, James B. and Potter, K., *Hate Crimes: Criminal Law and Identity Politics*, Oxford University Press, 1998.

83 Throughout this book 'UK' means the United Kingdom consisting of England, Scotland, Wales and Northern Ireland. 'British' means, England, Wales and Scotland. However, no consideration is given to Scottish law or legislation at any stage throughout this book. This

applies as a result of Scotland operating under a different legal system to that which applies in England and Wales. As such, this book is primarily concerned with the law and legislation of England and Wales.

84 See the discussion earlier within this chapter under the heading: 'What is Militant Racism?'. Also see: 'Fanning the Flames of Hatred' and 'The BNP in East London – Stepping Stone to Race War', *Searchlight*, September 1998.

85 Please note that the Convention on Human Rights and the European Convention on Human Rights are essentially one and the same, as a result of the Human Rights Act 1998 which incorporates the ECHR into UK law.

2 Action by Local Authorities

One of the recommendations of the Home Affairs Committee, in its report on racial attacks and harassment,[1] is that an individual suffering from harassment or molestation should consider taking civil action. Indeed, they went so far as to suggest that police should give to complainants details of local solicitors who might be able to assist[2] and even to produce leaflets in a range of languages drawing attention to the civil remedies available.[3] In making this recommendation it was recognised that in some cases the police may not be able to charge the perpetrator of a racial incident with a criminal offence either because of a lack of evidence, or because the harassment or molestation 'might fall below the level of a criminal offence'.

In its report, the Home Affairs Committee indicated that the main civil weapon used is the tort of trespass – with the assailant being pressed for an undertaking not to repeat past behaviour; alternatively an injunction might be sought. If the undertaking or injunction is broken, the assailant may be committed to prison for contempt of court, or may be liable to pay a fine or damages. In evidence submitted to the Home Affairs Committee, it was claimed that in Hounslow there had been no breaches of such undertakings in the previous few years, with the police therefore regarding civil actions as being very effective. However, as was recognised, there are drawbacks in that to obtain an injunction the cost is likely to exceed £1,000 – with many victims of racial harassment being frightened and lacking the finances to take such action. It is also the case that, without police assistance of investigation, it may be very difficult for a victim of racial harassment to establish a credible level of evidence for submission before a High Court judge. For example, assuming that a victim is a person who has recently moved to this country from say India, how can s/he be expected to identify, name and provide addresses for a group of individuals who may attack him/her, late one evening? Indeed, even if attacked in broad daylight, it is probable that any victim of crime would have identification problems when they are attacked by a group of people. Even if a victim could identify, given problems of language barriers etc., it can sometimes be difficult to present evidence before a High Court judge in an acceptable and convincing manner.

There may also be the problem of the suitability of the use of a civil injunction that is generally used to tackle individuals and organisations – rather than directed towards a group of racists. Even if the Court can be persuaded to grant an injunction, there must be some doubt that it would prove an effective legal weapon against a group of young racist villains who may be rebelling against society and its rules.

Not only is the idea of racial harassment victims bringing there own civil action prone to such tremendous evidential and practical difficulties, there is also a danger that the police, by sending complainants elsewhere, could give the impression (falsely or otherwise) that they have little interest in tackling complaints of racial harassment. In effect, this could even provide a green light for more racial harassment, since it may signify that the police will tolerate this kind of racial harassment – not being prepared to tackle it themselves.

Despite such criticism of this proposal of the Home Affairs Select Committee, as we shall see in subsequent chapters of this book, it is nevertheless a fact that the criminal law is often unable to tackle some forms of racial harassment and organised racism. As I shall demonstrate in the later chapters, the reasons for this are varied – but they are essentially due to the construction of the law and the requirement, in criminal cases, for proof beyond reasonable doubt.

One advantage of a civil legal remedy is that the proof required is lesser – being on the balance of probabilities. Although, many people suffering racial harassment and intimidation may understandably be too poor, nervous, or frightened to commence civil proceedings. Indeed, they may turn to the local authority, or voluntary groups,[4] for help and assistance. As I will show in this chapter, a local authority is under a statutory duty to eliminate unlawful racial discrimination, to promote equality of opportunity, and to develop good relations between persons of different racial groups. Quite how they fulfil this duty may vary from authority to authority. However, it seems reasonable to argue that it is implicit, from the nature of this statutory duty, that a local authority has a duty to tackle militant racism – which can be simply defined as incitement to/organised racial discrimination, harassment and/or attack. It also seems reasonable to suggest this can extend to having a responsibility to offer help and assistance to those suffering from militant racism. Obviously, this help and assistance can and will, take varied forms – sometimes legal, but more generally practical. It could even be carried out by an agency working with, or acting on behalf of, a local authority.

Powers of a Local Authority

Because of its nature, this chapter will generally be descriptive in style – looking at the powers of local authorities, together with the type of action they can and do take, in tackling militant racism. In doing so, it is important to recognise, from the outset, that there is a difference between a local authority acting under a discretionary power and under a statutory duty. When acting under a discretionary power, an authority is under no legal obligation to act – being very much governed by the availability of resources. In comparison, where central government imposes a statutory duty upon a local authority it may be legally obliged to fulfil or undertake a particular task.[5]

Parliament has provided local authorities with powers, under Section 111 of the Local Government Act 1972, to do 'anything which is calculated to facilitate, or is conducive or incidental to the discharge of any of their functions'. Clearly, this suggests a wide discretionary power without giving any definition of what precisely the functions of a local authority are. Indeed, there is no one Act that clearly defines all the functions of a local authority. However, there exist numerous statutes which impose a legal obligation on specific local authorities to carry out certain functions – just two examples of which are with regards to providing education or help for the sick and disabled.[6]

This apparent legislative vagueness (of functional definition) would appear to be consistent with the widely recognised convention that demands that local authority powers are multi-functional in nature.[7] To add support to this proposition, I need only refer to the multiplicity of powers and functions which central government have heaped upon the shoulders of local authorities throughout this century.[8]

A Statutory Duty under the Race Relations Act 1976

While the specific functions of a local authority cannot be found in one statute, Section 71 of the Race Relations Act 1976 requires authorities:

> To make appropriate arrangements with a view to securing that their various functions are carried out with due regard to the need:
>
> (a) to eliminate unlawful racial discrimination; and
> (b) to promote equality of opportunity, and good relations, between persons of different racial groups.

Not only does this impose, on local authorities, a statutory duty – it can also be argued it makes the elimination of racial discrimination and promotion of equal opportunities a key function of their work. It is a key function, because all other functions and responsibilities must be carried out in such a manner – i.e. with due regard to this need.

However, this imposition of a duty can, in certain circumstances, be of limited value – especially since along with this duty there is often no correlating provision of central government finance. For example, while one local authority may have a strong commitment to tackling racial discrimination, another authority may, due to finance limitations or even political priorities, be less committed. Clearly, an authority's commitment to tackling discrimination may and often will, vary due to the political will of the authority. Though, it is submitted that in order for central government to make a duty imposition viable they should introduce some form of ring fenced finance, possibly with some method of performance criteria. The current practice of central government simply imposing a duty upon a local authority, without any correlating finance, has been thrown into a state of potential uncertainty following the *Barry* case.[9]

In the *Barry* case the issues were not about race but about the statutory duty of a local authority to fulfil the social welfare needs of Mr Barry – an 81-year-old man who was suffering from a slight stroke with an history of heart attacks, poor vision, and having to use a walking frame due to a previous hip fracture. The local authority assessed his needs and decided that he required various Home Care services – including shopping, pension collection, laundry, cleaning and Meals-on-Wheels. However, due to a financial shortfall of £2.5m in their budget, they withdrew the cleaning and laundry facilities. Consequentially, Mr Barry sought a judicial review on the basis that the authority had a statutory duty[10] to provide the service. When the case reached the Divisional Court McGowan LJ found in favour of Mr Barry because of a failure to provide a reassessment of his need, although the judge observed that an authority would have an impossible task unless it could have regard to the size of the cake before deciding how to cut it. He argued, 'an authority is right to take account of resources both when assessing need and when deciding when it is necessary to make arrangements to meet those needs'.

When the case reached the Court of Appeal, it was held that 'in assessing or reassessing whether it is necessary to make arrangements to meet them [needs], a local authority is not entitled to take account of the resources available to the authority'. The reason for the apparent firmness of the Court of Appeal, being that a local authority is under a statutory duty[11] to assess the needs and, where it is necessary, to make arrangements to fulfil those needs. While this approach of the Court of Appeal may seem reasonable in the sense of requiring an authority to undertake something it is legally required to do – in extreme circumstances, it could mean that irrespective of its available finances, an authority must provide a statutory service.

Not surprisingly, when the *Barry* case reached the House of Lords this judgement of the Court of Appeal was overturned, it being held that an authority's obligation to fulfil a duty can be limited by its lack of resources. However, in deciding with the majority, Lord Nicholls rejected the assertion that by enabling a local authority to take into account its resources in carrying out a statutory duty he was demoting that duty to a (discretionary) power. He argued:

> The duty, it was said, would collapse into a power. I do not agree. A local authority must carry out its functions under section 2(1) [of the Chronically Sick and Disabled Persons Act 1970] in a responsible fashion. In the event of a local authority acting with Wednesbury unreasonableness, a disabled person would have a remedy.

Implications of the Barry Case for Section 71 of the Race Relations Act 1976

Applying these principles to the application of Section 71 of the Race Relations Act 1976, it seems clear that an authority remains under a duty to carry out all of its functions in accord with a commitment to equality of opportunity and to eliminating unlawful racial discrimination. However, where there are resource implications (which seems would inevitably apply to most situations), the duty is subject to rationing within the gambit of the local authorities' overall resource limitations. One resulting question – following the *Barry* case – which has not been considered by the courts, are the circumstances in which a local authority may fail to carry out a statutory duty due to limited resources – i.e. while choosing to spend available funds in an area that falls within discretionary powers. It may seem logical, on the basis of Lord Nicholls comment, to trust that such a decision could be challenged on Wednesbury unreasonable grounds. Indeed, support for this proposition can be gleaned from the comments of Lord Browne-Wilkinson, in the case of *R v East Sussex County Council ex parte Tandy*,[12] when he argued that a local authority in order to fulfil a statutory duty could, if it wished, divert money from other educational or other applications which were merely discretionary. In this case Lord Browne-Wilkinson distinguished the *Barry* case on the grounds that:

the statutory duty in *Barry* was to arrange certain benefits to meet the 'needs' of the disabled persons, but a lack of the benefits enumerated in the section could not possibly give rise to 'need' in any stringent sense of the word. The statute providing no guidance as to what were the criteria by which a need of an unusual kind was to be assessed ...

In comparison, in *Tandy*,

the council were not required to make any prior determination of Tandy's need for education nor of the necessity for making provision for such education. The state imposed an immediate obligation to make arrangements to provide suitable education. Moreover it then expressly defined what was meant by 'suitable education' by reference to wholly objective educational criteria.[13]

It is suggested this is an unfortunate if not irrational, distinction between the two cases. It suggests that where the statute clearly defines a statutory duty, with the use of objective criteria, that duty must be met. However, where the statute simply places a local authority under a statutory duty to investigate a 'need' and then to fulfil that 'need', they may have the discretion to leave some people's needs unmet? This is surely nonsensical because the purpose of the statute was to provide assistance to those in 'need'. The reason why the criteria is left open is because each case is required to be determined on its merit – due to a tremendous variety of 'needs' existing. Clearly an authority will be expected to prioritise within those 'needs' – but they should not be able to leave needs unmet – especially if they have determined that the need exists, and are simply choosing to leave the need unmet while spending resources elsewhere.

Duncan Forbes has proposed that the government should amend the Race Relations Act 1976 to impose a duty to use powers to eradicate racism and racial harassment. Forbes argues that this widened role should encompass a duty to monitor racial harassment and to adopt procedures for tackling it. He proposes minimum standards imposed by the Home Office, and the Department of the Environment, with wider powers given to the CRE to monitor such activities. He further suggests allowing individuals[14] a right to make a complaint to the county court for an agency's failure to comply with its statutory duty.[15] All this is fine, but following the decisions in *Barry* and *Tandy* the complainant may become embroiled in the difficult question of whether the local authority is acting with *Wednesbury unreasonableness*[16] in failing to carry out a statutory duty.[17] This question can only be fully answered if the authority can explain where it spends its resources, and why it may spend money in areas where it has a power to do so, while leaving unmet a statutory duty.[18] These issues relating to priorities and the spending of resources are surely decisions that any Court, let alone a County Court, may have tremendous difficulties in adjudicating upon. One answer, *on the basis of Tandy*, is for the legislators to provide clear objective guidance as to what duties and needs they require to be met.

Application of Section 71 Race Relations Act 1976

Even assuming that an authority has the will and resources to use its powers to tackle militant racism – it is clear, from the case of *Wheeler v Leicester City Council*,[19] that there are limitations upon the duty, which encompasses wide discretionary powers, which authorities have under Section 71.

Wheeler v Leicester City Council Leicester City Council was opposed to an English Rugby tour of South Africa, due to the support this implied for the apartheid regime. They were concerned that three players from Leicester Rugby Football Club were invited to join the national rugby team on its tour. Leicester City Council wrote to the Club asking them to reply to four questions:

1 did the Club support the Government opposition to the tour;

2 did the Club agree that the tour was an insult to a large proportion of the Leicester population;

3 will the Club press the Rugby Football Union to call off the tour;

4 will the Club press the players to pull out of the tour?

The Rugby Club replied that it agreed with the Council in condemning apartheid in South Africa, but that it could only advise its members and it was not unlawful for any member to join the tour. The Club did not answer any of the questions posed. The Council then passed a resolution banning the Club from using a Council-owned recreation ground for a period of twelve months. The Rugby Club sought to overturn this decision with both the High Court and Court of Appeal dismissing the application. However, the House of Lords unanimously allowed the appeal – essentially on grounds of procedure. It was held that the main purpose of Section 71 was for an authority, in relation to their various functions and exercising its discretion under statute, to pay regard to what it thought was in the best interests of race relations. However, the manner in which the Council had reached its decision was unfair. Having received a reply from the Club, the Council did not consider whether it was satisfactory, but instead passed a resolution banning the Rugby Club from use of the Recreation Club because affirmative answers had not been given to all four questions. Since the Club had done nothing unlawful, the Council could not use its statutory powers in order to punish the club. This did not mean that the Council was bound to allow its property to be used by racist organisations, or by any organisation, which by its actions or words infringed the letter or spirit of the Race Relations Act 1976 Act.

Implications of the Wheeler Case upon Section 71 Race Relations Act 1976

This important House of Lords' decision clearly suggests that correct procedure, consistent with the principles of natural justice, needs to be followed when local authorities reach decisions. Perhaps much wider than this, it suggests that in making its decisions, a local authority may need to show that it has taken into account its duty under Section 71. Indeed, if an authority completely fails to take account of Section 71 when reaching a decision, and has no mechanism for doing so, the decision could probably be successfully challenged in the courts.

Duncan Forbes argues that the *Wheeler v Leicester City Council* case provides grounds for withholding or withdrawing grants and discretionary facilities from organisations which:

1 are known to pursue unlawful practices including discrimination in employ-ment or in the delivery of services under the Race Relations Act 1976;

2 cannot show they are taking reasonable steps to ensure they do not discriminate or that racial harassment does not occur during activities over which they have some control;

3 have not established an equal opportunities policy;[20]

4 whose members are responsible for unlawful acts of racial harassment outside the organisation and which actively condone the acts.

Forbes also recognises that an authority would not be authorised, by Section 71, to withdraw grants and facilities when an organisation's members are responsible for unlawful acts of racial harassment outside of the organisation.

He argues that this also applies when the organisation fails to take steps to impose sanctions upon its members – or, because the organisation refuses to comply with a council's request to condemn racist views. However, Forbes does suggest that actions by the authority may be justified, by Section 71, if the organisation, whose members are responsible for unlawful acts or racial harassment outside the organisation, have no policy for dealing with such incidents and the organisation refuses to condemn acts of racial harassment.

Thus, a local authority may be able to use Section 71 of the Race Relations Act 1976 to persuade recipients of grants and discretionary facilities that they should follow an equal opportunities policy. However, they cannot expect that, in all circumstances, they must be forthright in declaring their opposition to racial harassment. Should reasonably prominent members of organisations, in receipt of grants or facilities, conduct potentially unlawful racist acts, or pursue policies inconsistent with good racial relations, it may be possible to insist that the organisation issue some form of statement condemning such acts.

To use another example which many local authorities face. On the basis of Section 71 of Race Relations Act 1976, it seems probable that a council could refuse to hire a hall to a political organization that it perceives as being racist – e.g. for one of its regular political meetings. The basis for this may exist where there is evidence of inconsistency between the council's equal opportunities policy and the declared aims of the racist organisation(s). However, authorities cannot refuse to make meeting halls available to political parties fielding candidates in an election.[21]

Action against Individual Perpetrators

While an authority may be able to deny organisations access to discretionary grants or facilities where they fail to show consistency with equality of opportunity, the position may be different concerning sanctions against individuals. If the authority provides the service to individuals under a statutory duty, it cannot be withheld unless the statute allows the conduct of the perpetrator to be taken into account.[22] However, where services are discretionary the authority is required to take into account Section 71 when it decides to provide a service. In doing so, it is important that the authority considers each case on its merits and does not fetter its discretion by applying a blanket policy. By way of example, this means that an authority could not refuse to provide education to a teenage activist prosecuted for racial harassment. The authority may, however, be able to deny him access to the school's youth club – e.g. provided the youth club is established under discretionary powers and the authority consider the decision to exclude on its merits.

Local Authorities and Legal Accountability

As I argued earlier in this chapter, a local authority has a statutory duty to eliminate unlawful racial discrimination and to promote equality of opportunity. This can involve various forms of action ranging from simply giving advice to victims of racial harassment to that of providing practical assistance such as fireproof letterboxes and rehousing. However, it is also important to recognise that having wide responsibilities does not mean local authorities are totally free to exercise their discretion with regards to the type of facilities they provide. All local authority decisions must be exercised in accord with the general principles of administrative law. For, without such, the validity and lawfulness of their actions may be challenged through judicial review or the invalidity of the decision may be used as a defence.[23]

The courts have identified three heads upon which they review the administrative acts of public bodies, including local authorities: (1) illegality; (2) irrationality; and (3) procedural impropriety.[24]

General principles of administrative law It is not the purpose of this book to consider in detail the principles of administrative law. However, it has relevance to the extent that it relates to decisions of public bodies in tackling militant racism. For these reasons I have identified, from the work of Duncan Forbes,[25] 14 general principles of administrative law relevant to this book.

1 The authority must have legal powers to make a decision. Given the statutory duty under Section 71 of the Race Relations Act 1976 it has already been demonstrated that an authority in carrying out its functions, must eliminate unlawful racial discrimination and promote equality of opportunity. As such, in general, it would give an authority powers to tackle incitement to/organised racial discrimination/militant racism.

2 The authority must have understood correctly the applicable legal powers and given effect to them.

3 The authority must act so as to promote and not to frustrate the policy and objects of the statute under which the decision is made.[26]

4 The authority must take into account all relevant matters before reaching a decision.[27]

5 The authority must disregard all irrelevant matters when making a decision.

6 The decision must not be made in bad faith or be dishonest.

7 The facts that form the basis of the decision must be correct and must provide a basis for the decision.[28]

8 The authority must not delegate decision making (i.e. if a local authority is given power by statute to make a decision it cannot adopt automatically the decision of some other person or body – e.g. a council cannot simply adopt automatically the decision of a political group).

9 The decision must be reached fairly in accord with natural justice.[29]

10 The decision must be made by full council – or by properly authorised committees/sub-committees/officers within the scope of their delegated authority.[30]

11 Any statutory procedural requirements must be followed.

12 The authority must not fetter its discretion (i.e. it must not refuse to exercise its discretion in an individual case by rigidly following a blanket policy).[31]

13 The decision must not be one to which no reasonable authority could reach.

14 Authorities must apply their policies consistently.[32]

Types of Anti-racist Actions a Local Authority could Undertake

In this section of this chapter, I will provide an indication of the type of activities that local authorities can take to tackle militant racism. It is not an exhaustive list. Indeed, requirements and activities will vary due to the specific demands of a particular person, problem or area. The purpose of this list is to briefly identify the type of actions local authorities can take, and quite frequently do take, when fulfilling a statutory duty and/or operating under discretionary powers. In undertaking these activities, as with all its activities, a local authority can (if the circumstances justify and a *prima facie* case exists) be open to judicial review. Their activities may also be subject to review by the Local Government Ombudsman or by the District Auditor.

- *Establishing a declaration against racism* This approach has been taken by the local authority in Hounslow and involves civic and community dignitaries – such as MPs, Councillors, Chief of Police, pop and football stars etc. – making a joint signed declaration against racism. This can be then posted at local authority locations such as schools and libraries, thereby demonstrating a common policy goal of opposing racism.

- *Offering practical assistance to victims of racial harassment* There are various ways that victims of racial harassment can be practically assisted. A local authority may provide mobile telephones, fireproof letterboxes, CCTV video surveillance etc.[33] Some of these practical steps may not only comfort the victim, but they can also save lives, with even a possibility that video cameras may deter crime. It is also possible that any film footage could be used as evidence.

- *Rehousing victims of racial harassment* Sometimes the racial harassment is such that a tenant suffering from racial harassment may need to be rehoused by the local authority. This approach has been taken in Hounslow, though it is clear this is very much a last resort solution, with the fear being that it may provide a victory for those committing the racial harassment. Despite such concerns, it may sometimes be better to move victims so that they can live nearer to friends and relatives.

- *Introduce a racial harassment clause into tenancy agreements* This issue will be discussed in more detail later in this chapter when I consider a local authority/landlord's ability to tackle militant racists. In simple terms, the insertion of a racial harassment clause into local authority tenancy agreements is a demonstration of intent to tackle problems of racial harassment. However, not only does it demonstrate that racial harassment is unacceptable, it also indicates that any violation of this clause can result in eviction from local authority housing.

- *'Rub-out racist graffiti' programme* In Hounslow the authority have established a 'Rub out Racism' hotline which consists of a place where the public can report racist graffiti. Once registered, the authority undertakes to try and remove the graffiti within 24 hours of it being reported. Obviously, they do not always succeed with this aim, but they do generally succeed in removing racist graffiti from their own premises within this period of time. This programme also involves officers working with owners of private property to try and encourage them to remove racist graffiti. In addition, the Chief Executive has written to all council staff instructing them that racism will not be tolerated and priority must be given to removing racist graffiti.

- *Establishing an Equal Opportunities Committee* A number of authorities now have Equal Opportunities Committees so that they can monitor their equal opportunities programmes. In Hounslow, the authority have established a subcommittee which forms a 'Racial Harassment Forum' where organisations, representing ethnic minority interests, meet and discuss problems of racism. At times, this may involve victims of racism appearing before the Forum relaying their specific experiences and seeking support or assistance from the authority. At these Forums, most of which are held behind closed doors, victims of racial harassment may discuss housing and evidential issues – with legal officers being present to monitor and advise on appropriate courses of action. Because of the confidential nature of the Forum it is difficult to be certain as to whether this approach is successful. However, elected members and officers from Hounslow Council generally appear to value this approach and the continued involvement of ethnic based organisations, such as the Hounslow Monitoring Project, does suggest some confidence in its workings.

- *Provide equal opportunities training for staff*[34] All good employers provide staff training. Many local authorities are keen to ensure that staff understand and follow the local authority equal opportunities policy. Over recent years equal opportunities policies have tended to become more detailed and less restricted to just issues of sex and race discrimination. This approach makes a great deal of sense given that discrimination law has now moved on to important areas such as disability.[35] It may also be the case that local authorities have a specific local definition of equal opportunities[36] that also includes issues of age, homophobia and religious discrimination. Clearly, a local definition of equal opportunities which expands that provided by statute will generally have only moral rather than legal force. However, where it forms the basis of a contractual agreement – such as a tenancy agreement – it should be possible to rely upon this definition when issues of contractual breach arise.[37] For these and other reasons it can be very important to ensure that staff are familiar with, and live up to, the authority's equal opportunities policy. As such, training can be very important.

- *Set up a committee, or mechanism, for police liaison* As a result of Section 6 of the Crime and Disorder Act 1998 a local authority, along with the chief officer of police whose police area is within the council's area, now has a statutory duty to establish a 'crime and disorder strategy'.[38] While the Act is not specific, it is clear that this must include a strategy for tackling racist crime. Indeed, this is consistent with the moral obligation to work with the police to establish a joint approach to tackling racial attacks and harassment which came out of the recommendations of the 1985/6 report of the Home Affairs Select Committee on racial harassment.

  While the 1998 Act sets up a formal arrangement it is clear that in the past the arrangements for a multi-agency approach have been both formal and informal, often depending upon the local arrangements. In the London Borough of Hounslow the approach has often been informal due to the role played by the Racial Harassment Forum. Indeed, the police used to attend the early meetings of the Forum, but representatives of organisations (like the Hounslow Monitoring Project) have argued that police presence at these public forums inhibits the freedom of expression of victims and their witnesses.[39] Thus, the local authority has decided to withdraw an open invitation to the police to these forum meetings. Clearly the police, in informal interviews, have expressed a desire to be involved – but they do respect the wishes of the local authority and they continue to work at officer level in tackling the issues.

- *Provide grants to organisations that seek to eliminate racism* While a local authority is under a statutory duty to promote equality of opportunity, it can decide upon the most suitable and indeed most cost-effective way of fulfilling this duty. One approach which a number of authorities take, is to work with voluntary groups by referring people to them so that they can obtain a specific type of assistance. They may also provide a grant to such organisations to enable them to carry out their functions. An example of this can be found in Hounslow with the support given to the Hounslow Monitoring Project – which enjoys funding to provide staff to tackle problems of racial harassment. Another less obvious example is the financial support given to the Citizens Advice Bureaux and Law Centres within the Borough. Many of these organisations, while using trained volunteers to undertake advisory work, provide a valuable service to people suffering racial harassment. The support can vary from assistance with filling in forms to legal advice and assistance. Many of these organisations depend upon the financial support of local authorities to carry out their tasks.

- *Using grants to develop equal opportunities in other organisations* Early in this chapter under the heading 'Implications of the *Wheeler* Case upon Section 71 of Race Relation Act 1976', I discussed the legal limitations upon a council's ability to withdraw grants from organisations that act inconsistently with the authority's own equal opportunities policy. As this discussion shows, a local authority has significant powers to encouraging organisations to which they are considering giving grants, to establish equal opportunities programmes and, where appropriate, to have a constitution which reflects this aim. Indeed, following the *Wheeler* case they may have reasonable grounds for refusing grants to organisations whose constitution contradicts equal opportunities.

- *The teaching of equal opportunities in schools* In carrying out its function under the Education Act 1944, a local authority has a legal duty to provide education for all children of school age. In carrying out this duty, and as a supplier of educational grants and services to local authority schools, a local authority is under a statutory obligation – via Section 71 of Race Relations Act 1976 – to promote equality of opportunity and eliminate unlawful discrimination. As we discussed earlier in this chapter, an authority may have discretion as to how it carries out this duty – but it remains a duty it is legally obliged to fulfil.[40] Indeed, the MacPherson Report into the murder of Stephen Lawrence recommended that consideration be given to amending the National Curriculum so as to value cultural diversity and prevent racism. In Hounslow, the local authority have encouraged schools to participate in the Heartstone Project, which is designed to educate young children on the consequences of racial harassment and school bullying. While it is difficult to be certain that such forms of anti-racist education are successful, it seems likely that, as with all education, it will have some impact upon the minds of young children. If this form of education only makes children aware of the issue and encourages them to think twice before becoming involved in such group activity, then it must be of value.

The Use of Injunctions to Tackle Militant Racism

Section 222 of the Local Government Act 1972 provides:

> Where a local authority considers it expedient for the promotion or protection of the interests of the inhabitants of their area they may prosecute or defend or appear in any legal proceedings and, in the case of civil proceedings, may institute them in their own name.

It follows that in any legal proceedings involving a local authority, they must be able to show they consider it expedient for the promotion or protection of the inhabitants of their area. They must also be able to justify their action as falling within the *general principles of administrative law*.

It is clear that Section 222 does provide powers for an authority to obtain an injunction restraining an identified perpetrator of nuisance or trespass from continued activity.[41] In order to obtain an injunction there must be an arguable civil case with the question of whether or not to grant an injunction, being at the discretion of the judge – 'on the balance of convenience'.[42] In cases involving racial harassment, the request for an injunction could be heard ex parte – with a general expectation that the balance of convenience would fall in favour of an applicant who is trying to prevent continued harassment. However, the discretion whether or not to grant an injunction rests with the judge and will be dependent upon the facts and issues of law.

The advantages of a seeking an injunction are that the burden of proof is limited to that of a balance of probability, with the person(s) named in the injunction being made aware that should they act in breach of its terms, they could face a charge of contempt. Indeed, such contempt of court can be punishable by imprisonment or a fine[43] – i.e. subject to proof, beyond reasonable doubt, of wilful and repeated disobedience of an order of the court.[44] These evidential requirements being necessary because the defendant could face a term of imprisonment for what is legally a contempt of court, but may in practice be a continued breach of civil law.

However, two disadvantages exist so far as injunctions are concerned. The first is that a breach of a civil injunction does not provide the police with immediate grounds of arrest for contempt. Indeed, the person (or in the case of a local authority, the authority) who obtained the injunction must generally go back to the civil courts with sufficient evidence to prove the contempt. Only then, on instructions from the court, can the police formally take action in relation to the contempt.[45] A second (and major) disadvantage, as far as tackling racial harassment is concerned, is that those committing acts of militant racism rarely act alone – they act as part of a group. It follows that while an injunction has legal force against those named, it only has indirect force upon a third party in circumstances whereby they aid and abet to break the court's injunction. In *Z Ltd v A–Z Ltd and AA–LL (Court of Appeal Case)*[46] Eveleigh LJ remarked:

> A third party who knowingly assists in a breach [and wilfulness is required] is liable for a contempt of court by himself. It is true that his conduct may very often be seen as possessing a dual character of contempt of court by himself and aiding and abetting the court by another, but the conduct will always amount to contempt of court by itself.

Indeed in 1897 it was said, in *Seaward v Patterson*,[47] that a third party is guilty of a criminal contempt since he is not party to the original action but is really impeding the court of justice. Despite such a legal position it is clear that any breach must be proved beyond reasonable doubt, with *wilful and repeated disobedience of an order of the court* generally a requirement. Indeed, in *Z Ltd v A–Z Ltd and AA–LL* the dictum of Eveleigh LJ indicates that judges, in dealing with contempt of an injunction by third parties, should consider whether they can be shown to have been 'contumacious' – which requires not just wilfulness, but insubordination *and* stubborn or wilful disobedience.

This clearly emphasises that courts will require a high level of proof before they are prepared to find a third party as being in contempt of an injunction. However, while these evidential requirements may seem onerous, they must be regarded as necessary given the fact that the case could result in imprisonment or a fine.

Obviously, such evidential requirements highlight that an injunction may not always be an ideal weapon to use in tackling racial harassment by a group of racists – particularly if the identity of many members of the group is unknown. Simply identifying and serving an injunction upon a few members from a group may not sufficiently deter the unknown committed group members (and any like-minded racist friends) from undertaking further harassment or attack. This particularly applies given that the victim of racial harassment will want the harassment to stop. As such, s/he is unlikely to be happy with the local authority pursuing a civil approach that requires further, and possibly repeated, harassment before further grounds for action may exist.

Despite such comment, these reservations should not be interpreted as meaning that injunctions might serve no purpose in tackling militant racism.

On the contrary, they can be valuable where there exists a neighbour dispute with racism a prominent issue. An injunction could also be of value in circumstances where the authority acts, as landlord, on behalf of tenants to tackle an identifiable group of racist individuals by restricting their trespass to an estate.[48] In such circumstances, the authority could seek the consent of the court to limit the identity of tenants (who are victims of harassment) who produce evidential statements.[49] In this way, it may be possible to reduce the potentiality of reprisal attacks.

Section 222 could also enable the authority to appear in civil proceedings, being brought by a victim of racial harassment – thereby giving additional support to the argument that racial harassment is unacceptable.[50] They could also help fund the cost of a victim's civil injunctive proceedings.

Various Types of Injunctions

There are various types of injunctions, with some more likely to succeed than others. For example, an authority should be able to obtain an injunction to restrain a tenant from breaching a tenancy agreement.[51] This could apply where a tenant was harassing a neighbour in contravention of a specific nuisance or racial harassment clause within the tenancy agreement.

Another form of injunction would be to prevent nuisance or trespass. This can be of value in dealing with neighbours and identifiable people visiting the area to undertake act(s) of militant racism. In making a decision to grant an injunction, the courts will generally consider the following points:

- whether damages are an appropriate remedy;[52]

- the motive of the perpetrator;[53]

- the behaviour of the authority;[54]

- the interests of the public;[55]

- whether the act is likely to be repeated.[56]

Obviously each case will need to be considered on its merits with the court balancing the advantage of the injunction with any detriment the respondent perpetrator may suffer. However, in cases involving racial harassment damages may not be an adequate remedy. The motive of the perpetrator will always be malicious and the public interest would suggest granting an injunction, as there will generally be a risk of repetition. In practice, injunctions are always subject to the discretion of the judge, though the court's may have limited grounds for refusing an injunction in this type of case because of the court's presumption that a person is entitled to prevent a trespass to his property. Though, they could choose to do so if they felt inclined to accept a written undertaking from the perpetrator of such acts that he would not undertake any further acts.

Injunctions for Nuisance on the Highway

The Highways Act (1980) gives local authorities specific powers to take action to protect and assert the public's right to use the highway. This includes a responsibility to prevent any obstruction of the highway that is prejudicial to the area[57] – this will include the ability to act to prevent a public nuisance on the highway. Public nuisance on the highway has been defined as 'any wrongful act or omission upon or near a highway, whereby the public are prevented from freely and conveniently passing along the highway'.[58] This very definition, by itself, emphasises the freedom of the public to pass along the highway and it is for these reasons that injunctions, which may interfere with such freedom, are not readily obtainable – i.e. without providing some firm evidence of a public nuisance which amounts to an 'unreasonable user'.[59] By way of example, it may be that it would be possible for an authority to use powers under the highway legislation to prevent the distribution of racist literature outside school gates,[60] or where racists, are congregating on a highway and harassing ethnic people living on an estate.[61]

In many ways some of the laws which have been used to deal with trade disputes may be applicable. For example, in the case of *Thomas v NUM (South Wales)*,[62] Scott J, in granting an interlocutory injunction, held that regular picketing of the home of a working miner, regardless of the number of people involved and regardless of the peaceful nature of their conduct, would constitute a common law nuisance. It surely follows that this principle should equally apply to a group of militant racists harassing people living on an estate. Although, as remarked by Lord Denning in *Hubbard v Pitt*[63] while using discretion to reject an application for an interlocutory injunction, if the grievance of a complainant is about the placards and leaflets they may not succeed due to a desire to respect freedom of expression. Interestingly, in *Hubbard v Pitt*, reference was made to the 'undoubted right of Englishmen to assemble together for the purposes of deliberating upon public grievances'.[64]

Racial Picketing

In many ways it may seem surprising that militant racists have not adopted the picketing strategy of trade unionists in some kind of 'Jobs for Whites' campaign. Any picketing by militant racists, protesting that an organisation employ a number of black or ethnic workers while white indigenous workers are on the dole, would undoubtedly appeal to the xenophobic tendencies of some sections of the media and public. Should they do so, it seems likely that the *Code of Practice on Picketing* (1992) would not be applicable since it is specifically designed to deal with trade disputes. Of course any form of 'racial picketing' would not attract the same protection under the law that legitimate trade disputes may possess.[65] Indeed, it could result in the plaintiff organisation seeking to bring an *interference with contract*[66] or *trade or business*[67] action against the pickets. Assuming a legal action is commenced, it may be relatively easy for the organisation to apply to the courts for an injunction to stop the picketing with the primary question being that of balance of convenience.[68] Though, of course, whether an injunction is granted is always a discretionary matter that may be indirectly influenced by the peaceful nature, or otherwise, of the racial picketing,[69] and whether or not unlawful means are used.[70] However, as I shall consider under the next heading the fact that any words, leaflets or placards, may be inducing an organisation[71] to act in contravention of the Race Relations Act 1976 must display the potential for establishing unlawful means.

Liability for Inducement of a Breach of a Statutory Duty?

One area where I consider that an interlocutory injunction is a remote possibility is with regards to the inducement of a local authority to breach its statutory duty under Section 71 of the Race Relations Act 1976. The general potential for this form of liability was first raised in *Meade v Haringey London Borough Council*[72] which was a case that involved plaintiff parents arguing that by closing a school during a caretakers' strike, the Education Authority was in breach of a statutory duty to provide education. While the Court declined to apply the interlocutory junction on these grounds it would have had the effect of making the unions liable for inducing the authority to breach its duty. For this to apply, according to *Deakin and Morris*,[73] the statutory duty must be independently actionable at the suit of the plaintiff.

Clearly, each incident would therefore depend upon the facts of a particular case – but it is difficult to imagine the circumstances where groups could be directly liable.[74] For example, although the local authority is under a statutory obligation to promote equality of opportunity, and racial tolerance, it is hard to imagine that any Court would readily wish to prevent a political party from campaigning in relation to the *discretionary* application of this statutory duty. Logically, much would depend upon the form of protest and whether or not there was interference by unlawful means.[75] Indeed, the requirement for unlawful means is surely necessary in order to keep the tort liability within manageable limits and the central principle, established in *Allen v Flood*,[76] that an act lawful in itself is not converted by a bad or malicious motive into an unlawful act leading to civil liability.

As discussed earlier, unlawful means can consist of trespass, nuisance, etc. However, if in conducting 'racial picketing' words are used which are calling upon the local authority to abandon its equal opportunities policy, there may be potential for establishing unlawful means in light of a breach of Section 31 of the Race Relations Act 1976. This could apply, depending upon the facts, because those picketing could be held to be inducing, or attempting to induce a person[77] to do any act that contravenes Part II of Part III of the Race Relations Act – i.e. to refuse to carry out a statutory duty. The persons being induced are elected members and officials responsible for the policy of the authority.

Injunctions in Relation to Criminal Offences

It may, in certain circumstances, also be possible for a local authority to seek an injunction to prevent the commission of a criminal offence. This extraordinary power, under Section 222 of the Local Government Act 1972, is rarely used and has only been applied in the specific circumstances of nominal fines being unlikely to deter the activity of commercial organisations.

An obvious example of the type of use of this injunctive power under Section 222, can be found in the way that local authorities have obtained injunctions against large companies in order to obtain fulfilment of the Sunday trading laws. A nominal fine of a few hundred pounds is hardly a deterrent to a company that may make huge profits from continued trading. The use of an injunction, in these circumstances, means that any breach technically results in a contempt of court – with potential serious consequences for the offender. The logic behind these injunctions is being one of providing a preventive remedy where fines fail to act as a deterrent. It follows that it must be unlikely an injunction would be granted for racial harassment – given that the police possess powers of arrest and any culprit brought before the courts could face a term of imprisonment.[78]

Appearance in Proceedings

Section 222 of the Local Government Act 1972 states that a local authority 'may … appear in any legal proceedings'. Forbes argues this phrase is open to two possible interpretations:

- that an authority can take part in proceedings in the same way as an individual, e.g. when joined as a third party in proceedings;

- that an authority may appear in proceedings to represent the local public interest.

It would seem that the phrase has not been considered in any decisions. However, a narrow interpretation of the powers under Section 222 would mean that an authority could only appear in proceedings of which it was directly interested. A wider interpretation means that local authorities have similar powers to that of the Attorney General who may appear in any proceedings with leave of the court to put forward the government's views on public policy.[79]

As Duncan Forbes persuasively argues, the 1972 Act gives no clue as to why the word 'appear' was included in the 1972 Act when it had not been included in the 1933 Act, from which Section 222 originated. Section 222 clearly provides local authorities with wider powers than those enjoyed by private citizens. As such, it is reasonable to argue that Section 222 does provide a local authority with powers to intervene in other proceedings. This would mean that a local authority might have power to appear in any civil or criminal proceedings involving acts of militant racism. This could have the advantage of ensuring the local public interest is placed before the court.

Section 222 also provides: 'Where a local authority considers it expedient for the promotion or protection of the interests of the inhabitants of their area, they may prosecute or defend or appear in any legal proceedings'. This clearly suggests that a local authority could bring a criminal prosecution, albeit that it is primarily the duty of the police to enforce the law, with criminal prosecutions being undertaken by the Crown Prosecution Service.

While a local authority may possess powers to bring a criminal prosecution, it would be advisable for them first to put all the available evidence before the police and invite them to investigate and try to persuade the Crown Prosecution Service to bring proceedings. To do otherwise, could be regarded as wasteful of local taxpayer funds.

However, where there exists a police policy of issuing cautions, or giving lower priority to certain types of crimes, it could be that a criminal prosecution by the authority would be justified. This though, could result in the Director of the Crown Prosecution Service making a decision, under Section 6(2) of the Prosecution of Offences Act 1985, to take over such a prosecution. One of the consequences of so doing, may be that the DPP then withdraws the case.[80] It surely follows that criminal proceedings by a local authority are unlikely to serve the purpose of obtaining a successful prosecution i.e. unless the CPS decides not to intervene, or, if they do so, they continue with the prosecution and obtain a conviction. Perhaps one advantage of a decision by a local authority to bring a prosecution is that because of its novelty, it would bring pressure to bear upon the police and/or Crown Prosecution Service to give a greater priority to certain types of cases (e.g. prosecute instead of giving cautions).

Prevention from Eviction Act 1977

One area where a local authority is given specific powers to prosecute a criminal offence is under the Prevention from Eviction Act 1977.[81] Although the Act is self evidently designed to deal with unlawful eviction and harassment of occupiers of housing, presumably by their landlord and/or agents. The terms of Section 1(3) provide:

> If any person with intent to cause the residential occupier of any premises:
>
> (a) to give up the occupation of the premises or any part thereof; or
> (b) to refrain from exercising any right or pursuing any remedy in respect of the premises or part thereof; does acts likely to interfere with the peace or comfort of the residential occupier or members of his household ...

For example, in situations where an identified perpetrator scrawls racist graffiti on the door of a Pakistani resident, a local authority could have powers to prosecute. This is because the words used by the perpetrator go some way towards helping to establish the required specific intent[82] to cause the occupier to give up the occupation of the premises. Any prosecutions brought under Section 1(3) of this legislation should be tried summarily with a term of imprisonment not exceeding six months, and/or a fine, or on indictment to a fine or to imprisonment for a term not exceeding two years or both.[83] Should a local authority decide to prosecute using this PEA legislation, Section 222 of the Local Government Act 1972 may also enable a prosecution for criminal damage based upon the same facts of racist graffiti. Indeed, in these circumstances, it may be appropriate for a local authority to bring criminal proceedings in an area (i.e. criminal damage) which would normally involve action by the police and Crown Prosecution Service.

Cooper and Qureshi[84] have indicated that local authority lawyers are reluctant to take action against racist perpetrators via the Protection from Eviction Act 1977 because of problems of proof, the reluctance of the courts to convict, and the lack of any protection it affords to victims against reprisals.[85]

This view may be oversimplistic due to the fact that lawyers are always likely to be hesitant about bringing prosecutions which require proof beyond reasonable doubt, in circumstances where the *mens rea* requirement is likely to be difficult to establish. This difficulty is made all the more problematic due to an understandable expectancy that the courts are unlikely to find guilt where an expected motive behind the legislation is not evident. This situation arises due to the fact that parliament clearly designed the Protection from Eviction legislation to deal with the unscrupulous landlord or his agent. It seems clear this legislation was not intended to deal with racial harassment undertaken by individual militant racists, and a question could well be asked, unconsciously or otherwise, as to why the police have not decided to use the new public order offence of harassment.

Given such anticipated difficulties of establishing guilt beyond reasonable doubt, local authority lawyers may be understandably reluctant to have to justify a 'racial harassment' prosecution as being: (a) expedient for the promotion or protection of the interests of the inhabitants of their area;[86] and (b) a reasonable use of local taxpayers' money. Indeed, bearing all this in mind and the financial pressures on local authorities, it is hardly surprising the local authority may prefer to liaise with the police to encourage their activity.[87]

One interesting aspect of a prosecution under the Prevention from Eviction Act 1977 is that Section 1(6) enables prosecution of a body corporate. This applies in circumstances where the body is vicariously liable for the actions of its employees. However, given that certain militant racist organisations are not body corporate it seems they could not be prosecuted under this legislation – thus would especially apply since they employ very few staff with most of the activity being undertaken by activists.

New Powers under the Crime and Disorder Act 1998

One area in which local authorities will have some clear and reasonably precise powers is that provided under Part 1 of the Crime and Disorder Act 1998. Under Section 1 of this Act a local authority has powers to apply to the Magistrates Court for an antisocial behaviour order in circumstances where it appears to the authority that a person (aged 10 or over) has acted in an antisocial manner, that is to say in a manner that caused or was likely to cause harassment alarm or distress to two or more persons not of the same household as himself.[88] The Act itself is not specific on the standard of proof required, but since the order is prohibitive it seems the Home Office expects that magistrates will determine whether a defendant has acted in a manner that has caused or was likely to cause harassment, alarm and distress on the balance of probability – i.e. unless the defendant can show that his act was reasonable in the circumstances.[89] Should the magistrates grant this 'antisocial behaviour order', it will have effect for a period of not less than two years. Should a person, without reasonable excuse, do anything that is prohibited by the 'antisocial behaviour order' he will then be liable for up to six months' imprisonment/ and or a fine on summary conviction and up to five years imprisonment/and or a fine on indictment.

While these new powers have not yet been fully tested in the courts,[90] it seems possible that local authorities will work with the police where known militant racists are active within the community. It may be possible for police officers to appear in court, as background witnesses, supporting local authority applications for antisocial behaviour orders. Likewise, where a known militant racist is charged before the Magistrates Court for matters like harassment, or even criminal damage arising from graffiti, we may see the local authority indirectly supporting the Crown's evidence by seeking an 'antisocial behaviour order' in an effort to influence the individual's future community behaviour.

A Local Authority/Landlords Ability to Tackle Militant Racists

One area where local authorities possess notable powers to tackle militant racism is in their responsibility as a landlord. These powers can be used to both assist victims of racial harassment and to invoke action against perpetrators of militant racism in circumstances where they are council tenants.

Eviction of Racists

As a landlord, a local authority can seek to influence the racist behaviour of tenants by education, persuasion, and by taking practical and even legal steps.[91]

For example, it is usual for landlords to include within tenancy agreements, a 'noise or nuisance to other tenants' clause – and it is certainly within the powers of a housing authority to include within its tenancy agreements terms and conditions designed to prevent racial harassment.[92]

One obvious advantage of a racial harassment clause, within a tenancy agreement, is that it educates tenants by giving notice that racial harassment is unacceptable and could lead to eviction.[93] As discussed earlier, it may also assist in providing the opportunity, where appropriate, for the authority to seek an injunction prohibiting future harassment.

Obviously an express clause within a tenancy agreement can provide grounds for possession[94] in circumstances where it is breached. However, this is not decided on simple contractual notice terms, but subject to proof that it is reasonable for the court to make an order for possession.[95] Indeed, it is possible to seek possession on the grounds of 'nuisance or annoyance'[96] even if there are no express clauses in the tenancy agreement.[97] It is also possible to extend the liability of the tenant to hold them responsible for the nuisance or annoyance by members of the family living with him or her.

For example, Hounslow Council has incorporated a clause within their tenancy agreements that specifically refers to racial harassment.[98] Should the Council seek to obtain possession specifically on grounds of a breach of this clause they would need to establish that the motive for the harassment was racial (or on grounds of sex, age, religion etc.). As will be discussed in the later chapter that deals with racial motive[99] – there can be significant problems in establishing motive because it involves reading the mind of the defendant. To this end, the authority may wish to seek possession on general grounds of a breach of nuisance or annoyance – where motive is not a necessary factor. It should still be possible to argue that the racial motive behind the nuisance is an aggravating factor supporting a possession order.[100]

While a housing authority may apply to the courts for possession, it is important to reflect that success cannot be judged upon the granting of an order. For example, it may be that, in any proceedings, the defendant tenant gives an undertaking that they will cease any further nuisance.[101] It may also be the case that the court, finding in favour of the authority, gives a suspended order for possession.[102] This situation arises when a tenant is allowed to remain in his/her home provided that s/he complies with any conditions imposed. In many ways, this may be regarded as a successful outcome since it signifies to the troublesome tenant that any continuance of the behaviour will enable the authority to apply for an immediate warrant of possession should the conditions be breached.[103]

Homelessness

Local authorities may not only have responsibility as a landlord but they are also likely to be under a legal duty to provide accommodation for the homeless. This can raise problems for local authorities that have succeeded with an eviction of a tenant. While the courts may grant possession of one property – the authority may find themselves with immediate responsibility to provide some form of accommodation for that same tenant.

Taking the example of the 'Silvester' family evicted in Hounslow for, *inter alia*, racial harassment. The local authority, in an effort to declare their opposition to racial harassment, sought publicity over the eviction. In doing so, the authority declared: 'They are deemed to be intentionally homeless so we don't have any intention of rehousing them'. Despite this understandable press statement Hounslow Council, as a housing authority, may have a statutory duty to fulfil a housing 'priority need' to categories of persons who are *homeless*. Clearly, this does not mean they must provide accommodation – but it does mean they must consider the merits of any application. The extent of preference given is discretionary and factors such as dependent children/pregnancy etc. must be taken into account and may even convert the application to one of priority.[104] What an authority cannot do is fetter its discretion by applying a blanket rule that a person evicted via court proceedings is intentionally homeless.[105] Indeed, any such blanket rule suggests a breach of the *general principles of administrative law* and could be open to challenge through the courts.[106]

In reality, this can mean that a tenant/family evicted for racial harassment may be able to show just cause for housing assistance from the local authority. This may result in a housing authority having an 'interim duty' to accommodate – often in 'temporary', private sector, bed and breakfast accommodation – while issues of need and liability are determined.[107] To this extent, eviction of militant racist tenants may not always be a desirable solution – due to the taxpayer being likely to have to pay for the financial cost of expensive alternative housing accommodation. It follows, therefore, that eviction should only be taken as a last resort – i.e. when all other means have failed and, despite various warnings, the racist activity continues. Certainly, eviction of tenants who themselves committed acts of racial harassment may be necessary.

Racism by Children

Despite some limited support for the eviction of racist tenants, there may be moral concerns about the occasionally applied practice of evicting tenants because of the racist activities of their children – with children as young as three reported, by the police, as being involved in racial harassment.[108]

An example of child racism, and the response of a local authority, can best by demonstrated by considering a news story from the *Feltham Chronicle*.[109] This story explains how Hounslow Council is prepared to take eviction proceedings against families where the children have been identified as perpetrators of racial harassment.[110] It seems that a group of seven children, aged between six and eleven who all go to the same school, have been held responsible for the racial harassment of two tenants living on a Feltham estate – with this leading to Hounslow Council speaking to the parents and publicly asserting:

> Parents are responsible for their children's actions and if children are harassing people, their parents will be called to interview to discuss their actions. If the harassment continues, and assuming the parents are council tenants, they may be in breach of their tenancy. They would then be given a chance to put matters right, but if the harassment continued it could lead to legal action [and/] or eviction.

Clearly, the local authority is acting within its powers – both in taking up the actions of the children with their parents and in deciding to take possession proceedings.[111] One possible alternative to using powers of eviction, is to use Social Services' powers in relation to child protection, with the argument existing that a child involved in racial harassment attacks is 'at risk and likely to suffer significant harm'.[112] Obviously, this kind of approach to tackling child racism may be open to challenge[113] via judicial review,[114] although the local authority could defend its position on the basis that while carrying out its child protection function[115] it remains under a statutory duty[116] to eliminate unlawful racial discrimination.

One advantage of using child protection powers to tackle child racism is that all children, irrespective of whether their parents live in the private sector or are council tenants, can be treated alike. What is more, it is not about punishment but about working in partnership with the family and the school[117] to address the problem.

On grounds of morality the use of eviction powers in relation to child racists seems wrong, simply because it treats those that live in rented accommodation differently from those whose parents own their property. Another option – which prevents discrimination on the basis of social background – would be to use the new powers under Section 1 of the Crime and Disorder Act 1998 to obtain an antisocial behaviour order in the circumstances where racial harassment is evident and the child is aged 10 or older.[118] In addition, it should be noted that Section 34 of the Crime and Disorder Act 1998 abolishes the presumption of *doli incapax*,[119] resulting in children under 10 being regarded as not criminally responsible, whilst those over 10 are.[120] This means that children, as young as ten, could face criminal proceedings for any illegal acts, though in practice they may initially be given a reprimand and/or warning by the police as per Section 65 of the Act.[121]

In Conclusion

A local authority has a multiplicity of functions ranging from schooling to responsibility for cemeteries. However, in carrying out its functions – some of which it carries out under a discretionary power and others under a statutory duty – it has a statutory duty to eliminate racial discrimination while promoting equality of opportunity and good relations between persons of different races. I have described this duty as a key function of a local authority – in the sense that all other functions must be carried out with this in mind.

In this chapter I have considered the various activities, powers and duties a local authority can use to tackle racism. Possibly, the problem giving most concern must be the reports of children, some as young as three, being involved in racial harassment. Obviously, the criminal law has only limited value so far as child racist activity is concerned, with other measures more likely to be appropriate. However, I have expressed moral concerns about local authorities using eviction powers in cases involving child racism, preferring instead the use of child protection procedures. At least this way the authorities could work with the parents – instead of punishing them and the rest of the family – when tackling the problem. This form of solution may also require some form of anti-racist education at the children's schools.

I have also suggested that the statutory duty, under Section 71 of the Race Relations Act 1976, should be more fully defined – agreeing with Duncan Forbes that the duty should encompass a requirement to monitor racial harassment and to adopt procedures for tackling it. Forbes proposes minimum standards being imposed by the Home Office, and Department of the Environment, with wide powers for the Commission for Racial Equality to monitor such activities. I have agreed with this argument, but have reservations about providing a complaint mechanism to the County Court for an agency's failure to comply with its statutory duty. My reservations in this area, stem from the *Gloucestershire County Council Case* which signifies that a lack of resources may be an adequate defence for not fulfilling a particular statutory duty. To this end, it is my submission that along with a statutory duty there should be some ring fencing of finance, possibly performance related, in order to ensure that a duty is fulfilled. At least this way, it may be easier for the courts to determine whether or not an authority is acting in accord with its statutory duty.

In this chapter, I have highlighted a few of the actions local authorities have taken, and could take, to tackle militant racism – though it is clear they may be able to do more if central government tied finance to the statutory duty. Future chapters of this book will examine issues of racial motivation and how to tackle militant racism by introducing some amendments to the public order legislation – at the same time we may come across other examples of local authority action.

Notes

1   *Racial Attacks and Harassment*, Third Report, Session 1993–4, Vol. 1, p. XV.
2   It was noted in the *Racial Attacks and Harassment* report that a project in the Hounslow Division of the Metropolitan Police has been successful in this regard.
3   This practice has been followed in a joint project between Leicester City Council and Leicestershire County Council.
4   Many of these voluntary groups may also be dependent on local authority funding to carry out their work. An example of which is the Hounslow Monitoring Project discussed later in this chapter.
5   An example of this is the duty imposed under Section 2 of the Chronically Sick and Disabled Persons Act 1970 to assess and where necessary make arrangements to provide for those categorised as being in need. However, following the House of Lords' decision in *R v Gloucestershire CC and the Secretary of State ex parte Barry* [http://www.parliament. the-stationary-office.co.uk (21–3–97)] a local authority is entitled to take into account its available resources in deciding to provide such services. In a majority judgement, Lord Nicholls suggested that in the event of a local authority acting with Wednesbury unreasonableness a disabled person would have a remedy. This principle must equally apply to all statutory duties. The *Gloucestershire* case will be discussed more fully later in this chapter.
6   Some examples of the introduction of functions can be found in legislation such as the Education Act 1944 and the Chronically Sick and Disabled Persons Act 1970. However, it would be very difficult to provide a full list of local authority functions since they may vary from authority to authority – though it is reasonable to suggest they can range from a duty to provide schooling to a responsibility for cemeteries.
7   Ian Loveland (*Constitutional Law – A Critical Introduction*, Butterworths, 1996, p. 393) claims that the multi-functional nature of local authority powers was well established in the 1990s.

8 It is only really since 1979 that there has been a central government desire to limit or reduce the functions of local authorities, with opting out of schools but one example of a more recent approach.

9 *R v Gloucestershire County Council and the Secretary of State for Health ex parte Barry.*

10 Under Section 2 of the Chronically Sick and Disabled Persons Act 1970.

11 Via Section 2 of the Chronically Sick and Disabled Persons Act 1970.

12 *The Times Law Reports*, 21 May 1998. This House of Lords case resulted in a 16 year old girl having her home tuition restored after a local authority had cut her tuition hours due to financial pressures.

13 *R v East Sussex CC ex p. Tandy*, case report *NLJ* [1998] 781.

14 Possibly with CRE assistance.

15 In the same manner as a complaint can currently be made of discrimination.

16 This was suggested by Lord Nicholls in the *Gloucestershire County Council* case.

17 There may also be the difficult question of whether or not an authority has fully carried out its duty, or has mitigated its liability by partly carrying it out so far as resources allow.

18 This may become an especially difficult argument given the issues of ring fencing etc.

19 [1985] 2 All ER 1106, HL.

20 Before any grant is given, Hounslow Council requires a tenants' association or voluntary group to have an equal opportunities policy statement within their constitution.

21 As per Section 95 of the Representation of the Peoples Act 1983. The purpose of this section is to facilitate the holding of a public meeting during an election. However, it may be possible for an authority to deny use of a meeting hall if they have proof that only a section of the public may be allowed access. This could especially apply if the meeting was for party members or was restricted to ticket holders only.

22 e.g. where a perpetrator is homeless and applying for housing.

23 *Wandsworth LBC v Winder* [1985] AC 461. This case involved Wandsworth Council suing tenants for nonpayment of rent and the tenants raising the defence that rent increases raised by the Council were *ultra vires*.

24 *Council of Civil Service Unions and others v Minister for Civil Service* [1984] 3 All ER 935, HL. For fuller consideration of judicial review and the general principles of administrative law see Oliver, D., *Government in the United Kingdom*, Open University Press, 1991, ch. 7; Bradley and Ewing, *Constitutional and Administrative Law*, Longman, 1993, chs 29 and 30; also, Wade, H.W.R., *Administrative Law*, Oxford, 1988.

25 *Action on Racial Harassment: Legal Remedies and Local Authorities*, London Legal Aid Action Group and London Housing Unit, 1988.

26 *Padfield v Minister of Agriculture, Fisheries and Food* [1968] AC 997, HL.

27 *Associated Provincial Picture Houses v Wednesbury Corp.* [1947] 2 All ER 680, CA.

28 *Secretary of State for Education and Science v MB Tameside* [1976] 3 All ER 665, HL per Lord Wilberforce at p.671.

29 *Re HK* [1967] 1 All ER 226.

30 Section 101 Local Government Act 1972.

31 *British Oxygen Co. v Board of Trade* [1971] AC 610.

32 *R v Home Office ex p. Ruddock and Others* [1987] 2 All ER 518.

33 Much of this can be achieved by developing a working relationship with the local police. For an example of this, see 'Met Launches Units to Combat Victimisation', *Surrey Comet*, 11 June 1999.

34 This can be done in consultation with the Commission for Racial Equality (it could also be undertaken as part of a package involving disability and sexual discrimination).

35   Disability Discrimination Act 1995.

36   For example in Hounslow, a clause in the local authority tenancy agreement says that tenants must not harass any neighbour of other local resident(s) on grounds of their race, sex, age, religion, mental or physical disability, for being lesbian or gay.

37   Issues relating to the consequences of breaches of tenancy agreements will be discussed later in this chapter.

38   This needs to be done, as per the Crime and Disorder Act 1998, in cooperation with any police authority, probation committee or health authority.

39   'Witnesses' here is used in the wide context of the family and friends of victims who come to provide details of racial harassment and victimisation. It is also important to reflect that at times they may also be critical of police activity – or lack of it – presumably it is easier to criticise if no police are present.

40   Recommendation 68 of the MacPherson Report (HMSO, February 1999) stressed that Local Education Authorities and school governors have a duty to create strategies and implement strategies in their schools to prevent and address racism. These include recording all racist incidents and reporting these to the pupils' parents/guardians, school governors and LEAs.

41   In the report of the Home Affairs Select Committee, *Racial Attacks and Harassment*, Third Report, Session 1993–4, reference was made to the success of civil actions with regards to the tort of trespass in dealing with racial attacks. It was claimed in the Borough of Hounslow, where the police encourage this practice, there has not been one breach of such undertaking in the previous few years.

42   *American Cyanamid Co v Ethicon Ltd* [1975] 1 All ER 504, HL.

43   Rules of the Supreme Court, Order 52.

44   *Churchman v Joint Shop Stewards Committee* [1972] 3 All ER 603. For a general discussion of this area see Borrie, G. and Lowe, N., *Law of Contempt*, 2nd edn, Butterworths, 1996; Stone, R., *Textbook on Civil Liberties*, Blackstones, 1994, ch. 6.

45   The police can of course act if they have reasonable grounds for believing that a criminal offence is at issue.

46   [1982] QB 558. This case was concerned with the defrauding of a company, with a Mareva injunction being granted against 36 defendants to stop any disposal or dealings with the assets. In particular, the case concerned the liability of banks and other third parties that held the assets. Clearly a Mareva injunction is a specific form of injunction, but it is clear from the nature of the discussion in the Court of Appeal that the principle of contempt applies to all types of injunctions.

47   [1897] 1 ch. 545.

48   This may be particularly appropriate if those identified do not live on the estate. However, if the racist individual(s) live on the estate an injunction in such terms is unlikely to be suitable. This applies because of an implied term in a tenancy agreement of a right of access to one's property (not that this gives a right to harass another tenant – but it can mean that evidential problems may develop, particularly if trying to establish any contempt). Later in this chapter I will discuss, in more detail, an authority landlord's ability to tackle militant racism.

49   See Section 11 of the Contempt of Court Act 1981 which gives jurisdiction to a judge to order that the name of a witness should not be disclosed in proceedings if there is a danger that the lack of anonymity would deter such witnesses from coming forward. Note that the Contempt of Court Act does not codify all of the law of contempt.

50 The issue of an authority appearing in proceedings as a result of Section 222 will be further discussed later in this chapter.

51 The court has limited grounds for discretion – see *Doherty v Allman* (1878) 3 App Cas 709 HL.

52 See *London and Blackwell Railway Co. v Cross* (1886) 31 ChD 354.

53 See *Hollywood Silver Fox Farm v Emmett* [1936] 1 All ER 825.

54 See *Hubbard v Vosper* [1972] 2 QB 84, CA.

55 *Miller v Jackson* [1977] QB 966, CA.

56 *Proctor v Bailey* (1889) 42 ChD 390.

57 Section 130(3) Highways Act 1980.

58 *Jacobs v London CC* [1950] AC 361 – Lord Simonds.

59 *Lowdens v Keaney* [1903] 2 IR 82; *R v Clark (No 2)* [1964] 2 QB 315, CCA. In *Hubbard v Pitt* [1976] QB 142 Forbes J observed that 'unreasonableness' was established if it can be shown that passage was obstructed.

60 Material was distributed outside Isleworth Primary School in Hounslow – though, this cannot really be described as racist literature.

61 This example could also apply to any other form of protest by any other persons – e.g. trade dispute etc.

62 [1985] 2 All ER 1.

63 [1975] 3 All ER 1.

64 A general right to freedom of assembly is to some extent recognised within the Public Order Act 1986, in that under Part 1 the police do not have powers to ban an assembly. However, following the introduction of Section 14A (via the Criminal Justice and Public Order Act 1994) the police have powers to apply to the council of the district for an order, for a specified period, to prohibit a trespassory assembly where there is considered to be, *inter alia*, serious disruption to the life of the Community. Following *DDP v Jones (NLJ* reports, 7 February 1997, p. 289) this restriction would apply to a trespass to the highway within an area designated by the order.

65 An act done by a person in furtherance of a trade dispute may, in certain circumstances, not be actionable in tort – Section 219 of the Trade Union and Labour Relations (Consolidation) Act 1992. To this limited extent, it can be argued that certain trade disputes can operate within the law. For a fuller consideration of the liability of Trade Unions and their members see Smith and Wood, *Industrial Law*, 5th edn, Butterworths 1993, ch. 11.

66 *Merkur Island Shipping Corp v Laughton* [1983] IRLR 218 HL.

67 In *Allen v Flood* [1898] AC 1 HL it was held that an act lawful in itself is not converted by a malicious or bad motive into an unlawful act leading to civil liability. It follows that for tort liability to be determined, i.e. in relation to interference with trade or business, an unlawful activity would need to be established. It could certainly be argued that any action of militant racist protesting about the employment of black workers is unlawful in the sense of being discriminatory and in breach of the Race Relations Act 1976 and/or likely to stir up racial hatred as per the Public Order Act 1986.

68 *American Cynamid Co v Ethicon Ltd* [1975] 1 All ER 504 HL.

69 Some evidence of this comes from the judgement of Lord Denning in *Hubbard v Pitt* [1975] 3 All ER 1 who was prepared to respect the right to peaceful assembly and protest when he said: 'Finally the real grievance of the plaintiffs is about the placards and the leaflets. To restrain those by an interlocutory injunction would be contrary to the principle laid down by the court 85 years ago in *Bonnard v Perryman* [1891] 2 Ch. 269 and repeatedly

applied ever since. That case spoke of the right of free speech. Here we have to consider the right to demonstrate and the right to protest on matters of public concern. These are rights which it is in the public interest that individuals should possess; and indeed, that they should do so without impediment so long as no wrongful act is done'.

70   In the case of *Middlebrook Mushrooms v TGWU* [1993] IRLR 232 CA. The plaintiff sought to prevent the union from distributing leaflets outside supermarkets supplied by the plaintiffs asking customers not to buy their mushrooms. Plaintiffs sought an injunction on grounds of inducement to breach a contract but this failed because the action was not directed at the supermarkets (who were the contractual partner with the plaintiffs) but their customers. Consequentially, the act was *indirect* and therefore requiring unlawful means that was not established on the facts.

71   An organisation can breach the Race Relations Act under Part II by discrimination in employment and under Part III in relation to the provision of goods, facilities, services and premises. It is also unlawful, under section 31 to induce or attempt to induce a person to do any act that contravenes Part II or III.

72   [1979] ICR 494.

73   Deakin and Morris, *Labour Law*, Butterworths, 1995. This argument is based upon the case of *Associated British Ports v TGWU* [1989] IRLR 305.

74   This is primarily because it is hard to imagine circumstances whereby a local authority would act in breach of a statutory duty as a result of inducement from such far right groups. However, it may be possible that they would act in breach as a result of pressure from other groups, be they tenants' associations, trade unions or political parties such the Conservatives, Labour, Liberal Democrats, SNP or Plaid Cymru.

75   The need for unlawful means was suggested as being necessary in *Associated British Ports v TGWU*.

76   [1898] AC 1 HL.

77   Assuming the racial picketing is directed towards council policy it would seem that an elected councillor might logically be a person to whom the inducement is directed.

78   Section 4A(5) of the Public Order Act 1986 (as amended by the Criminal Justice and Public Order Act 1994) provides for a term of imprisonment, not exceeding six months or a fine not exceeding level 5 on the standard scale or both, for intentional harassment alarm or distress.

79   *Adama v Adama* (Attorney-General intervening) [1970] 3 All ER 572.

80   This scenario, of the CPS taking over a private local authority criminal prosecution, was made clear in correspondence, dated 19 July 1993, from the Office of the Attorney General to Cllr Jagdish Sharma (Deputy Leader of Hounslow Council).

81   See Section 6.

82   See *R v Moloney* [1985] 1 All ER 1025.

83   Section 1(4).

84   New Ethnicities and Education Group of the University of East London, *Through Patterns not our Own*, 1993 – a study of the regulation of racial violence on the council estates of East London.

85   A possible approach to assist is the use of an injunction. Though, as discussed earlier, injunctions have limitations when a victim faces racial harassment by a group of racists. See the section in this chapter, 'The Use of Injunctions to Tackle Militant Racism'.

86   As per Section 222 Local Government Act 1972.

87   Though, this may need to be action under Part III of the Public Order Act 1986 (i.e. assuming sufficient evidence is available).

88 Section (1)(b) of the Crime and Disorder Act 1998 also enables the granting of an order where such an order is necessary to protect persons in the local government area in which the harassment, alarm or distress was caused or was likely to be caused. For a discussion on the first use of an Anti-Social Behaviour Order by a local authority see Rowan, M. 'Crime and Disorder – ASBOs', [1999] *NLJ* 1051.

89 Anti-social Behaviour Orders came into effect on the 1 April 1999. See Plowden, P., 'Love thy Neighbour', [1999] *NLJ* 479. This article also discusses the burden of proof issue.

90 The only reported case in 1998 involved a 'sex offender order' under Section 2 of the Crime and Disorder Act 1998, resulting in a eight-year long night curfew being imposed on a convicted rapist. The application was made by the Chief Officer of Police and granted on grounds that it was 'necessary to protect the public from serious harm'. See 'Rapist is Put under Curfew for Eight Years', *The Times*, 24 December 1998.

91 See 'Council Evicts Racist Tenants', *Searchlight*, April 1995, for some examples for local authority actions against racist tenants. In Dundee a family were evicted for racial harassment of neighbours.

92 Housing Act 1985, Section 21.

93 Issues in relation to the educational effectiveness of the law will be discussed in general terms later in this book.

94 Housing Act 1985, Schedule 2, ground 1. An example of such an eviction is the possession granted to Hounslow Council after a man disturbed his neighbours for two years with constant loud noise and offensive language. The neighbours had kept a diary to monitor the nuisance ('Noisy Neighbour Evicted by Council', *Hounslow, Feltham and Hanworth Times*, 19 April 1996).

95 Housing Act 1985, Section 84(2).

96 This term has its ordinary meaning – see e.g. *Tod-Heatley v Benham* (1888) 40 ChD 80.

97 Housing Act 1985, Schedule 2, ground 2.

98 'You must not abuse, harass, or intimidate any neighbour or other local resident(s) because of their race, sex, age, religion, mental or physical disability, for being lesbian or gay, or encourage any other person to do such acts' – Hounslow Council (Housing Department) Tenancy Agreement (1993).

99 Chapter 7, 'Racial Motivation and Hostility'.

100 When Hounslow Council sought possession from a family in Isleworth various grounds were submitted – with harassment included along with noise, nuisance, rent arrears etc. However, the resulting publicity associated with the evicted centred upon the Councils attempts to 'Wipe out Racism from the Borough – Evicted after 3 years of hate', *Hounslow, Feltham and Hanworth Times*, 17 May 1996). See also Hounslow Council, *Housing News*, July 1996, where it was reported that the eviction was for 'nuisance' – making no reference to racial harassment.

101 For an example of this see – 'Noisy Neighbour Evicted by Council', *Hounslow, Feltham and Hanworth Times*, 19 April 1996. While the main story relates to an eviction for noise; a supplementary story indicates a suspended order for possession with a Feltham man being ordered to promise in writing not to cause further nuisance to his neighbours. See also Hounslow Council, *Housing News*, July 1996.

102 A suspended order for possession can last indefinitely – *Yates v Morris* [1950] 2 All ER 577.

103 Such an application can be made without notice being given to the tenant.

104 For example, under Section 189(1)(a) of the Housing Act 1996 a pregnant woman – or a person with whom she resides or might reasonably be expected to reside – has a priority housing need for accommodation.

105 Housing Act 1996 Section 191 – provides that a person become homeless intentionally if: 'he deliberately does or fails to do anything in consequence of which he ceases to occupy accommodation which is available for his occupation and which it would have been reasonable for him to continue to occupy'.

106 See *A-G ex rel. Tilley v Wandsworth LBC* [1981] 1 WLR 854. Also Wade, H.W.R., *Administrative Law*, 6th edn, Clarendon Press, Oxford, 1989, pp. 205 and 370, with regards to the potential for a local authority to act unlawfully by fettering its discretion by applying a blanket rule in relation to homeless persons.

107 Section 188 of the Housing Act 1996.

108 Police reported that this incident occurred on the Butts Farm Estate in Hounslow: 'Racist Child Outlaws', *Hounslow, Feltham and Hanworth Times*, 12 January 1996.

109 'Parents Face eviction over Race Attack by Children', *Hounslow Chronicle*, 25 July 1996. See also comments of Peter Jepson, 'Morally Unjust to Evict Families due to Child Racism', *The Chronicle*, 26 September 1998.

110 A case which provides a precedent for taking action against tenants even when it is their children who are perpetrating racial violence is *London Borough of Camden v McIntyre* (*Making the Law Work against Racial Harassment*, Report of the Legal Action Group Research Project [1990]).

111 A local government official suggested publicly at a People's Tribunal on Racial Harassment that Hounslow Council could make use of child protection powers when dealing with racial harassment involving children.

112 The Department of Health provide guidelines – *Working Together* – for child protection registration and these suggest that the basis for child protection is that of a child suffering, or is likely to suffer significant harm. The cases of *R v Harrow LBC ex parte D* [1989] 3 WLR 1239 and *R v Norfolk CC ex parte M* [1989] 2 All ER 359 recognised *Working Together* as the authoritative guide for Social Services Departments when dealing with child protection registration.

113 Section 26 of the Children's Act 1989, and also the *Working Together* guidelines, provide for a complaints procedure being established by the local authority. It is generally considered that this complaint procedure should be exhausted before seeking judicial review – though there seems to be no legal requirement to this effect.

114 An example of this is the case of *R v Norfolk CC, ex parte M* [1989] 2 All ER 359 which emphasised the importance of authorities complying with the principles of natural justice.

115 Section 47 of the Children Act 1989 provides on a local authority a duty to investigate where they have reasonable cause to suspect a child is suffering, or is likely to suffer, significant harm.

116 As per Section 71 of the Race Relations Act 1976 – this was discussed earlier in this chapter under 'Powers of a Local Authority'.

117 In Hounslow the Heartstone Project provides education on racism and bullying within schools. Though, involvement is at the discretion of the Head and governors of the school.

118 See discussion earlier in this chapter under the title 'New Powers under the Crime and Disorder Act 1998'.

119 *Doli incapax* represented a legal attempt to recognise the variable development of individual children and their capacity to appreciate the wrongfulness of different types of actions.

The presumption of *doli incapax* could only be rebutted by the prosecution proving that the child knew what he had been doing was seriously wrong (not just naughty or mischievous).

120 For a discussion on the abolition of the presumption of *doli incapax* see Lang, R., Taylor, R. and Wasik, M., *Blackstone's Guide to the Crime and Disorder Act 1998*, p. 55.

121 Under the Crime and Disorder Act 1998, a child (or adult) – who has not had a prior conviction for an offence – can be given only one reprimand and then one warning. This is recorded and any offender who is given a warning must be brought before the courts if he offends again within two years. In such circumstances, a conditional discharge is then removed from the options available to the court. For a discussion on reprimands and warnings see Lang, Taylor and Wasik, *Blackstone's Guide to the Crime and Disorder Act 1998*, p. 81.

3 Racist Speech and Literature

In this chapter I will examine issues of both racist speech and literature. In order to conduct this examination, I have produced two evidence assessment sheets. The first is of what can loosely be determined as a collection of *racist materials*, consisting of 'jokes' given to an audience, racist material sent via a Book Club and other materials that are anti-Semitic. The second assessment sheet relates to *material distributed in the London Borough of Hounslow* by political parties. From these evidence assessments, I will consider the examples, relating and applying them to the appropriate sections of the Public Order Act 1986, along with the Malicious Communications Act 1988 and The Post Office Act 1953. In examining racist material, using the evidence assessment sheets, I will not give consideration to the Protection from Harassment Act 1997, since to establish an offence under the legislation it is necessary to prove that the conduct, which amounts to harassment, has occurred on at least two separate occasions. The racist material referred to in this chapter may well have been part of a sustained campaign of harassment, but without such evidence it is inappropriate to make such assumptions. However, towards the end of this chapter, I will examine the potential for using the Protection from Harassment Act 1997 as a means of tackling racist speech and conduct that may amount to harassment.

I will also, later in the chapter, consider the issue of racist graffiti and fly posting, relating this both to existing planning laws and the Criminal Damage Act 1971. Finally, I will consider the issue of racist chanting at football matches, and the Football (Offences) Act 1991.

Possibly, this approach can be criticised as an analysis of racist material that is based upon laws preceding the introduction of the Crime and Disorder Act 1998. However, the reason for this is fundamental to an understanding of how anti-racist crime laws work in Britain. Indeed, such an approach is necessary because the Crime and Disorder Act 1998, while establishing new alternative offences for racist crime, only provides an alternative charging and sentencing policy. It does not make it easier for criminal acts to be punished. By way of illustration, the Crime and Disorder legislation provides a new alternative offence of racial criminal damage (with an enhanced sentence) –

but issues of racial motivation or hostility are only applicable if the courts *first* determine that the accused is guilty of criminal damage. This emphasises that the basic offence remains fundamental to any finding of guilt, since a person cannot be found guilty of a racial element unless guilt has first been established in relation to the basic offence. It is for these reasons that this chapter concentrates on the potentiality for establishing criminal charges in relation to racist literature and material.

The issues associated with harsher sentencing for racist crime will be considered later in this thesis, in chapter 7, 'Racial Motivation and Hostility'.

Racist Material

Before considering the first evidence assessment sheet, it is important to reflect that while these assessments are of value as an academic exercise, they provide an incomplete picture. For example, I often have no knowledge of specific circumstances of the distribution, previous record of the accused etc. As such, the assessment relates to a cold analysis on the basis of the information from within the literature. However, this is of value, since it is probably the way that most people receive the material – usually through their letterboxes.

Evidence assessment sheet 1 consists of eight items of '*racist material*'. The first involves a few common racist 'jokes'. Others are items of racist material that were sent via a book club to members of a group, while there are two items of anti-Semitic material sent through the post to Jewish Synagogues. The last item was an extract from a book written by Lady Birdwood that resulted in a prosecution under Section 19, Public Order Act 1986.

Public Order Act 1986

Nearly 50 per cent of racial incidents that get taken to court involve the Public Order Act 1986.[1] In order to bring a prosecution in relation to racist speech or literature under this Act, it is essential that the words used are 'threatening, abusive or insulting'. This requirement applies to all relevant sections of the legislation. The fact that the words may be 'racially offensive' is certainly not sufficient to bring a prosecution. The words must be more than 'offensive' – they must be 'threatening, abusive or insulting'.

Table 3.1   Evidence assessment sheet 1

Racist material.	BM	Book club items				Anti-Semitic		
Appendix ref:	1	2	3	4	5	6	7	8
Public Order Act 1986 (*The answer to Question A must be affirmative to establish a prosecution under this Act*)								
A Were the words used threatening, abusive or insulting?	Y	Y	Y	Y	Y/?	Y/?	Y	Y
B With intent to cause harassment, alarm or distress (Section 4A)?	?	?	?/Y	Y	Y	?	?	Y/?
C thereby causing any person harassment alarm or distress (Section 4A)?	?/Y	?	?	?	Y/?	Y/?	Y/?	Y/?
D Within hearing/sight of a person likely to be caused h, a, or d (Section 5)?	Y	#	#	#	#	#	#	#
E Intent/aware his words/writing – threatening, abusive or insulting (Section 6)	Y/?	#	#	#	#	#	#	#
F Use words/display material – intent/likelihood to stir up racial hatred (Section 18)?	?	Y/?	Y/?	Y/?	Y/?	Y/?	Y/?	Y
G Publish/distribute material – intent/likelihood to stir up racial hatred (Section 19)?	#	?	Y/?	Y/?	Y/?	Y/?	Y/?	Y
Malicious Communications Act 1988 (*sending of letters etc. with intent to cause distress or anxiety*)								
H Is the message indecent, grossly offensive or a threat (Section 1)?	#	Y?	Y/?	Y	Y	Y/?	Y/?	#
I Purpose to cause distress or anxiety to recipient (Section 1(b))?	#	N	N	N	N	Y	Y	#
Post Office Act 1953 (*prohibition on sending by post of certain articles*)								
J Was the item sent via the post office? (can only proceed under Act, if yes)	#	?/Y	?/Y	?/Y	?/Y	Y	Y	#
K Words/designs which are grossly offensive or indecent (Section 11)?	#	Y?	Y/?	?	Y/?	Y/?	Y/?	#
L Were the remarks racially offensive?	Y	Y	Y	Y	?	Y	Y	Y
M Can a racial motive be inferred?	N	Y	Y	Y	Y/?	Y	Y	Y

Y = yes, N = no, ? = possible/doubtful, # = not applicable.

While the statute does not provide a specific definition of what these three words mean, the case of *Brutus v Cozens*[2] lays down some principles from which it is possible to establish a meaning or understanding. This case arrived in a Magistrate's Court out of an anti-apartheid demonstration at the Wimbledon Tennis Championships. Brutus had stepped onto the tennis court blowing a whistle and throwing leaflets. He was arrested and charged with insulting behaviour under Section 5 of the Public Order Act 1986. At first instance, the Magistrate's held that his behaviour had not been insulting and dismissed the information without calling him to give evidence. On appeal, by the prosecutor, the Divisional Court ruled that 'insulting behaviour', under the Act, was *behaviour which affronted other people and evidenced a disrespect or contempt for their rights, and which reasonable persons would foresee as likely to cause resentment or protest.* Thus, insulting behaviour, by Brutus, would likely be established.[3]

Brutus appealed to the House of Lords, which disagreed with the Divisional Court and held that the meaning of an ordinary word of the English language is 'not a question of law, but of fact'. In doing so, Lord Reid commented:

> I cannot agree with that. Parliament had to solve the difficult question of how far freedom of speech or behaviour must be limited in the general public interest. It would have been going much too far to prohibit all speech or conduct likely to occasion a breach of the peace because determined opponents may not shrink from organising or at least threatening a breach of the peace in order to silence a speaker whose views they detest. Therefore vigorous and it may be distasteful or unmannerly speech or behaviour is permitted so long as it does not go beyond any one of three limits. It must not be threatening. It must not be abusive. It must not be insulting. I see no reason why any of these should be construed as having a specially wide or specially narrow meaning. They are all limits easily recognisable by the ordinary man. Free speech is not impaired by ruling them out. But before a man can be convicted it must be clearly shown that one or more of them has been disregarded. We were referred to a number of dictionary meanings of 'insult' such as treating with insolence or contempt or indignity or derision or dishonour or offensive disrespect. Many things otherwise un-objectionable may be said or done in an insulting way. There can be no definition. But an ordinary sensible man knows an insult when he sees or hears it.

Section 4A of the Public Order Act 1986

Section 154 of the Criminal Justice and Public Order Act 1994 amends the Public Order Act 1986 to establish a new and more severe offence in relation to harassment. This new Section 4A does not replace the old Section 5 of the Public Order Act 1986, but is intended to run as complimentary to it. Indeed, Section 5 only carried a fine at a maximum of Level 3 on the Standard Scale, while Section 4A can result in a maximum term of imprisonment of six months and/or a fine not exceeding Level 5 on the Standard Scale.

As with most relatively new laws, it will take many years for the impact of Section 4A to be fully recognised. What the legislation does make clear, is that an offender must have *intent* to cause harassment, alarm or distress, using threatening, abusive or insulting words or behaviour, or disorderly behaviour[4] – thereby *causing* that or another person harassment, alarm or distress.

Thus, applying such legal principles to jokes, it is likely that the so-called *jokes* could be considered as 'threatening and/or insulting'. It is sufficient to establish that *any* person present was caused harassment, alarm or distress – even if the *jokes* were directed towards another.

To prove *intent* to cause a person 'harassment, alarm or distress' may not be so clear-cut. Any expresser of such jokes may argue that his intent was to make the audience laugh. However, this should prove an unsatisfactory defence given the 'threatening or insulting' nature of the words used. Such *intent* would be decided, as per *R v Moloney*,[5] as a matter of fact and according to the ordinary usage of the word.

It is certainly possible that any jury would have sympathy for any well-known entertainer who was fulfilling his stage act.[6] The use of racist words that are 'threatening and insulting', and directed towards a coloured individual within the audience, could certainly indicate intent to 'embarrass'. However, the law requires intent to cause 'harassment, alarm or distress'. Given that a prison sentence could be the outcome, it may be difficult for the prosecution to convince a jury beyond reasonable doubt. Indeed, it is possible that any jury could be sympathetic towards a defendant once elements of reasonable doubt are raised.

So far as the book club items are concerned, the strongest case would seem to exist with regard to where it is clear that 'threatening and abusive' words have been used. It can also be argued that the words used, together with instructions on how to make a bomb, establishes a clear intent to cause harassment, alarm or distress to somebody. The real legal question is whether *it has thereby caused any person harassment, alarm or distress*. Presumably, if a person who had sight of the publication were to complain that the words used had caused him alarm or distress then the *actus reus* would be fulfilled. As already mentioned, the fact that the intention was not to cause alarm or distress to that person would not be an adequate defence.

Section 5 of the Public Order Act 1986

It can be seen from evidence assessment sheet 1 that only the joke material is applicable with regards to establishing a prosecution under Section 5 of the Public Order Act 1986. This is because there is no evidence that Appendices 2 to 8 involves use of 'threatening, abusive or insulting' words/display of writing/sign etc. 'within the hearing or sight of a person likely to be caused harassment, alarm or distress'.[7]

Section 5, although dealing with harassment, is constructed differently to Section 4A. Indeed, Section 4A does not entail this limitation of being within the 'hearing or sight'. Thus, Section 4A could apply to the use of 'threatening, abusive or insulting' words in a leaflet that has been produced and handed out to people, say at a bus stop.[8] Should one of the recipients then pass the leaflet on by leaving it on the bus, the person who had produced the leaflet could have committed an offence, if this new reader was caused alarm or distress (i.e. assuming an intent existed to cause a person [any person] harassment, alarm or distress). By comparison, under Section 5, the person who produced and handed out the leaflet could only be liable in connection with the people at the bus stop – since he would not be within the 'hearing or sight'[9] of people who subsequently got on the bus (and read the leaflet) at another bus stop.

It can also be noted that Section 4A is specific, in that it requires a person to be 'caused' harassment, alarm or distress. Whereas, Section 5 only requires a person to be 'likely to be caused' harassment alarm or distress. A question therefore arises as to whether the likelihood has to be a reasonable one, or one that a reasonable person could foresee. While there is no specific case under the Public Order Act 1986, the case of *Jordan v Burgoyne*[10] dealt with a similar issue. This case involved a fascist expressing support for Hitler and condemning Jews. The question of law being whether the public speech was 'likely' to cause a breach of the peace. Jordan argued free speech and that the violent reaction of Jews amongst the audience, to his speech, was unreasonable. In the Divisional Court, Lord Parker remarked:

> Once a speaker uses threatening, abusive or insulting words or behaviour...that person must take his audience as he finds them, and if those words to that audience are likely to provoke a breach of the peace, then the speaker is guilty of that offence.

Also, the prosecution does not have to prove that a person was caused harassment, alarm or distress, as long as the consequence was likely. In *Lodge v Andrews*,[11] it was sufficient that an unidentified driver of a car might have been alarmed by the sight of someone walking down the middle of the road late at night.

Section 5 – Mens Rea Requirement

The case of *DPP v Clarke*[12] establishes that, like an ordinary citizen, a police officer is capable of being harassed, alarmed or distressed. This case also illustrates the *mens rea* requirement for Section 5 under Section 6(4) of the Public Order Act 1986. Clarke was among demonstrators outside an abortion clinic. The police requested the demonstrators not to display posters of an aborted foetus. The magistrates found that the pictures were abusive and insulting and that their display caused alarm and distress to one of the police officers present. However, under Section 6(4) the magistrates found that the demonstrators did not intend the pictures to be 'threatening, abusive or insulting', nor were they 'aware' that they might be. They were therefore acquitted.

Clearly, this case can be criticised for its logic, in that the purpose of the posters must have been both to inform and distress the public. The picture of the foetus was present in order to grab attention and to shock people into supporting their opposition to abortion. If the protesters were not themselves distressed by the abortion of a foetus, and thus aware that it could cause distress, what were they protesting about?

Whatever the arguments over the Clarke case, it is clear that any entertainer/comedian could argue that while the words used were 'threatening, abusive or insulting' and that while it is 'likely' that a member of the audience could feel 'harassed, alarmed or distressed' by the jokes, he had no intention to 'threaten, abuse or insult' anyone. He was not aware that it may do so, with his intent being to establish joy and laughter.

As was remarked in Clarke, even if this lack of awareness defence of any entertainer/comedian was successful, it could only be used once, since subsequently he would be aware that such jokes may 'threaten, abuse or insult' certain groups and individuals. To this extent, the police could also consider the issuing of a formal written caution. Thereby keeping on record the extent of any knowledge of the accused with regards to the offence concerned.

Sections 18 and 19, Public Order Act 1986

So far as Section 27(2) of the Public Order Act 1986 is concerned, all sections from 18 to 23 create one offence. Thus a person cannot be penalised under say Section 19 for the distribution of 'threatening, abusive or insulting' literature which may 'stir up racial hatred', and also be penalised under Section 23 for possession of that same material.

It is also clear from evidence assessment sheet 1 that Section 19 is not applicable for dealing with racist speech, with this section being designed to deal with the publication or distribution of written material.

As can be seen from the assessment sheet, Section 18 is specifically designed for dealing with insulting words, or behaviour, or the display of any written material which is 'threatening, abusive or insulting, with a person guilty of an offence if he intends to stir up racial hatred, or having regard to all the circumstances racial hatred is likely to be stirred up thereby'.

Thus, with regards to the racist 'jokes', it is clear that there could be a case under Section 18 of the Public Order Act 1986.

However, before a prosecution could be brought a number of obstacles would need to be overcome. The first, of which, is that it is the police who have a duty:

> to investigate a suspected offence, obtain evidence and form the view that a prosecution should be commenced. Then the matter will be reported to the Crown Prosecution Service. If the CPS, having reviewed the available evidence, wish to prosecute such a Part III offence they will then ask the consent of the Attorney General (once consent is granted then the case will be conducted by the Crown Prosecution Service), with each application considered personally by the Attorney General or Solicitor General.[13]

Obviously, the Attorney General would need to consider the available evidence and decide if a prosecution is in the public interest. Clearly, a key issue to be considered in deciding whether to prosecute, must be the likelihood of success. Thus the first question to determine is, did any person telling the jokes use 'threatening, abusive or insulting words'? In *Brutus v Cozens*,[14] a case which arose out of an anti-apartheid demonstration, it was held that the word *insulting*[15] must be given its natural meaning – and therefore is a matter of fact not law. Given such a situation, it would not be surprising if the words used in the jokes could be found to be both 'threatening and insulting'. It also seems reasonable to determine that the person telling the jokes must have either intended, or been aware, that his words were insulting.[16]

Racist Jokes and Intent to Stir up Racial Hatred?

The question of whether a person telling jokes intended to stir up racial hatred or, having regard to all the circumstances, racial hatred was likely to be stirred up thereby, is therefore of critical importance.

Any entertainer/comedian could argue that given that he had no intention to commit an offence. He may also suggest that laughter signifies enjoyment and not hatred.

As a counter to this argument, it is clear that the words used are arguably an indication of both being insulting to black people. Given the overall tone of the jokes it may be possible for the jury to infer racial hatred, but it is not a clear-cut case that it is intended to stir up racial hatred or that this was the likely outcome of the jokes.

Possible Private Prosecution?

On balance, despite the precedent of an 'incitement to stir up racial hatred case' in *R v Edwards*[17] for racial comedy, it seems unlikely that the Attorney General would proceed with prosecution against any entertainer/comedian, under Section 18 of the POA 1986. One consequence of taking no action is that any aggrieved individual could seek to bring a private prosecution. This right is specifically preserved under Section 6(1) of the Prosecution of Offences Act 1985. However Section 6(2) of the 1985 Act does permit the Director of Public Prosecutions to take over such a private prosecution and one of the consequences of so doing may be that the DPP then withdraws the case.[18]

Book Club Items – A Loophole under the Public Order Act 1986

Evidence assessment sheet 1 shows a potential for prosecution under sections 18 and 19 of the Public Order Act 1986[19] with regards to the Book Club items.[20] However, this does not reveal the loophole, evident within the public order legislation, which enables groups to skate around the law by sending their racist material to individual members rather than to the public.[21] To this extent, the evidence assessment, with regards to the book club items, shows a 'Y/?', which reflects an opinion that the words/material can be regarded as having an 'intent/likelihood to stir up racial hatred', but it is doubtful as to whether a successful prosecution is possible due to the fact that a defendant could avoid Section 19 by claiming that the material was exclusively 'published' for 'distribution' to individual members of a Book Club, and not to the public.

Despite such, it could still be argued that a potential for prosecution might still exist under Section 18. – in that the literature involved the use of 'threatening, abusive or insulting' words which reflect an 'intent/likelihood to stir up racial hatred'. The problem for the prosecution may be in establishing just where the words were used – since the legislation provides a defence of being 'inside a dwelling and having no reason to believe that the material would be seen by anyone other than inside that or another dwelling'. Assuming that the racist material is sent, via a book club, to a member inside a dwelling[22] then an appropriate defence should exist.

The anti-Semitic items certainly indicate a potential for prosecution under Section 19 of the Public Order Act 1986. The material conveys words which have the potential for being *insulting*,[23] with the material being distributed via the post to members of the public at a Jewish Synagogue. Those receiving the material are not members of any book club, but members of a section of the public. It is clear that the potential exists for believing that an intent existed, on behalf of the person producing the material, to stir up racial hatred, with the words self evidently intended to insult the memory of Jews murdered in the war.

Given the extreme sensitivity of the Holocaust, grounds should also exist for believing that publication or distributions will likely result in stirring up racial hatred, with an increase in racial tension a possible outcome.

Racist Literature and the Malicious Communications Act 1988

The case of *Chappell v DPP*[24] held that it is not appropriate to bring a prosecution under Section 5 of the Public Order Act 1986 where a letter, deposited through a letter box of a dwelling-house, contains 'threatening, abusive or insulting' words. This is because Section 5(2), as does Section 18(2), provides that while an offence can take place in a public or private place, it excludes conduct taking place within a dwelling. Thus, a person displaying a poster in his own home that gives an abusive message to those in the street, may commit an offence. However, a delivery of a 'threatening or abusive' letter to a person within his own home, where he reads it and is alarmed by its contents, could not be an offence within the ambit of the Public Order Act.

Surprisingly, it seems this same situation is inherent in the new Section 4A of the Public Order Act 1986.[25] Despite being designed to deal with harassment of a racial or more general nature, the new legislation still retains an exemption for conduct inside a dwelling. Thus, a person harassing an individual by depositing leaflets through a letterbox could avoid prosecution under the public order legislation.[26]

In *Chappell,* Mr Justice Potter concluded that the conduct of pushing a letter through a dwelling letterbox falls fairly and squarely within the provisions of the Malicious Communications Act 1988. Section 1 of that Act provides:

> 1(1) Any person who sends to another person:
> (a) a letter or other article which conveys – (i) a message which is indecent or grossly offensive; (ii) a threat; or (iii) information which is false and known or believed to be false by the sender; or
> (b) any article which is, in whole or part, of an indecent or grossly offensive nature, is guilty of an offence if his purpose, or one of his purposes, in sending it is that it should, so far as falling within paragraph (a) or (b) above, cause distress.

However, it is clear that a strong defence can be made in relation to Question I, which relates to a purpose to cause distress or anxiety to the recipient.[27] The defence being: *since the material is sent via a Book Club, the recipient will have ordered the material and be a member of the club/ organisation.* To this extent, it is unlikely that the distributor of the items intended to cause distress or anxiety to the recipient. Thus, given this likely defence, prosecution under the Malicious Communications Act for Book Club items is not really appropriate.

The same defence could not apply to material sent to members of the public. For example, anti-Semitic items were sent through the post (not via a Book Club). Further, as per Section 1 of the Malicious Communications Act 1988, it is certainly arguable that both these items could be considered as being 'grossly offensive'. In the sense that the items were sent to Jewish Synagogues with a message of denial of the Holocaust – calling it a 'Holohaux'. Quite whether the words are 'grossly offensive or just 'offensive' is an issue to be determined by the jury.[28] It seems that no judicial guidance should normally be given as to meaning, though by analogy, it is worth noting that 'indecent' is objectively determined taking into account the relevant circumstances.[29] For example, touching a woman's breast may be indecent – but if done by a doctor, as part of a relevant medical examination, it might not be.

Likewise, a jury could determine that the material is 'grossly offensive' and the purpose of sending such anti-Semitic material was to cause distress or anxiety to the recipient.

The Post Office Act 1953

Because certain items were sent via the post it may be that Section 11 of the Post Office Act 1953 would also apply – that is provided evidence exists of who sent the item(s).

Both items show some evidence of a publisher, but the sender of the material would be prosecuted and not necessarily the publisher.[30] The police could also be lucky and obtain finger print or even DNA evidence from either the envelopes or the leaflet.

If sufficient evidence exists of the sender of the material, this legislation could be applicable. Indeed, it may also be of value with regards to racist material sent via Book Clubs through the Post Office.[31]

However, to bring a prosecution, as per Section 11(1)(c), the words, marks or designs must be 'grossly offensive or of an indecent or obscene character'.

As EAS 1 shows, the words used are clearly 'racially offensive'. But, is that the same as 'grossly offensive'? As argued, under the section dealing with the Malicious Communications Act 1988, strong grounds exist for believing that sending this anti-Semitic material to a Jewish Synagogue should be considered as 'grossly offensive' – though the decision would be objectively determined by a jury.[32]

Similarly with regards to the Book Club items. While it seems that most of the Book Club material was sent via the Post Office, there was no direct knowledge that these particular items have been. Thus, EAS 1 signifies a '?/ Y' in relation to Question J, with it worth noting that only material sent via the Post Office is subject to the Post Office Act 1953 legislation. Material sent via private couriers is not covered by the Act, though the Malicious Communications Act may apply.

Racist Material – An Overall Assessment

The evidence assessment sheet 1 signifies the varied circumstances upon which sections 18 and 19 of the Public Order Act may be applicable for dealing with racist material. It has the capability for dealing with racist speech and literature – i.e. assuming the use of 'threatening abusive or insulting' words with intent/ likelihood to stir up racial hatred. The legislation is diverse and flexible, in the sense that it can deal with books, leaflets, posters, plays, videos, tapes, broadcasts,[33] and should also apply to electronic messages placed on the Internet.

There are, though, limitations when it comes to dealing with racist material. This same evidential limitation may also exist with regards to the Malicious Communications Act 1988. This limitation derives from the fact that the legislation is intent on dealing with individuals – while the racist material is directed not towards individuals, but towards specific groups within society. It follows, therefore, that proving specific intent can be difficult. Take the Malicious Communications Act 1988 as an example. The majority of literature showed the characteristics of being 'grossly offensive' or a 'threat'. However, it was not possible to show that it was intended to cause anxiety or distress to the particular recipient. A similar problem is also evident with regards to Section 5 of the Public Order Act 1986, with a requirement for the use of words within the 'hearing or sight' of a person likely to be caused harassment, alarm or distress.

To a certain extent, this Section 5 limitation is dealt with under the new Section 4A of the Public Order Act 1986, with the legislation applying where not just in circumstances whereby the particular person to whom the material may be directed is alarmed or distressed – but *any* person is so affected.

However, even with the new Section 4A, the legislation would not be applicable if the leaflet was deposited through a letterbox of a dwelling house. This seems a strange anomaly, given the purpose of the legislation is to deal with harassment – with many incidents of harassment occurring when people are in their homes. The obvious explanation, of the alternative of a prosecution under the Malicious Communications Act 1986, may not be sufficient – particularly when dealing with the most extreme cases of racially motivated harassment. Indeed, the MCA 1988 only provides for a fine, whereas prosecution under Section 4A of the Public Order Act 1986 could result in up to six months imprisonment and/or a fine.

Of all the material analysed in EAS 1 only one item has resulted in any prosecution, with a conditional discharge for the publication of literature in contravention of Part III of the Public Order Act 1986. This may seem surprising given the conclusions which can be drawn from EAS 1, with other items not showing significantly different characteristics than that which was prosecuted. Despite such, no prosecutions have, to my knowledge, been formally commenced. This clearly does not signify a strong and firm commitment, on behalf of the Attorney General,[34] to deal with racist material.

Material Distributed in the Borough of Hounslow

Evidence assessment sheet 2 (see Table 3.2) examines literature which has been distributed in the Borough of Hounslow, most of which has been the subject of complaint. Hounslow Council and the Metropolitan Police in Hounslow supplied certain items – with elected Councillors having made complaints about others. In comparison, further items are copies of stickers removed from lampposts on just one road in Hounslow.

Before examining the evidence assessment sheet it is perhaps important to reflect upon the multicultural society which exists within Hounslow. The Borough, in West London, has a population of approximately 205,000 people, of whom 24.4 per cent are from black and ethnic minority communities.[35] In one electoral ward, 50 per cent of the population are from an ethnic minority background,[36] thereby indicating the multicultural aspect of Hounslow. Quite clearly, because of this variance in the population of specific electoral wards, certain areas are more sensitive to racist activity than others.

Evidence assessment sheet 2 will not be examined in the same specific detail as EAS 1, but will be given a more general and overall assessment.

In doing so, it is important to recognise a significant difference between EAS 1 and EAS 2. While certain items in general showed a potential for prosecution under the Public Order Act because of the use of 'threatening, abusive or insulting' words, the same does not apply with other material. Indeed, by looking at EAS 2 we can establish a clear general theme of an answer of 'No' to Question A. The only item which signifies a '?' is Item 18, and only because it suggests that unless immigrants are returned to their country of origin, a racial war could break out on the streets of Britain. Obviously, this has the potential for being 'threatening', but it is not clear-cut.

The obvious consequences of this evidential assessment, is that prosecutions against the party concerned, on the basis of this sample literature, would fail under the Public Order Act 1986. This may cause some concern to the Leader of Hounslow Council who complained to the Chief Superintendent of Hounslow Police[37] about another item. In his correspondence, Cllr John Chatt emphasised he did not wish to stifle or censure political debate, but that he was of the opinion that 'this kind of literature' was intended to stir up racial hatred.

While the Councillor's opinion may be justified, it is clear from EAS 2 that I do not consider the leaflet provides grounds for prosecution.[38] The law requires the use of 'threatening, abusive or insulting' words and then asks whether the publisher/distributor 'intended to stir up racial hatred – or is racial hatred likely to be stirred up thereby'.

The leaflet is 'racially offensive', but it seems to contain no 'threatening, abusive or insulting' words.[39] The candidate argues for spending on education, care for old folks, with opposition to VAT on heating charges. He uses the words 'Keep Feltham White', arguing against spending on an 'Asian Women's Centre', and on 'Ethnic Alcohol Counselling'. It is possible[40] that there exists intent to stir up racial hatred, but it is unlikely the use of such words would thereby stir up racial hatred (thus, '?/N').

In all the circumstances, to prosecute for expressing such views could impede political and election campaigning, something which may be undesirable in a democracy unless a clear breach of the criminal law exists.[41] Given the absence of 'threatening, abusive or insulting' words, it is argued that grounds do not exist for a Section 19, Public Order Act 1986 prosecution.

By comparison, it is clear that some items are potentially much more likely to stir up racial hatred.[42] One example, for instance, talks of being in danger of being swamped by waves of immigrants and so called refugees, with native-born British people fast becoming second class citizens in their own country. Likewise, another item refers to a racial war breaking out on the streets of Britain unless immigration is stopped and immigrants currently living in Britain are returned to their country of origin. It is certainly the case, that if the language used had been clearly 'threatening, abusive or insulting', while conveying this racist theme, the grounds for prosecution would exist under Section 19 of the Public Order Act 1986.

With regards to prosecution under the Post Office Act 1953, it seems that this literature is distributed door to door. As such, it is not possible to prosecute under The Post Office Act. It is, though, possible to prosecute under the Malicious Communications Act 1988, where the message is 'indecent, grossly offensive or a 'threat', with a purpose to cause distress or anxiety to the recipient. In a number of instances, EAS 2 shows doubt as to whether the message is 'indecent', 'grossly offensive' or a 'threat', but signifies that it may cause distress or anxiety to the recipient. This point is made, because a legal immigrant living in this country may be anxious or be caused distress by a leaflet calling for repatriation.

Finally, in relation to this material, it is clear that in general this literature does not break our existing laws. Despite such, it is clear from EAS 2 that a racial motive can be inferred and that in the vast majority of instances the remarks within the material are 'racially offensive', with reports that an increase in racial harassment/attacks often follow the distribution of this racist material.

Table 3.2   Evidence assessment sheet 2

BNP/NF material distributed in the Borough of Hounslow

	Appendix ref:	9	10	11	12	13	14	15	16	17	18
	Public Order Act 1986 *(The answer to Question A must be affirmative to establish a prosecution under this Act)*										
A	Were the words used threatening, abusive or insulting?	N	N	N	N	N	N	N	N	N/?	?
B	With intent to cause harassment, alarm or distress (Section 4A)?	N	N	N	N	?	Y/?	Y/?	?	Y/?	Y
C	thereby causing any person harassment alarm or distress (Section 4A)?	N/?	N/?	N/?	N/?	?	?	?	Y	?	?
D	Within hearing/sight of a person likely to be caused h, a, or d (Section 5)?	#	#	#	#	#	#	#	#	#	#
E	Intent/aware his words/writing – threatening, abusive or insulting (Section 6)?	#	#	#	#	#	#	#	#	#	#
F	Use words/display material – intent/likelihood to stir up racial hatred (Section 18)?	?/N	N	?/N	N	?/N	Y/?	?/N	N	?	?
G	Publish/distribute material – intent/likelihood to stir up racial hatred (Section 19)?	?/N	N	?/N	N	?/N	Y/?	?/N	N	?	Y/?
	Malicious Communications Act 1988 *(sending of letters etc. with intent to cause distress or anxiety).*										
H	Is the message indecent, grossly offensive or a threat (Section 1)?	N/?	?	?	?	?	?	?	N/?	#	#
I	Purpose to cause distress or anxiety to recipient (Section 1(b))?	?	?	Y/?	?	Y/?	Y/?	?	?	#	#
	Post Office Act 1953 *(prohibition on sending by post of certain articles).*										
J	Was the item sent via the post office? (can only proceed under Act if yes).	#	#	#	#	#	#	#	#	#	#
K	Words/designs which are grossly offensive or indecent (Section 11)?	#	#	#	#	#	#	#	#	#	#
L	Were the remarks racially offensive?	Y	Y	Y	Y	Y	Y	?	N	Y	Y
M	Can a racial motive be inferred?	Y/?	Y	Y	Y/?	Y/?	Y	Y/?	N	Y	Y

Y = yes, – N = no, – ? = possible/doubtful, # = not applicable.

Racist Graffiti and Fly Posting

In many parts of the country, and particularly in Hounslow, racist graffiti and fly posting is a problem, both to the environment and to the local authorities who are deemed responsible for clearing up the mess.[43]

Clearly, racist graffiti, as with any graffiti daubed on walls without the permission of the property owner, would amount to an offence under the Criminal Damage Act 1971. The problem often is one of establishing the evidence to bring a prosecution.

The words used are abusive and as such the offender (if caught) could face charges under both the Section 5 of the Public Order Act 1986 as well as under the Criminal Damage Act 1971. While the words could amount to an intent or likelihood to stir up racial hatred, given the reluctance of the Attorney General to prosecute under Part III, it seems unlikely a Section 18, POA 1986 prosecution would be brought.

However, it is not just graffiti that causes problems. Another major concern has been one of fly posting. That is, the displaying of posters without planning consent. While planners have not generally been concerned by the content of the advertisement posters, it is argued that racial motive may be relevant – controversially in relation to a decision to commence proceedings and also in relation to sentencing.

The case of *London Borough of Merton v Edmonds and Tyndall*[44] involved Tyndall (Chairman of the BNP) and Edmonds (South London Regional Organiser). It was established that a BNP poster had been displayed on Vestry Hall, the home of the Merton Ethnic Minority Centre.

The court found on the facts that Edmonds was responsible for the printing of BNP literature. However, both Tyndall and Edmonds argued that they had no knowledge and had not consented to the advertisement poster. It was established, in the Appeal, that the defendants had knowledge from the Council's letters that the advertisements were being displayed. If after being told of this display, the defendant who benefits from the publicity does nothing to remove it, then a Magistrate or Crown Court may have very little difficulty in concluding that it continues to be displayed with his consent. This issue, if raised by the defence, is to be decided on the facts.

The net result of this case is that the leaders of the BNP were found guilty,[45] because of a failure to remove the posters. The precedent which the case establishes should not be underestimated – since it affirms the powers of planning authorities to take action to deal with fly posting. Further, it is argued that the Courts should penalise any racial motive behind such posters, with this being particularly applicable to racist stickers.

Applying such principles to items discussed, it would clearly be possible for Hounslow Council to seek to bring proceedings with regard to the display, without planning consent, of such racist stickers. Given that these types of stickers are often found attached to lampposts, the potential for prosecution must be immense. Obviously, these types of stickers are commonplace, with also anti-racist and even party political stickers often displayed. To this extent, since the prosecution is brought on planning grounds, the Council could be open to a criticism of not being even handed in its planning enforcement and even politically motivated in a decision to bring proceedings.

While this kind of criticism may undoubtedly have some credence, it is important to acknowledge that racially motivated and offensive speech reflects an unacceptable form of debate in any open democracy. It is inconsistent with the public interest goals evident within society and, as such, any resulting technical breaches of law deserve to be punished.

Racist Speech – Chanting at Football Matches

Section 3(1) of the Football (Offences) Act 1991 makes it an offence to take part at a designated football match in chanting of an indecent[46] or racialist nature, with a maximum fine at scale 3 applicable. For definition purposes,[47] 'chanting' means the repeated utterances of any words or sounds in concert with one or more others. With the words 'of a racialist nature' defined as 'consisting of or including matter which is threatening, abusive or insulting to a person by reason of his colour, race, nationality (including citizenship) or ethnic or national origins'.

Research by Brian Holland[48] showed that black players were receiving a disproportionate amount of abuse, racial abuse and 'monkey' chanting, being burdened up to 150 times more than white players. Figures produced by the Football Unit of the National Criminal Intelligence Unit, covering the 1991–92 season, showed that in total 88 arrests had been made under Section 3 of the Football (Offences) Act 1991.

In *R v Phillip, Newcastle Magistrates Court*,[49] acquitted a football fan arrested for racial abuse. Phillip was charged under Section 3 of the Football (Offences) Act 1991 after he had been making monkey noises – 'Ooh ooh, ooh' and monkey gestures towards three coloured Watford players. However, the Magistrates dismissed the charges when no evidence was provided which established that Phillip was chanting in concert with others.

According to Holland, the lesson is that individual fans arrested for racist behaviour would probably have to be charged under Section 4 of the Public Order Act 1986, rather than the 1991 Act if a conviction were to be successful.[50] It is submitted this is an over simplification of the law since both Section 4 and Section 5 of the Public Order Act 1986 are constructed differently from Section 3 of the Football (Offences) Act 1991.

Racist Chanting – A Need to Prove Intent?

Under Section 3 of the Football (Offences) Act 1991 there is only a need to establish the *actus reus* of the chanting.[51] There is no *mens rea*, or intent requirement. Whereas, Section 4 of the Public Order Act 1986 specifically provides for the a*ctus reus* of the use of 'threatening, abusive or insulting words or behaviour', with:

> intent to cause that person to believe that immediate unlawful violence will be used against him or another by any person, or to provoke the immediate use of unlawful violence by that person or another, or whereby that person is likely to believe that such violence will be used or it is likely that such violence will be provoked.

Generally, there is unlikely to be any evidence of intent to use unlawful violence from the football terraces to a player. Thus, Section 4 Public Order Act 1986 prosecutions must be inappropriate for dealing with incidents of racist chanting.

A prosecution under Section 5 of the Public Order Act 1986 (which is a lesser charge and a maximum fine under scale 3) would be far easier to establish, with a person guilty if he uses 'threatening, abusive or insulting words or behaviour, or disorderly behaviour'[52] within the hearing or sight of a person likely to be caused 'harassment, alarm or distress'.

Clearly, many acts of racial chanting could fall into this public order category, which deals with abuse. Although, as we considered earlier, Section 5 of the Public Order Act 1986 has a *mens rea* requirement of either 'intent', or the defendant being 'aware'[53] that his words or behaviour may be 'threatening, abusive or insulting'.

Holland has also questioned the wisdom of prosecuting fans for racist chanting, making reference to one Police Commander emphasising the concept of education rather than the punishment of fans. This same Police Commander, also expressed that he felt that the Public Order Act 1986 was more than adequate to deal with racial chanting, with the 1991 Act being an optional 'luxury'. Whatever, the merits of his view, it seems that three other Police Commanders, interviewed by Holland, were full of enthusiasm for the Football (Offences) Act 1991 believing it to be extremely useful because it was 'clear and specific'.

While not sharing their enthusiasm, I consider that, as Holland's research indicated, the core of the chanters are a distinct and vociferous minority. If these are in any way politically motivated, it is unlikely that such equal opportunity measures will succeed in reforming them. Thus, there is a need for both education[54] and punishment, with the role of the National Criminal Intelligence Unit, using video evidence techniques, of importance.

To this end, the combination of both Section 3 of the Football (Offences) 1991 Act and Section 5 of the Public Order 1986 Act, may be of limited assistance in dealing with the extreme orchestrators of racist chanting – with education being of value in dealing with the less committed racist supporters.

Protection from Harassment Act 1997

Earlier in this chapter, I considered Section 4A and Section 5 of the Public Order Act 1986 in relation to harassment. What seems clear from the wording of the legislation is that just one single incident can amount to harassment, alarm or distress. The legislator enables the courts to get around the plurality[55] associated with 'harassment', by including the words 'alarm or distress' – allowing the court to find one, and/or another.

By comparison, the Protection from Harassment Act 1997 establishes a new criminal offence of harassment that involves conduct that must have occurred on at least two occasions. Accordingly, no single and isolated act of distributing a racist leaflet, or expressing a racist message, can in itself amount to harassment under the 1997 Act. The legislation requires two incidents of conduct. Thus, it is certainly possible that the repetition of racist conduct, or a combination of, for example say pushing a racist leaflet through a person's door, followed by a verbal expression of racism directed towards that same person, could result in a prosecution.

What is more, the terminology used need not be 'threatening, abusive or insulting'. Indeed, as remarked by Lawson-Cruttenden and Addison,[56] repeatedly sending a rose to a person's place of work is not 'threatening, abusive or insulting' but has the potential to cause harassment. Quite whether delivering a rose can amount to harassment is decided on the facts by the magistrate or jury.[57]

This provides a very clear distinction from the Public Order Act 1986 legislation in that there is no requirement for the use of 'threatening, abusive, or insulting' words. Obviously, this could have enormous consequences for the majority of the material considered in the evidence assessment sheets – in that while, as representative of individual incidents, the material, or expression, may not amount to a criminal offence – done repeatedly, or in combination, it could do so.

Taking the racist jokes as an example: the actual content of the joke is 'racially offensive', and I considered the words used were 'threatening abusive or insulting'. However, the problem of ensuring conviction,[58] should any charges be brought, is one of proving intent to cause harassment, alarm, or distress under Section 4A – or, of him being aware that his words used were 'threatening, abusive or insulting' under Section 5 of the Public Order Act 1986.

By contrast, should a comedian pick on a member of his audience and repeat racist jokes directed towards that individual (which a number of comedy acts often do) it seems possible that he could face prosecution under the Protection from Harassment Act 1997. This is applicable even in circumstances where there is no use of 'threatening, abusive, or insulting' words – or no intent to cause 'harassment, alarm or distress'. This applies because a person must not pursue a course of conduct – which amounts to harassment of another, and which he knows or ought to know amounts to harassment of the other.[59] However, to comply with the PHA 1997 the conduct must occur on at least two occasions, with much depending on what the courts consider is reasonable in the particular circumstances. Quite whether two or more jokes – told in the course of one act – amounts to conduct on at least two occasions is not clear from the legislation. Assuming that the jokes were a one off event, it seems likely that there would be no real grounds for prosecution – but if it were repeated there could be.

Given the potential for a wide definition of harassment – i.e. due to a variety of situations being decided upon the facts – it would seem the Protection from Harassment Act 1997 legislation could be of value in relation to a whole host of militant racist activities. For example, suppose a political party were to leaflet a sheltered housing scheme specifically catering for elderly people from the ethnic communities – the leaflets containing messages of 'start repatriation'. Clearly, one such leaflet would not amount to harassment.

However, should these leaflets repeatedly be put through the door, it may be possible that it could amount to harassment – or, it could be concluded that the defendants 'ought to know' that it could amount to harassment. Under the terms of Section 1 of the Protection from Harassment Act 1997 this can amount to an offence since: 'A person must not pursue a course of conduct which amounts to harassment of another, and which he knows or ought to know amounts to harassment of another'.

If the material were part of an election campaign, there may exist a reasonable defence of legitimate political campaigning. However if, on the facts,[60] the material is perceived as a means of harassment, the courts may reject such a defence.

This also raises another interesting legal problem – the legislation is specific to a person. It says a 'person must not pursue a course of conduct'. As a political party is an organisation, it follows that it cannot face a criminal prosecution. In the case of *London Borough of Merton v Edmonds and Tyndall*[61] it was held that national/regional BNP officials Edmond and Tyndall, were liable in relation to a BNP poster displayed on a door, by virtue of them having consented to its display. While there was no direct evidence that Tyndall and Edmonds had themselves displayed the poster, their consent was established due to the ongoing situation. Tyndall and Edmonds were found, on the facts, to have failed to take down posters when advised by Merton Council that BNP handbills had been displayed in breach of planning regulations.

It is submitted that the case, which found leaders of the organisation liable for the organisation's posters, should not readily be a precedent to suggest that as national/regional leaders, Tyndall and Edmonds would be automatically liable in relation to any offending BNP leaflets. This logically applies because, in the planning law *BNP Merton* case, the defendants could have removed the posters within the authority's seven-day notice period. By comparison, if they are not personally liable for instructions in relation to the distribution of leaflets, it is difficult to see how they can be found guilty in relation to their repeated distribution. As Judge Buckley pointed out, in the *BNP Merton* Case:

> there are practical difficulties that arise in these cases, and Mr Tyndall has drawn our attention to them on behalf of himself and his Party, for example he says: It is well known that they have opponents, if not enemies. There may be mischief-makers who, on coming into possession of handbills, (and indeed the advertisement in this case was a handbill not a poster), might quit deliberately, display these in all sorts of places in order to make trouble for Mr Tyndall.

> Can it sensibly be suggested that the moment Mr Tyndall becomes aware that has happened, and I am assuming, without his consent that he should automatically be guilty of a criminal offence? The obvious answer in our judgement to that is 'no'.

This requirement, for some form of *mens rea*, is generally always necessary in criminal cases. In the circumstances of the *BNP Merton* case the Appeal Court remitted the case to the Crown Court to consider the issue of consent. Ultimately, it was decided that Tyndall and Edmonds had consented to the advertisement display in breach of regulations because they had failed to take the BNP posters down when requested to do so by the authority. These circumstances are very different to that of leaflets being delivered to people's homes or handed out in the street. If the deliverer is not known and no evidence exists they are working directly on behalf of individuals such as Tyndall and Edmonds, there exists no likelihood of evidence, beyond reasonable doubt, as to their guilt.

Although, it would seem that any election candidate, and or election agent, could be liable. This must apply because they are perceived as being responsible for the conduct of their election campaign. Each and every leaflet distributed in an election campaign, requires the authorisation of the agent who acts on behalf of the candidate. Accordingly, they must be personally responsible and liable in relation to the conduct of their campaign. Despite such a situation, it is to be hoped that the Crown Prosecution Service will recognise the importance of the need for freedom of expression for candidates during an election campaign – with widespread leafleting by all political parties. As such, unless there is some evidence of malice aforethought, the CPS could decide that it may not be in the public interest to instigate criminal proceedings in relation to election leaflets that are not 'threatening, abusive, and/or insulting' – yet may cause a limited level of harassment. However, this discretion need not apply outside of an election campaign – i.e. in circumstances where the facts suggest that the repeated conduct of leafleting establish harassment. What is more, this CPS public interest discretion can only apply in relation to criminal proceedings. Indeed, the Protection from Harassment Act 1997 also provides for a civil approach. In effect, this means that any individual who feels he is being harassed by any repeated (more than one) conduct could apply to the courts for an injunction[62] to cease the distribution of the material.[63] Again, should the defendant, without reasonable excuse, do anything he is prohibited from doing by the injunction, an application can be made for a warrant for the arrest of the defendant[64] with the possibility of up to five years imprisonment.[65]

This issue of legal interference with political campaigning raises a serious issue of freedom within a democracy. It is obvious that any political candidates/ agents could find themselves the subject of a civil action in relation to political literature that is perceived as providing harassment. Obviously, the courts will consider the merits of each and every individual case – with the facts and circumstances differing accordingly. Although, in general, it must be recognised that since I am not talking about literature that is 'threatening, abusive or insulting', this new Protection from Harassment Act 1997 provides the potential for a significant interference with the concept of freedom of expression as we know it. Indeed, it seems inevitable that the courts could experience defences associated with freedom of expression, now that the government has taken steps to incorporate the European Convention of Human Rights into UK Law via the Human Rights Act 1998.

In Conclusion

This chapter has also shown that there exist various laws that can be of limited value in tackling militant racism. The Criminal Damage Act 1971 can deal with graffiti, with planning laws able to deal with unlawful fly posting. The Malicious Communications Act 1988 can be of value in dealing with material which is a 'threat' or 'grossly offensive', but it is limited by the fact that the law requires specific intent, with literature often directed not towards the individual – but a group.

Of particular concern must be the limitations of penalty enforcement under the Malicious Communications Act 1988. A simple fine maximum, is hardly sufficient to deter the committed militant racist. To this end, it is disappointing that the new Section 4A of the Public Order Act 1986 (which can result in a fine and/or six months imprisonment) was not adapted to include material deposited through letterboxes and into a dwelling house. After all, a great deal of racist harassment is directed at victims living in their homes.

So far as prosecutions under Part III of the Public Order Act 1986 are concerned, by looking at the two evidence assessments, it is clear that racist material avoids the prospect of prosecution because the words used are not, in themselves, 'threatening abusive or insulting'. By comparison, the racist material, sent via book clubs or of an anti-Semitic nature, has much greater potential for prosecution under the Act – simply because the language can be considered to be not just offensive, but possibly 'threatening, abusive or insulting'.

Assessing all the material, it seems that nine out of 19 show some potential for an intent/likelihood to stir up racial hatred. However, only one has resulted in a prosecution. Obviously, this could indicate a lack of commitment from the Attorney General (whose consent is needed for prosecutions) to tackling militant racism and dealing with the problem of racist material which is likely to stir up racial hatred.

Perhaps another and better explanation, is that those producing the material are wise as to the law and are deliberately producing material which may stir up racial hatred by using words which are obviously 'racially offensive', but not directly 'threatening, abusive or insulting'.

The fact that following distribution of racist literature, racial harassment/attacks are reported to have increased is obviously of concern. If this increase is not directly due to the actions of party members, it must indirectly be due to the impact of their literature. Given that 'racially offensive' literature may increase tensions in a multicultural area, it is not unreasonable to make this deduction. To this end, in the next chapter I will examine changes to our current public order laws which will help deal with the problem of 'racially offensive' literature. Inevitably, such legal changes will impact upon freedom of speech, which will also need some detailed consideration.

Despite the limitations of existing legislation, it is pertinent to look at the positive elements of existing laws. The Protection from Harassment Act 1997 provides not just a criminal means but also a civil means of tackling militant racism. It is clear the Football (Offences) Act 1991 provides the potential for dealing with instances of any extreme orchestration of racist chanting – but it does not and cannot produce a solution. What is needed, and what is provided by the Football Association,[66] is an education programme that deals with the less committed racist supporters. Indeed, it is a combination of education and the law, which helps provide a relevant solution. Obviously, both approaches have indirect implications upon each other – in the sense that education may limit the eventual need for prosecution. Likewise, a lack of an education programme could result in the need for more prosecutions.

Notes

1   Figures produced by the Crown Prosecution Service for year ending 31 March 1998 show that 48 per cent of criminal charges, in relation to racial incidents, are public order offences (see *Racial Incident Monitoring Report for 1997–1998*). These figures are based upon the ACPO definition of a racial incident.

2   [1972] 2 All ER 1297.

3   The Magistrates, Court would still have needed to hear the case.

4   Or, as per 4A(1)(b) displays any writing, sign or other visible representation which is 'threatening, abusive or insulting'.

5   [1985] AC 905 HL.

6   Though, it must be recognised that a jury's sympathy is likely to vary depending upon the defendant. For example, they may accept racist jokes told by a well-known entertainer far more easily than they would accept the same jokes told by a skinhead.

7   Items 2 to 5 were sent via a book club. Thus, the words/writing was not used within the hearing or sight of a person: the anti-Semitic items 6 and 7 were sent via the post – see *Chappell v DPP* [1989] 89 Cr. App. R which suggests that the Malicious Communications Act 1988 (or even Post Office Act 1953) is applicable – not the Public Order Act 1986. Item 8 involves statements in a book. For further discussion of *Chappell v DPP* see 'Racist literature and the Malicious Communications Act 1988' later in the chapter.

8   Both Section 4A and Section 5 apply to a public or a private place. However, under both sections no offence can be committed in a private dwelling (see below in this chapter).

9   In *Chappell v DPP* [1989] 89 Cr. App. R., at 89, Lord Justice Watkins said: 'I fail to see how a person writing and/or delivering a letter to another, who opens it in the absence of the sender, can, on any reasonable reading of Section 5, be said to be a person who "uses ... words or behaviour ... within the hearing or sight of a person ..." who receives it'.

10 [1963] 2 All ER 225.

11 *The Times*, 26 October 1988.

12 [1992] Crim LR 60.

13 As signified by Attorney General's Chambers in correspondence to Hounslow Council, 17 August 1993.

14 [1972] 2 All ER 1297.

15 And, therefore, presumably the words *threatening* and *abusive*.

16 Under Section 18(5) this applies where an intent to stir up racial hatred is not established, but a likelihood exists.

17 [1983] 5 Cr. App. R. (S)145. Edwards had aided, abetted, counselled or procured the publication of a magazine called *The Stormer*, which was threatening, abusive or insulting in circumstances in which racial hatred was likely to be stirred up against Jews, Asians and Coloured people in Great Britain.

18 See *R v Bow Street Stipendiary Magistrate, ex p. South Coast Shipping Co. Ltd* [1993] 1 All ER 219. Also, advice from Attorney General's Chambers in correspondence to Hounslow Council – 17 August 1993. The irony of this situation is that the Home Affairs Select Committee have called for the DPP to be responsible for such prosecutions, instead of the Attorney General. Presumably starting a private prosecution could achieve this end – though, of course, the DPP may still liase with the Attorney General. Further, as per Section 9(3) of the Prosecution of Offences Act 1985, the Attorney General may request the DPP to report to him on such matters as he may specify.

19 As per Section 27 of the Public Order Act 1986, being found guilty in relation to any of the sections within 18 to 23 constitutes one offence. Thus a person cannot be found guilty of displaying written material that may stir up racial hatred (under Section 18) and also in possession of the same material (under Section 23) in relation to the same incident.

20 I.e. Appendices 2 to 5. It is also possible that the publishers of Item 5 could be prosecuted under Section 3(a) of the Explosive Substances Act 1833. Though, this area of Criminal Law is not the subject of this book.

21 The very fact that such members are individuals who are more likely to be influenced by the racist material is of no evidential concern.

22 See *Chappell v DPP* [1989] 89 Cr. App. R. which will be discussed in this chapter under 'Racist Literature and the Malicious Communications Act 1988'.

23 For a discussion in relation to 'insulting', see earlier in this chapter and the section 'Public Order Act 1986' and the case of *Brutus v Cozens* [1972] 2 All ER 1297.

24 (1989) 89 Cr. App. R.

25 Notably, the Protection from Harassment Act 1997 does not contain a similar 'dwelling' exemption. However, as I shall discuss later in this chapter, this Act requires two incidents of conduct to establish an offence.

26 A person prosecuted and found guilty under the new Section 4A Public Order Act 1986 faces a term of imprisonment of up to six months and/or a fine up to Level 5 on the standard scale. By comparison, if found guilty under the Malicious Communications Act 1988 a fine to the maximum at Level 4 would apply.

27 Section 1(b) Malicious Communications Act 1988.

28 *R v Stamford* [1972] 2 All ER 427.

29 *R v Court* [1987] 1 All ER 120 CA. Also, Smith and Hogan, *Criminal Law*, 6th edition, p. 449.

30 Though, of course, depending on the particular circumstances and facts of a specific case the publisher could be solely or equally responsible for both the publication and distribution of the material.

31 Though this legislation would not be applicable for any delivery by a private courier.

32 I.e. assuming the defendant opts for trial by jury.

33 While this book deals with racism, I will not examine issues associated with plays (Section 20), recordings (Section 21), or Broadcasts (Section 22) of the Public Order Act 1986. However, the broad legal principles of sections 18 and 19 are equally applicable to these sections.

34 As per Section 27(1) Public Order Act 1986, the consent of the Attorney General is required for all Part III prosecutions (i.e. sections 18–23).

35 Source: 1991 Census.

36 Hounslow Heath – 50 per cent, Hounslow West – 49 per cent, Cranford – 48 per cent, Hounslow Central – 47 per cent, Heston Central – 44 per cent, Heston West – 44 per cent, Heston East – 41 per cent. This compares with areas like Feltham South – 7 per cent, Hanworth – 8 per cent and Chiswick Homefields 9 – per cent.

37 The offending leaflet was distributed in a local by-election in Feltham South.

38 The police came to the same conclusion after consultation with the Crown Prosecution Service.

39 To be determined as a matter of fact – *Brutus v Cozens* [1972] 2 All ER 1297.

40 Since the election Hounslow Council have cut back spending in this area.

41 This will be discussed in more detail later in this book.

42 Though the words used were not 'threatening, abusive or insulting' (thus no offence committed).

43 Hounslow Council run a 24-hour 'Rub Out Racism' hotline, the aim being to remove racist graffiti from all public property within 24 hours. Council Officers will also negotiate with private property owners concerning the removal of any graffiti on private property.

44 This case involved four court hearings (Magistrates, Crown and Appeal Court). Finally resolved in case CO/1722/92 Divisional Court, 28 June 1993.

45 They were fined £100. Tyndall was ordered to pay costs of £468, Edmonds £472.

46 No definition of *indecent* is given under the Act. Although not the subject of this book, R v Courts [1988] 2 All ER 221 deals with motive and indecent assault cases. See also, Smith and Hogan, *Criminal Law*, 6th edition, p. 449.

47 Section 3(2) of the 1991 Act.

48 For a summary see Appendix 23. Home Affairs Committee, *Racial Attacks and Harassment*, Vol. II, Session 1993–94.

49 *The Times*, 12 December 1991.

50 It is possible this is a mistake and he means Section 5 of the Public Order Act 1986.

51 On 5 January 1999 the Home Office confirmed that the government were considering amendments to Section 3(2) of the Football Offences Act 1991 (which defines chanting as meaning 'the repeated utterance of any words or sounds in concert with one or more others') so as to enable prosecution of just one person shouting alone. Under section 3(1) of the Football Offences Act 1991 the chanting must be of a indecent or racialist nature at a designated football match, to establish an offence.

52 Section 5(1)(a) or Section 5(1)(a) displays any writing, sign or other visible representation.

53 Section 6(4), Public Order Act 1986. Also *DPP v Clarke* [1992] Crim. LR 60. This was discussed above.

54 *Let's Kick Racism out of Football* is an example of a FA approach. See 'Racism in football alive and kicking', *Searchlight*, November 1997, which gives examples of racist incidents at football matches and also tells of the work that is being done by football stars, like Alan Shearer, Gianfranco Zola and Ryan Giggs, to combat racism at football grounds.

55 In general, a lack of a statutory definition means that the word can be given its natural everyday meaning. *The Concise Oxford Dictionary* 'defines harassment as 'to trouble and annoy continually or repeatedly'.

56 *Blackstone's Guide to the Protection from Harassment Act 1997*, p. 14.

57 *Lodge v DPP* (*The Times*, 26 October 1988) determined that criminal harassment is to be determined by the magistrates' on the basis of the facts and only to be interfered with by an Appeal Court if the decision is totally perverse.

58 See Evidence assessment sheet ·1.

59 Section 1 of Protection from Harassment Act 1997.

60 *Lodge v DPP* (*The Times*, 26 October 1988) held that criminal harassment is an issue determined on the basis of the facts only to be interfered with by an appeal court if the decision it totally perverse.

61 See 'Racist Graffiti and Fly Posting' within this chapter.

62 As I demonstrated in chapter 2, 'Action by Local Authorities', this injunction could be directed towards individuals and organisations.

63 This will be determined on the balance of convenience – *American Cyanamid Co v Ethicon Ltd* [1975] 1 All ER 504, HL. For a fuller discussions see chapter 2, 'Action by Local Authorities'.

64 Section 3 (3) (b).

65 Section 3 (9).

66 i.e. a voluntary programme in consultation with the Commission for Racial Equality.

4 'Say No to Racism' – Part One: The Legal Options for Change

In chapter 3, I discussed the fact that offensive literature, which may stir up racial hatred, will not in itself provide grounds for a prosecution under British law.[1] The literature must be 'threatening, abusive or insulting' to establish an offence under the Part III of the Public Order Act 1986.

I argued that there is anecdotal evidence which shows that following the distribution of racist literature, an increase in racial harassment/attacks may be found. Clearly, if this is not due to the direct actions of militant racists, it must indirectly be due to the impact of their racially offensive literature contributing to an increase in tensions in a multi-cultural area. It follows, that so far as criminal law is concerned, two obvious approaches exist:

(a) prosecute where evidence exists of racial harassment/attack;
(b) prosecute those who stir up racial discrimination or hatred through the use of material that is threatening, abusive, insulting and/or offensive.[2]

So far as (a) is concerned, various criminal laws exist which can be deployed to enable the police to tackle such militant racism,[3] with the Crime and Disorder Act 1998 providing enhanced sentencing where a person is found guilty of racially-aggravated crime.[4] While (b) could be tackled by amending Part III of the Public Order Act 1986 to make it an offence to stir up racial discrimination (as well as hatred) and by adding 'racial offence' to those of 'threat, abuse or insult' as a prerequisite to a prosecution.

The previous chapters have considered various laws applicable to (a) – i.e. militant racist activity that results in racial harassment or attack. Accordingly I will not be treading further down this path, but intend to examine (b) on the basis that to develop such reforms will make it more difficult for militant racists to distribute racist materials. In order to consider (b) I will break the proposals into two options. Option 1 will deal with the relatively straightforward proposal of making it an offence to '*stir up racial discrimination or hatred*', while Option 2 will give consideration to including '*racial offence*', along with '*threat, abuse or insult*', as a prerequisite to a prosecution under Part III of the Act.

Option 1 – 'Stirring up Racial Discrimination or Hatred'

The Public Order Act 1986[5] states:

> A person who uses threatening, abusive or insulting words or behaviour, or displays any written material which is threatening, abusive or insulting is guilty of an offence if:
> (a) he intends thereby to stir up racial hatred, or
> (b) having regard to all the circumstances racial hatred is likely to be stirred up thereby.

However, statute provides no guidance as to what 'to stir up' means, and as such it is given a natural meaning. Indeed, there appears to have been no serious problems with its application, though Bailey, Harris and Jones[6] report that there have been some difficulties with regards to the prosecution of offenders who send material to clergymen or Members of Parliament, since such public figures are thought to be less likely to be stirred up to racial hatred. Conceivably this could be a difficulty, though a prosecution could still be established under Section 18(1)(a) with regards to an intent to stir up racial hatred. This must apply, because although it may be unlikely that the clergy would be stirred to racial hatred by a leaflet, the intent could still have been for the material to do so.

It seems reasonable to argue that the words 'to stir up' are broadly synonymous with the term 'incite'.[7] On this basis, the 'stirring up of racial discrimination or hatred' in Option 1 can be considered as synonymous with 'incitement to racial discrimination or hatred'.

However, it does seem probable that 'stirring up', 'inciting' or encouraging 'racial discrimination' would be evidentially easier to determine than 'inciting racial hatred'. To racially discriminate is 'to treat less favourably' on racial grounds,[8] while 'racial hatred' can be interpreted as being to 'dislike intensely'[9] a group of persons because of their race, nationality etc.

Applying these definitions, it follows that treating another less favourably involves, some form of treatment that can be objectively measured as providing disadvantage to a person, or group of persons, on the grounds of race or nationality.[10]

By comparison, encouragement to 'dislike intensely' is potentially much more problematic, since it involves a consideration of the mental process involved. What degree of emotion is necessary to determine 'intense dislike'? Since a synonym is also 'violent or forceful'[11] – does this need to be fulfilled to reach the natural meaning of 'intense dislike'? The answer to these questions is left to the discretion of the jury or magistrates – with a combined statutory and natural meaning of the words 'racial hatred' being applicable. While the courts can and do currently grapple with the difficulty of determining racial hatred, changing the law so as to tackle the stirring up of racial discrimination should produce a more readily definable threshold.

It also follows that to introduce Option 1 must broaden the scope of the law. By way of illustration, we can examine a leaflet which says 'Keep Feltham White'. The leaflet does not stir up racial hatred, but it can stir up racial discrimination, with it being clear that it proposes that black and Asian families are kept out of Feltham.[12] As this demonstrates, changing the criminal law to penalise the stirring up of 'racial discrimination' will inevitably extend the opportunities for prosecution. One superficial concern, may be that the proposals suggest criminalising acts related to racial discrimination, while racial discrimination itself is considered to be a civil offence under the Race Relations Act 1976. However, there is a definite difference between acts of racial discrimination and the stirring up of racial discrimination. The difference being that those applications in relation to 'racial discrimination' are generally claims for compensation arising from an organisation's racial discrimination. In terms of the stirring up of racial hatred, I am talking about society penalising a person who incites others to pursue a course of conduct that the rules of society consider is unacceptable. While 'incitement to racial discrimination' suggests a purposeful decision to encourage others to treat others less favourably, it should be noted that intent need not be proven, since the legislative proposals could provide for guilt in circumstances whereby a likelihood exists that racial discrimination will be stirred up thereby.[13]

Option 2 – A 'Racial Offence' Prerequisite

As chapter 3[14] demonstrated, a great deal of literature which in all likelihood has the potential of inciting racial hatred is 'racially offensive', but not 'threatening, abusive or insulting'.

Evidence suggests that militant racists carefully produce literature that will give 'racial offence', but which avoids prosecution under the *existing* law.[15] This is in effect, an attempt to stir up racial discrimination and possibly even hatred, without being in breach of the Public Order Act 1986. This argument is strengthened by examining the analysis of the racist material developed earlier in this book.[16]

As already acknowledged, there is no evidence that 'racially offensive' material directly incites conflict or violence within communities. However, it is certainly possible that 'racially offensive' material may lead to the raising of racial tensions.[17] Clearly, any rise of racial tensions can have serious community consequences with incidents of violence a possible consequence. Thus, in order to maintain the peace it is important that racial tensions are not significantly inflamed.

It is also appropriate to consider the extent to which 'racially offensive' material has the potential to incite racial discrimination. To stir up racial discrimination, material must encourage others to treat an individual or group of people, defined by race, less favourably than people from other more accepted groups. Applying such a criterion, it is important to recognise that it is almost symptomatic of 'racially offensive' material that it undermines support for a racial group's existence within the community and thereby treats people from that group less favourably. Naturally, depending upon the nature of the leaflet, the resulting discrimination can take various forms ranging from abuse, directed towards members of that group, to them simply being ignored and frozen out of the general life of the community. Whatever form of action may, or may not, result, 'racially offensive' material is often inherently discriminatory. While this may suggest that an intention to discriminate/stir up hatred often exists, intent is not a necessary ingredient since the offence can be committed if 'having regard to all the circumstances racial hatred [discrimination] is likely to be stirred up thereby'.[18] Despite such an objective approach, the law returns to subjectivity with regards to words used that are '[racially offensive] insulting, threatening or abusive' – with a requirement that for a person who is not shown to have intended to stir up racial hatred he is not guilty unless he intended, or was aware that, his words/behaviour might be '[racially offensive] threatening, abusive, insulting'.[19] However, while it is clear that the words 'threat, abuse and insult' require elements of subjectivity there may also be objective elements that help a jury measure the subjectivity. For example, in subjectively determining words like 'threatening' we often apply certain objective criteria to determine the extent of the threat – was there an indication of violence etc. Again with 'abusive' – did the words involve swearing, in what way were they abusive? By comparison, 'insulting' is clearly more subjective, with few objective criteria to help clarify. The same can be said for 'racially offensive', with offence being almost entirely subjective and objectivity arising from a determination as to whether the words are 'racial'.[20]

Racist Speech and its Audience

In order to discuss matters further, I intend to examine the practical implications of a combination of Options 1 and 2, by looking at the impact they would have in relation to first racist speech and then racist literature or materials. In considering speech, it is important to reflect that in determining incitement[21] to racial discrimination or hatred, the words themselves are not the sole criteria for determining incitement – what should generally be of importance is to whom they may be directed, or by whom they may be heard. For example:

- *Suppose Tom – while mixing with a group known to hold extreme racist views – shouts to Mohammed, in extreme racist terms*

This situation could result in a prosecution, because Tom must[22] have been aware that his words could give 'racial offence' and a likelihood of incitement to racial discrimination or hatred exists. This derives from the fact that Tom could incite other members of the group to discriminate or hate people because of their colour. The same would apply even if those observing, and likely to hear the words shouted, were just members of the public – because a likelihood exists that the words expressed by Tom could incite others to discriminate or hate on grounds of race, nationality, etc. The intent of Tom to incite may matter little since, having regard to all the circumstances, the stirring up of racial discrimination or hatred, is likely thereby.

What this illustration demonstrates is that Tom may be relatively free[23] to express 'racially offensive' words, but in doing so he must ensure that he does not incite others. This principle can be related to that advocate of individual freedom John Stuart Mill, who argued:

> An opinion that corn-dealers are starvers of the poor, or that private property is robbery ... may justly incur punishment when delivered orally to an excited mob assembled before the house of the corn dealer, or when handed out among the same mob in the form of a placard.[24]

In a sense, this combination approach helps qualify the subjectivity of 'offence', since 'racially offensive' words in themselves could not lay grounds for a criminal offence, they need to be combined with inciting others to 'racial discrimination or hatred' to provide a basis for prosecution.

This approach is consistent with the philosophy of J.S. Mill and can also be found in the *existing public order law* in relation to 'insult'. Indeed, under Part III of the Public Order Act 1986, a person who uses insulting words is guilty of an offence if:

(a) he intends thereby to stir up racial hatred, or,
(b) having regard to all the circumstances racial hatred is likely to be stirred up thereby.

Problems Associated with Incitement in Relation to Sole Recipients

This clearly penalises the incitement of others. Indeed, the existing public order legislation seems to enable a prosecution where racial hatred can be stirred up within a sole recipient; i.e. notwithstanding that racial hatred is defined as meaning hatred *against a group* of persons – by reference to race etc. – and not against an individual.[25] Thus, a person using insulting words on a verbal one to one basis,[26] could commit an offence if it can be proven that he intended to, or it is likely that racial hatred will be stirred up thereby. Obviously, problems of evidence would exist with it being one person's word against another. However, assuming the problem of evidence could be overcome, there is no reason why a person could not be successfully prosecuted. Though there could be a few problems that could arise. By way of illustration:

• *Suppose in a private conversation Tom turns to a woman, and fellow indigenous citizen, called Lis and says: 'Don't go with any of those people, they are infested with AIDs'*

This involves Tom using an insult to incite Lis to have some level of resentment or hatred towards a particular group.

In theory at least, grounds may exist for a prosecution in that the words used may be insulting and incite Lis to racial hatred (or discrimination under Option 1). While that is the theory, the practicalities of formulating the evidence could result in problems for bringing a prosecution. Given that it is a private conversation, where would the evidence of any offence come from? Obviously a third party may have a complaint that Tom incited Lis to racial hatred/ discrimination, but given that it is a private conversation between Tom and Lis where would the evidence come from and how reliable could it be?

Let us assume that Lis is unhappy with the remark of Tom. Consequently, she complains to the police that Tom has used an insulting remark to stir her into racial hatred (or discrimination under Option 1). If we also assume that Tom admits he made the remark (but pleads not guilty to incitement), evidence would exist of a comment that is potentially insulting and to a racial group and thus could lay the foundations for a Section 18, Public Order Act 1986 prosecution under the existing law. The problems for the prosecution are numerous. First, they must establish, beyond reasonable doubt, that the words are 'insulting' – which is determined as a matter of fact and not law.[27] Secondly, they would need to prove an *intent*, or that it is *likely*, that racial hatred would be stirred up thereby. Further, if the prosecution is brought upon the basis of a *likelihood of stirring up racial hatred*, they must prove an intent or awareness, on behalf of the accused, that the words might be insulting.

In the case of *Jordan v Burgoyne*,[28] Lord Parker held that 'Once a speaker uses insulting words, that person must take the audience as he finds them'.[29] In this illustration concerning Lis, the defence argument could be – assuming that no intent is evident – that the audience was not likely to be stirred into racial hatred. Proof of this comes from the fact that the audience, consisting solely of Lis, complained to the police about the remark of Tom – rather than being incited into racial hatred. While this seems to be the logic of the *Jordan* ratio, it can be criticised because such an interpretation nullifies the impact of the legislation and serves to undermine the complainant's legal rights.

Should the Public Order law be changed as proposed in Option 1 – i.e. establishing incitement to racial discrimination – the prospect of prosecution could be stronger. This is because the words: 'Don't go with any of those people, they are infested with Aids', show the potential for insult and provide a clear indication of a likelihood of inciting others (Lis) to treat particular groups less favourably – with incitement to discrimination demonstratively easier to establish than incitement to hatred. To this extent, changing the law to tackle racial discrimination as well as hatred broadens the scope for prosecution, with the case of *Jordan* serving to limit the prospect in circumstances where the complainant is the sole receiver of the message.

Let us consider another illustration, albeit that this one does not readily signify the broadening of the scope for prosecution:

- *Suppose Tom, sitting alone with Mohammed, turns to him and makes a remark which implies that members of his ethnic group are infested with AIDs*

Should Mohammed complain to the police, and Tom admit he made the remark (but plead not guilty to incitement), it seems that grounds may exist for bringing a prosecution under the existing Section 18 of the Public Order Act 1986. Again, the problem for the prosecution is one of establishing that stirring up of racial hatred is likely or intended. Assuming the court determines that Tom is aware his words might be insulting, there remains a problem of determining a likelihood of stirring up racial hatred. Is it likely, beyond reasonable doubt that Mohammed would be stirred up into hating his own race? Or, is Mohammed likely to be stirred up to hate Tom, and people of the same race and nationality as him? This may be possible, but it seems problematic – because it suggests that the hatred develops as a result of the unlawful use of insulting words (rather than likely thereby). This would be the equivalent of arguing that any criminal act by a person of one race on another, inevitably would likely result in the stirring up of racial hatred between the races.

Likewise, with regard to the intent of Tom to stir up racial hatred, it clearly is possible that a court could determine, on the facts, that Tom intended to stir up hatred between the races, though much will depend upon the reasons that he may give for making the remark. Did he express the words as part of a warning about safe sex – or as a means of antagonism levelled towards Mohammed? Even if he was antagonistic towards Mohammed, did he intend to stir up racial hatred?

If we were to move from the existing public order law to that proposed In applying Option 1 – did he intend to incite racial discrimination? The answer to this last question involves the difficulty of Mohammed being incited to discriminate against other people of his own race (which he may do, if he was to believe the claim and does not wish to risk catching AIDS). It certainly seems unlikely that Mohammed could easily be incited to racially discriminate against members of his own race. To this extent, the proposed changes in the law would not extend the boundaries in relation to incitement to sole recipients.

Indeed, such sole recipient cases raise difficult issues for a jury to determine on the basis of fact, essentially because it is likely to be one person's word against another. Even if the facts can clearly be established, the case of *Jordan v Burgoyne* seems to undermine the prospect of a successful prosecution, due to the fact that the sole recipient would be demonstrating that they are unlikely to stir up racial hatred or discrimination by virtue of being the complainant. For such reasons, it seems probable that the Crown Prosecution Service, and/ or Attorney General, may decide that – unless there is an admission/evidence as to intent – it is inappropriate to bring charges where the complainant is the sole recipient.

Racially Offensive Literature

In considering Option 2 in relation to verbal speech, I have argued that expressing 'racially offensive' words, in themselves, should not constitute a criminal offence. However, the use of 'racially offensive' words in combination with incitement to racial discrimination/hatred provides some justification for amendments to current legislation.

Clearly, this form of division may be relatively easy to determine when verbal words are involved, with the existence of persons within hearing of the 'racially offensive' words being expressed, a critical requirement. Thus, a person would be free to verbally express 'racially offensive' views so long as they ensure that the words cannot and do not incite others.

However, this simple division cannot apply to 'racially offensive' literature since there can rarely be a guarantee that the literature will be seen by just the one reader. Indeed, a leaflet given wholesale distribution is designed for public consumption and thus once it is established that the words used give 'racial offence', it must be possible that it would incite others to racial discrimination and/or hatred. To consider this point further, I intend to consider the practicalities associated with a leaflet designed to advocate a further restriction on immigration.

Advocating Immigration Controls under Options 1 and 2

I use immigration as an example, because it emphasises a potential conundrum so far as 'racially offensive' literature is concerned. In effect, material arguing for immigration controls can easily give racial offence, since by its nature it generally advocates treating persons of certain races differently, and often less favourably, than those of indigenous origin. To this extent, such material would be openly advocating racial discrimination, quite whether this would amount to an offence of stirring up racial discrimination would obviously depend upon the facts in relation to words used.

However, materials that discuss immigration – in the limited terms of people coming to the United Kingdom – should not lead to a prosecution for stirring up racial hatred/discrimination. By way of illustration,

- *Suppose a political party extends the leaflet to say: 'We will stop Pakistanis from immigrating into the UK'*

While these words may, or may not, give racial offence and stir up racial discrimination, they should not provide grounds for a prosecution due to Section 17 of the Public Order Act 1986 which defines 'racial group' as meaning hatred against a group of persons in Great Britain. Thus, by definition, since the immigrant group referred to will be outside of Great Britain there can be no offence.

Discussing Issues Associated with Repatriation

Should a policy leaflet go a stage further and argue for repatriation, there could be grounds for a prosecution. By way of example:

- *Suppose a political party's leaflet were to say: 'We have too many Pakistani immigrants, they should all be sent back home'*

This refers to Pakistani immigrants who are currently resident in the United Kingdom, as such the statement is discriminating against a group of persons in Great Britain defined by race, nationality etc. Accordingly, grounds could exist for a prosecution under the proposed legislation incorporating Options 1 and 2.

The first thing to establish is do the words give racial 'racial offence', as per the proposed Option 2? Obviously, the legislature could provide a statutory meaning of 'racial offence', while requiring that the accused *intended* or is *aware* that his words may give *offence*.[30] However a more preferable way forward may be to take a combined statutory and natural meaning approach, with a statutory definition applying for the term 'racial' and a natural meaning applicable for the term 'offence'. This may mean slight amendment to Section 17 of the Public Order Act 1986, refining it to read: 'In this part 'racial offence', 'racial hatred' or 'racial discrimination' derives as a result of expression referring to a group of persons in Great Britain defined by reference to colour, race, nationality (including citizenship) or ethnic or national origins'. This would leave the definition of 'offence' to the courts to determine in accord with the 'ordinary usage – natural meaning – methodology' already established in *Brutus v Cozens*.[31] Inevitably, this would result in 'offence' being interpreted according to its natural meaning – which is 'a wounding of feelings'[32] – and determined as a matter of fact. Indeed, this approach is preferable because it would retain a consistency of legal approach concerning the words 'threatening, abusive, insulting' and the proposed 'racially offensive'.

Simply expressing 'racially offensive' words would not in itself amount to an offence. Indeed, the words also need to stir up *racial discrimination (or hatred)*. So far as stirring up *racial discrimination* is concerned, it would be necessary to determine that those responsible for the leaflet intended to stir up racial discrimination, or the words were likely to stir up racial discrimination. Obviously, without a confession, intent is difficult to determine with any degree of consistency and for these reasons it can be difficult to determine beyond reasonable doubt. By comparison the 'likelihood' approach is easier to determine, since the jury are able to reason from their own understanding of the words and the circumstances surrounding the use. It could certainly be argued that a leaflet, with its words 'We have too many Pakistani immigrants they should all be sent back home' discriminates against Pakistani people. But that in itself is not enough to constitute an offence under the proposals, since the words need to incite others to discriminate to establish a criminal offence. It could certainly be argued that the leaflet by its use of words is urging people to be less than welcoming to Pakistani people – which in effect means that they are inciting people to treat them less favourably than other nationals. To this extent, a jury could – on the facts – determine that the words are inciting racial discrimination (though this is far from certain).

Despite such, there still remains one additional hurdle for the prosecution to overcome, albeit one that is so limited in height it hardly constitutes an hurdle. This requirement claims its foundations from Section 18(5) of the Public Order Act 1986 and, as amended by Option 2, determines that where the defendant is not shown to have intended to stir up racial discrimination, he would be not guilty if he did not *intend* or was not *aware* that the words used *might be racially offensive* (threatening, abusive or insulting). On the basis of the illustration, a defendant may have difficulties in convincing a jury that he was not aware that Pakistani people might be racially offended by the words 'We will stop Pakistanis from immigrating into the UK'.

However, even if it is felt that the words amount to the use of threatening abusive, insulting and/or racially offensive words that stir up racial hatred or discrimination the Crown Prosecution Service and/or Attorney General may still consider it is not in the public interest to bring a prosecution. In deciding whether to prosecute, two questions are generally asked. The first, whether reasonable grounds exist for believing that a court will establish guilt, with the second being whether it is in the public interest to instigate a prosecution.

So far as the public interest question is concerned, this is clearly not easy to determine and can often be dependent upon a number of factors including the consequences of bringing an action that may fail. Also relevant must be the need to respect the intent of genuinely being involved in political debate about government legislation. How can a political party discuss and promote its policies on an important issue, if to do so may put it in breach of the criminal law? As a counter to this argument, it is also important to recognise that some extreme parties may have little desire for genuine political discussion and be more inclined to use the issue of immigration as a disguise for promoting their offensive and racist views. Given such circumstances, it could be that a noticeable failure to bring prosecutions against political organisations would undermine respect for anti-racist legislation and even the law.

Let us now consider a new illustration.

- *Suppose a party produces a further leaflet that says, 'We have too many immigrants, they should all be sent back home'*

This leaflet is very similar to the previous leaflet, in that its words call for repatriation and thus most of the previous arguments apply. However, a key difference is that it does not call for a specific group of nationals to be repatriated, it applies to all immigrants. This new illustrated leaflet does discriminate against immigrants, but it does not directly seem to fall within the criteria of 'racial group' as per Section 17 of the Public Order Act 1986. This applies because the legislation refers to hatred 'against a group of persons … by reference to race, colour, nationality (including citizenship) or ethnic or national origins' – it does not refer to 'races' (plural). The words of the party are not specific in terms of colour, citizenship or national identity and as such they do not readily fall within the category of race. Indeed the only way that such an offensive leaflet could be considered to fall within the definition of race, is on the grounds of a purposive interpretation of the law, with ethnic origins equated to persons whose origins are other than indigenous. For such an approach to be legally acceptable, it may be necessary to amend Section 17 of the Public Order Act 1986 to enable the jury to determine such issues purposively, with this having the added advantage that religious terms that are shorthand for racial descriptions, could also be encompassed.[33]

However, a purposive interpretation in relation to criminal law seems an adventurous leap – with this term only recently having been developed in civil law.[34] Though, in support of such a leap it can be argued that, in effect, the government requires the courts to give a purposive interpretation to legislation in order to give effect to Section 28(3) of the Crime and Disorder Act 1998. This section relates to racially aggravated crime and is designed to enable the law to penalise hostility that may also be based upon religion. Indeed, the wording of Section 28(3) specifies:

> It is immaterial … whether or not the offender's hostility is also based, to any extent, on (a) the fact or presumption of that any person or group of persons belongs to any religious group, or (b) any other factor not mentioned in this paragraph.

Certainly, this Crime and Disorder Act requires the courts to determine the purpose and/or motive behind both the activities of the accused and to a limited extent requires the court to establish if this purpose falls within the definition provided by statute. This, it is argued, does require a limited form of purposive interpretation in order to give effect to the statute. While this may not be an exact replica of the purposive approach taken in relation to the interpretation of EU directives and UK domestic laws, it is nonetheless a form of purposive interpretation. This demonstrates that in order to give effect to legislation, parliament expects that it may be necessary to look at the purpose behind the legislation and apply the facts within a case, so as to comply with the legislation. This signifies some form of recognition, that the traditional literal interpretation of legislation is not always appropriate.

The Impact of Options 1 and 2 on Militant Racist Materials

Having considered some theoretical examples, I intend to consider the proposed changes, to Part III of the Public Order Act 1986 by examining materials distributed by a political party in the Borough of Hounslow.[35] In order to fulfil this task, I have produced evidence assessment sheet (3) (see Table 4.1). It can be seen from the earlier evidence assessment sheet (2), shown in chapter 3, that none of this material provides grounds for a prosecution under the existing Part III of the Public Order Act 1986. Obviously, these assessments are to a large extent subjective and thus open to question. However, the assessment has been produced by applying the appropriate

Table 4.1 Evidence assessment sheet 3

Material distributed in the Borough of Hounslow.

Appendix ref:	9	10	11	12	13	14	15	16	17	18
Part III of the Public Order Act 1986 – [options, or proposed changes, shown in brackets]										
A Were the words used threatening, abusive or insulting?	?	N	N	N	N	N	N	N	N/?	?
B Were the remarks/words racially offensive? [Option 2]	Y	Y/?	Y	Y	Y	Y	?	N	Y	Y
C Intent/aware his words/writing – threatening, abusive or insulting (Section 18 (5))?	#	#	#	#	#	#	#	#	#	#
D Intent/aware his words/writing – racially offensive? [Option 2]	Y	Y/?	Y/?	Y	Y	Y	N	#	Y/?	Y
E Use words/display material – intent/likelihood to stir up racial hatred (Section 18)?	N	N	?	N	N	Y/?	?	N	?	N
F Publish/distribute material – intent/likelihood to stir up racial hatred (Section 19)?	N	N	?	N	N	Y/?	?	N	?	Y/?
G Intent/likelihood of inciting racial discrimination/hatred? [Option 1]	Y	Y/?	Y	Y	Y	Y	N	N	Y	Y
M Can a racial motive be inferred?	Y/?	Y	Y	Y/?	Y	Y	Y/?	N	Y	Y

Y = yes, N = no, ? = possible/doubtful, # = not applicable.

questions of law and serves as a valuable aid to determining if grounds could exist for bringing a prosecution.

Indeed, evidence assessment sheet 3 (Question A) demonstrates that none of the material was considered to be either threatening, abusive or insulting. Thus, the prerequisite for a prosecution under the existing Public Order Act 1986 has not been fulfilled, and a prosecution would not be applicable. However, from Question B we can see that, in eight out of ten cases, grounds exist for believing that the material is 'racially offensive'[36] and, as such, capable of fulfilling the prerequisite for an Option 2 (racial offence) public order prosecution.

Question D also signifies that in all cases where 'racially offensive' words have been used, it is possible that an intent or awareness that the material may be 'racially offensive' could be established. Clearly, any answer to this question must be potentially erroneous because we have not heard the defence of any accused. However, it is difficult to imagine how a person may not be aware that comments like, 'Keep Feltham White', have the potential of being 'racially offensive'. No doubt, militant racists would argue that it is 'racially offensive' that foreign people are offered accommodation in Feltham – but this kind of comment simply provides justification for a prosecution.

What is especially interesting about evidence assessment sheet 3 is that even after introducing the Option 2 prerequisite of 'racial offence' to the Public Order Act 1986, we will not see a significant increase in prosecutions. This is because in only two out of the eight instances of the material being potentially 'racially offensive', is it possible to conclude that grounds may exist for either a Section 18 or Section 19 (stirring up racial hatred) prosecution.

By examining EAS 3 Question G, we can see that by also adopting Option 1, and making incitement to racial discrimination/hatred a criminal offence, it opens up the potential for a prosecution in all instances where words have been used which are 'racially offensive' (i.e. eight out of the ten instances).[37]

What the assessment also demonstrates is that, in order to make Option 1 – incitement to racial discrimination/hatred – a viable new offence, it may be necessary also to include Option 2, i.e. 'racial offence' along with 'threatening, abusive or insulting'. Indeed, as EAS 3 shows, in all eight instances where racial discrimination/hatred appears evident, there are no grounds for arguing that the words used were 'threatening, abusive or insulting'. As such, it would not be possible to bring a prosecution unless the legislation was changed to include 'racial offence' as a prerequisite.

This clearly suggests that simply changing Part III of the Public Order Act 1986 to include 'incitement to racial discrimination', would not produce a significant impact. Though, it would make prosecutions for a likelihood of incitement to racial discrimination easier to determine than currently exist in relation to the stirring up of racial hatred.

Evidence assessment sheet 3 further indicates that grounds may also exist for believing that some level of racial motivation may be inferred in nine out of the ten examples given. Such motivation should not in itself provide evidence to justify a finding of guilt, but it may result in a judge determining that some element of racial hostility exists which could justify a tougher sentencing policy.[38]

Wider Implications in Relation to a Racial Offence Prerequisite

Obviously, a more detailed and thorough analysis of 'racially offensive' literature might be appropriate before firm conclusions could be made on the need for changes to our existing law. An analysis of just 10 items of racist material cannot be regarded as sufficient. However, it is worth noting that the materials used are typical of the type of racist material distributed by militant racists.[39]

What is also clear from the EAS 3 analysis, is that none of the material was considered to be in breach of the existing public order laws. In applying Option 1 (incitement to racial discrimination), no additional items of literature would be in breach of any amended legislation – principally because the existing prerequisites of 'threat abuse or insult' act as a shield to prosecution. By applying just Option 2 (racial offence), two additional items of literature could likely be considered as being in breach of the proposed legislation – with the remainder[40] failing to be considered in breach due to the stirring up 'racial hatred' criterion. However, by amending the public order legislation to include both Options 1 and 2 – i.e. to make it illegal to use racially offensive words to stir up racial discrimination – a total of eight items are considered as being in breach (see Figure 4.1).

From Figure 4.1, it is clear that the application of Option 2 alone[41] has only a limited impact upon racist materials – with some 20 per cent of racist materials likely to result in a criminal prosecution.[42] However, such a partial approach still displays a potential for some limitation upon the concept of freedom of expression[43] and will leave United Kingdom law inconsistent with the CERD convention, which requires nations to tackle incitement to racial discrimination.[44]

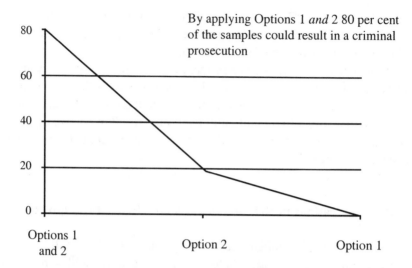

Figure 4.1   Area chart 1 showing the potential effect of Options 1 and 2 on racist material

By comparison, as the area chart demonstrates, the application of Options 1 and 2 certainly shows a wider potential for tackling militant racist material.[45] However, this gives rise to the problem that the combination may be so wide as to limit what may morally be considered to be legitimate discussion of racial issues. This can be considered by considering a hypothetical leaflet in relation to Kosovo refugees.[46]

- *Suppose a political campaigning group produces a leaflet that says: 'We should not be accepting so many Kosovo refugees. The Serbs don't want them – why should we have them? They are immigrants who are exploiting our good nature. They are quick to claim state benefits and are a drain on our country's resources. They should be flown back home to Kosovo as soon as possible'*

Such discussion is commonplace, and illustrates a political debate amongst UK citizens. The words used may not indicate an intent to give 'racial offence', but it is clear that an awareness of a likelihood of giving 'racial offence' could exist.[47] This inevitably would mean that such a leaflet could possibly fall foul of any new legislation that contains Options 1 and 2, since the words used suggest that indigenous people should not welcome Kosovo refugees and they should be sent back home.[48]

Irrespective of one's opinion on the uncharitable nature of such comments, it is worrying that simply expressing such views could result in a person committing a criminal offence. To this extent, the illustration helps indicate that the combination of Options 1 and 2 may seriously threaten freedom of expression. Indeed, such is the interference with freedom of expression, it may become unlawful for a political party to publicly debate, and give specific detailed information of its policies, on a vitally important issue like refugees and asylum seekers. The consequences for our society can be judged by the comments of Feldman:[49]

> It is impossible to imagine a properly functioning democracy in a country where people by and large are not guaranteed freedom of expression, a free press, a right to vote, a right to petition Parliament, freedom of protest, and freedom from arbitrary arrest and detention by government agencies. Such rights are fundamental to the notion of democracy, and could not be abrogated by democratic decision-makers in the public sphere without undermining the very democracy which is said to legitimise public decision making.

While some limitations already exist in many of these areas – e.g. on freedom of protest under the Public Order Act 1986[50] – on the whole such freedoms are respected in the United Kingdom. Obviously, introducing the limitations in Options 1 (incitement to racial discrimination) and 2 (racial offence prerequisite) will not amount to the abrogation of the right of freedom of expression – though it would add to limits already imposed by various laws ranging from defamation to race relations.

As Area Chart 1 shows, separately Options 1 and 2 do not appear to produce an overtly restrictive impact upon racist materials. However, the combination of the two can, in certain circumstances, have a direct and negative impact upon the democratic process. It clearly cannot be considered as acceptable that morally legitimate debate, on an issue of such political importance as Refugee and Asylum seekers, may in part become unlawful, with a minefield existing as to what is, and is not, a statement that leads to criminality. To this end, *it is argued that the combination of Options 1 and 2 could seriously undermine freedom of expression and may not be considered as acceptable in a democratic society.*

The CERD Convention

Despite such strong reservations, it is clear that International Conventions[51] do commit the UK government to take action to introduce legislation that tackles Option 1 – the incitement of racial discrimination. Indeed, in 1969 UK Ministers, under Crown prerogative powers, ratified the International Convention on the Elimination of All Forms of Racial Discrimination (the CERD Convention).

Article 2(1) of the CERD Convention requires state parties to 'condemn racial discrimination and undertake to pursue by all appropriate means and without delay a policy of eliminating racial discrimination in all forms ...', with Article 7 encouraging the use of 'teaching, education, culture and information, with a view to combating prejudices which lead to racial discrimination ...'. More pertinent to this book is:

- *Article 4.* State parties condemn all propaganda and all organisations which are based on ideas or theories of superiority of one race or group of persons of one colour or ethnic origin, or which attempt to justify or promote racial hatred and discrimination in any form, and undertake to adopt immediate and positive measures designed to eradicate all incitement to, or acts of, such discrimination and, to this end, with due regard to the principles embodied in the UDHR and the rights expressly set forth in Article 5 of this convention (a catalogue of rights including freedom of opinion, and expression and peaceful assembly and association), *inter alia*:

  (a) Shall declare an offence punishable by law all dissemination of ideas based on racial superiority or hatred, incitement to racial discrimination, as well as all acts of violence or incitement to such acts against any race or group of persons of another colour or ethnic origin, and also the provision of any assistance to racist activities, including the financing thereof:

  (b) Shall declare illegal and prohibit organisations, and also organized and all other propaganda activities, which promote and incite racial discrimination, and shall recognize participation in such organisations or activities as an offence punishable by law:

  (c) Shall not permit public authorities or public institutions, national or local, to promote or incite racial discrimination.

The United Kingdom is among 16 of 150 countries[52] that have ratified the CERD Convention, expressing a reservation or declaration concerning Article 4. In particular, the UK has stated that it interprets Article 4 to require the adoption of further legislation, for subparagraphs (a), (b) and (c), 'only in so far as it may consider with due regard to the principles embodied in the UDHR and set forth in Article 5 of the Convention' (in particular the right to freedom of opinion and expression and the right to freedom of peaceful assembly and association). The government accepted that some legislative changes were required for the achievement of the purpose set forth in the first paragraph of Article 4, namely to eradicate all incitement to, or acts of, racial discrimination.[53]

Despite this British legislative change, it is evident that over the years, academics and officials of CERD have criticised the UK and claimed that it has failed[54] to implement fully Article 4. Oyediran claims that the UK position on legislation to restrict racist speech and organisations, stands halfway between that of the United States and the rest of Europe. The traditional US approach, with its strong commitment to freedom of speech, only regards restrictions in this area as legitimate if they guard against a likely breach of the peace. British law will restrict racist speech (that is 'threatening, abusive or insulting'), if it is likely to stir up racial hatred on the grounds that racial hatred can, in the long term, lead to a breakdown in public order. By contrast in France, Italy and Austria, laws criminalise the expression of views that merely insult or vilify racial groups.[55]

While this view of Oyediran is no doubt justified and balanced, I would critically argue that the British approach is insular. It is typical of the British 'we know best' approach, which is likely to stick in the craw of the Convention members. The UK has only ratified the CERD Convention on its own terms, with its reservation indicating that it will decide the parameters of the 'with due regard' clause. In effect, this signifies the sovereignty of the UK parliament and a refusal to accept the jurisdiction of the CERD Convention. This situation is exacerbated by an 'intent/likely to stir up racial hatred' clause[56] which requires the personal approval of the Attorney General and has resulted in an average of fewer than two convictions per year.[57]

A further example of this British insular approach, is demonstrated by the definition of racial hatred provided in Section 17 of the Public Order Act 1986. According to British legislation, racial hatred means hatred against a group of persons in Great Britain defined by reference to colour, race, nationality etc.

- *This means that it is lawful for Tom to express: 'Kill the blacks in South Africa', but it may be unlawful for him to say: 'Kill the blacks from South Africa'*

Given that the first statement may, indirectly, stir up racial hatred towards blacks from South Africa living in Britain, this seems a strange anomaly. One logical explanation for this UK/British approach, is that the government considers that expressions of hatred towards peoples in other nations may at times be justified. For example, the government may find it easier to justify a war with another country by stirring up racial hatred towards that country and its leadership.[58] Whatever the justification for this anomaly, it is worth noting that a purpose behind the UN international treaties, is to avoid hatred between nations. The British definition of racial hatred does not fully comply with this grand international ideal, indeed it enables hatred to be stirred up towards groups living in other nations.

Clearly amendment to UK legislation so that the law penalises incitement to racial discrimination is justified on the basis of the CERD Convention. However, it also seems that additional support for such change can be found in the ratification by the UK[59] (again under Crown prerogative powers) of the 'International Covenant on Civil and Political Rights (ICCPR)'. Article 20 of this Treaty includes a requirement that 'any advocacy of national, racial or religious hatred that incites racial discrimination, hostility or violence shall be prohibited by law'. As already argued, UK law currently fails to tackle incitement to racial discrimination and the proposals within Option 1 would clearly fulfil this international commitment.

The Need to Tackle Religious Terminology that Stirs up Racial Discrimination/Hatred

The issue of religious discrimination is outside the scope of my book and as such I will not be considering this area in detail. However, where religious terminology is used by militant racists as a camouflage for their racist activity, it clearly must have some relationship to my research. For example, clearly relevant to my research is a slogan painted on a London tube station wall which says 'Kill a Paki for Christmas' – with grounds existing for a Part III Public Order prosecution,[60] since the words are threatening and capable of stirring up racial hatred towards a racial or ethnic group. However, an almost identical slogan that says, 'Kill a Muslim for Christmas'[61] would not, since Muslims are considered to be a religious and not an ethnic group.[62]

This apparent anomaly stems from parliament's decision to exclude religion from both the Race Relations Act 1976 and the Public Order Act 1986. The approach to encompassing Sikhs as an ethnic group stems from the case of *Mandla v Dowell Lee*,[63] which defines an ethnic and racial group on the basis of seven characteristics determined by Lord Fraser:

(1) They have a long shared history of which the group is conscious as distinguishing it from other groups, and the memory of which keeps it alive,

(2) A cultural tradition of their own, including family and social customs and manners.

In addition to these two *essential* characteristics, the following were also considered to be *relevant* in determining an ethnic group:

(3) Either a common geographical origin or descent from a small number of common ancestors,

(4) A common language, not necessarily peculiar to that group,

(5) A common literature peculiar to the group,

(6) A common religion different from that of neighbouring groups or from the community surrounding it,

(7) Being a minority or oppressed by a dominant group within a larger community.

A group defined by reference to enough of these characteristics would be capable of including converts, for example, persons who marry into the group, and of excluding apostates.[64] Provided a person who joins the group feels himself or herself to be a member of it, and is accepted by other members, then he is, for the purposes, of the Act, a member.

Applying this criterion, gypsies have been held to be an ethnic group,[65] Jews a racial and religious group,[66] but Rastafarians are not protected, being regarded as a religious sect.[67] However, an Industrial Tribunal decision confirming that Muslims are a religious group,[68] and cannot be directly considered as a racial or ethnic group, has developed a state of perplexity. Logically, the tribunal decision appears consistent with the ratio of *Mandla v Dowell Lee,* with Muslims not possessing a clear-cut 'common geographical origin' due to them being too broadly based as a worldwide religion.[69] While this may, on the basis of Lord Fraser, be only a relevant (rather than essential) characteristic, it is clear that Lord Templeman, while agreeing with the conclusion that Sikhs did constitute a racial group, took a much firmer line than Lord Fraser. Indeed, Lord Templeman discussed whether Sikhs were a race and reasoned that a racial group *must* have the characteristics of a race, namely 'group descent, a group of geographical origin and a group history'. As a result of these arguments, it may be difficult to disregard the relevance of a 'common geographical origin', albeit that one of the consequences is that a religious term like 'Muslim' is often depicted, and considered, as being synonymous with a person of foreign descent (i.e. foreign to the UK).

Sadly, the net result of the 'categorisation of Muslims as being a religious group and not an ethnic group', is that militant racists have become significantly involved in stirring up racial discrimination/hatred through anti-Mosque campaigns,[70] applying a warped racially political message that turns the term 'Muslim' into a shorthand description for ethnic foreigners who are not welcome. In fact, materials seized by the police have been considered to be insulting, but the Crown Prosecution Service has declined to prosecute a BNP activist who was allegedly found in possession.[71] The basis of this refusal being *inter alia,* that the material – although stirring up racial hatred – uses religious terminology, with the term 'Muslim' relating to religion rather than race.

This situation is made all the more problematic when you consider the possibility of a 'religious conflict' between Sikhs and Muslims[72] within Britain, resulting in a Muslim distributing a leaflet saying: 'Stab a Sikh'. These words would provide grounds, on the basis of *Mandla v Dowell Lee*, for a prosecution in relation to the stirring up of 'racial hatred', since Sikhs are considered to be an ethnic group. However, an almost identical leaflet produced by a Sikh that said, 'Stab a Muslim' would not.

This religious/race anomaly is censoriously emphasised by the fact that a leaflet which says 'Stab a Muslim' could amount to racial discrimination, notwithstanding the ratio of *Mandla v Dowell Lee*. This applies because *Mandla v Dowell Lee* simply suggests that the term Muslim refers to a religious rather than a racial group, it does not rule out the possibility that indirect racial discrimination may arise.[73]

In its *Second Review of the Race Relations Act*, the Commission for Racial Equality criticised the law saying:[74] '... it cannot be any more acceptable to stir up hatred against people because they are seen to be Muslims than to do so because they are seen to be Pakistanis'.

This CRE statement, in expressing that Muslims should not be discriminated against, seems to be advocating the need for a new law to tackle religious discrimination. While not wishing to undermine such an aim, it is not necessary to plug the legal religious/racial loophole in the public order legislation.[75] An alternative approach is to amend Section 17 of the Public Order Act 1986 in accord with the approach taken in Section 28(3) of the Crime and Disorder Act 1998.[76] This involves enabling a purposive approach to determining guilt. In simple terms, this would probably involve amending Section 17 of the Public Order Act 1986 so that it would read 'it is immaterial for the purposes of this section whether or not the offender's hatred or discrimination is also based, to any extent, on the fact or presumption that any person or group of persons belongs to any religious group'.

Such legislative change should give the criminal courts an element of discretion in assessing whether the words used relate to religious discrimination, or are used as a means of getting around the racial sections of the public order legislation. In effect, it would require a purposive interpretation and thereby enable the court to consider the motivation behind the words used. If the courts consider that the words used were influenced by race, they would be entitled, on the facts, to determine a guilty verdict, notwithstanding the use of religious terminology.

Additional support for some legislative change, can again be found in Article 20 of the International Covenant on Civil and Political Rights which includes a requirement that 'any advocacy of national, racial or religious hatred that incites racial discrimination, hostility or violence shall be prohibited by law'.

An Overall Analysis

On the basis of compliance with obligations under the CERD Convention, there does exist a ground for introducing legislation to tackle Option 1 (stirring up of racial discrimination). However, as the analysis of the evidence assessment sheet (3) shows, simply changing Part III of the Public Order to include Option 1, would not produce any real impact upon militant racist materials, since the requirement for the words to be threatening, abusive and/ or insulting acts as a shield to prosecution. Indeed, it seems likely that those who are responsible for such materials will continue to avoid prosecution by producing material which stirs up racial discrimination or hatred and which is purposely not quite 'threatening, abusive or insulting'. In other words, they will continue to produce literature that is 'racially offensive'.

In comparison, producing legislation which tackles Option 2 *alone*, does extend the ability of the law to tackle racially offensive material. However, such a legislative change – while still impacting upon freedom of expression – fails to bring UK law in line with the CERD Convention requirement to tackle material that incites racial discrimination.

A combination of Options 1 and 2 fulfils such an objective. The problem is that such an approach displays a clear potential to undermine freedom of expression. As highlighted by the illustration on refugee and asylum seekers, it seems inevitable that by expressing a detailed view that refugees should not overstay their welcome there will be some level of racial offence given, with a possibility existing that the words expressed may stir up racial discrimination. One way of ensuring that such important debate could take place (i.e. assuming the law was changed to include Options 1 and 2) without fear of prosecution, would be to provide an exemption under the law for either political parties or in relation to information concerning immigration, refugees and asylum seekers. The exemption for political parties must be considered as unacceptable on a number of grounds. The most obvious being the difficulty of justifying giving political parties a privileged position in society – with democracy also implying that critics of political parties should have the right to debate and criticise any party policy. A further obvious problem being, that to give a carte blanche immunity for political parties, would not fulfil the aim of tackling militant racism; with the application of the laws to certain parties and not others, likely to be considered as discriminatory and politically unacceptable.

However, this should not be taken to mean that the example of refugees and asylum seekers completely undermines Options 1 and 2. Indeed, as I will show in the next chapter 'Say No to Racism – Part Two: A Counter-Message', it may be possible to introduce laws, which tackle the stirring up of racial discrimination or hatred through the use of racially offensive words, without seriously undermining freedom of expression. As I will argue in the next chapter, this can be achieved not through exemption – but as a result of the refinement of Option 2.

Notes

1   British means England, Wales and Scotland.
2   In practical terms it would be sufficient to add the term 'offence' to the prerequisites in relation to Part III of the Public Order Act 1986. This is because since the term is by necessity combined with incitement to racial hatred (discrimination) there is little practical difference between 'offence' and 'racial offence'. This must logically apply since due to the combination requirements 'race' must be an element of any 'offence' that is given – i.e. in order to establish criminality under the proposed section. Hence in future within

this book, I will make reference to the term 'racial offence'. In reality, due to the combination requirement, whether the word(s) 'offence' or 'racial offence' was to be used by any legislative draughtsmen should have little practical and legal difference.

3   Some examples of laws are the Public Order Act 1986, Protection from Harassment Act 1997, Criminal Damage Act 1971 etc. These and other laws were discussed in detail in chapter 3.

4   See chapter 7.

5   See sections 18–23 of the Public Order Act 1986.

6   *Civil Liberties Cases and Materials*, Butterworths, 1995, p. 666.

7   See the *Oxford Thesaurus*, 1991. It is also worth noting that 'incite' is synonymous with 'stir', 'to stir up' and 'encourage'.

8   This represents a paraphrase of the definitions given in Section 1 of the Race Relations Act 1976. It also reflects a natural meaning as given in *The Concise Oxford Dictionary*, 1990.

9   Section 17 of the Public Order Act 1986 does not define 'hatred'; it follows therefore that the natural meaning applies. As per *The Concise Oxford Dictionary*, 'dislike intensely' can be considered applicable.

10   A magistrate or jury should be able to determine such an issue, on the basis of the facts, without too much difficulty.

11   In *The Concise Oxford Dictionary* these are given as synonyms in relation to 'intense'.

12   Thereby treating black and Asian people less favourably on grounds of race.

13   This proposal is consistent with the law as it currently stands in relation to the stirring up of racial hatred (see Section 18(1)(b) of the Public Order Act 1986). It should be noted, however, that Section 18(5) establishes that any person who is shown not to have intended to stir up racial hatred is not guilty of an offence if he did not intend his words or behaviour, or the written material, to be, or was not aware that it might be, threatening, abusive or insulting.

14   'Racist Speech and Literature'.

15   Within the BNP web site (http://www.bnp.net/) published 20 September 1997, the British Nationalist home page editors produced an article 'Freedom of Speech in Britain – A Brief Legal Primer' which explains BNP support for the European Convention on Human Rights and gives a legal summary of Section 18, 19, and 23 of the Public Order Act 1986. In effect, they criticise those in the nationalist ranks who argue for abusive language in publications, arguing that the POA 1986 prevents such language stating: 'the legislation can work entirely to our advantage, if only a tiny minority of people would just stop sending out abusive and illegal material anonymously'. The whole context of the article emphasises that language used should not be 'abusive, threatening, or insulting' and that 'in general, there is nearly always a way of saying what you want to say without breaking the law'.

16   See evidence assessment sheets 1 and 2 in ch. 3, 'Racist Speech and Literature'.

17   For arguments that the distribution of racist literature can lead to the raising of racial tensions see 'Fanning the Flames of Hatred', *Searchlight*, September 1998.

18   See Part III of the Public Order Act 1986.

19   As per Section 18(5) Public Order Act 1986.

20   'Racial grounds' are determined under Section 17 of the Pubic Order Act 1986.

21   'Incitement' is again being given a natural meaning which can include encourage.

22   'Might' have been aware is sufficient under Section 18(5) Public Order Act 1986.

23 That is in criminal law terms.

24 *On Liberty*, J.S. Mill.

25 Section 17 Public Order Act 1986.

26 This would apply only in a public or private place – but not within a dwelling unless heard or seen by a person outside that dwelling (Section 18 (2)).

27 As per *Brutus v Cozens* [1972] 2 All ER 1297. The word 'insulting' must be given its natural meaning – a matter of fact not law.

28 [1963] 2 All ER 225. The question of law being whether the public speech was likely to cause a breach of the peace.

29 A.T.H. Smith argues in 'Offences against the Persons Act (1987)', p. 14, that notwithstanding Lord Parker's statement there is room for a *reasonable man test* in determining whether the words are insulting in the first place.

30 This requirement of 'intent or awareness' is consistent with Section 18(5) of the Public Order Act 1986 and will be discussed a little later in this chapter.

31 As discussed in chapter 3, 'Racist Speech and Literature', *Brutus v Cozens* [1972] 2 All ER 1297 involved an anti-apartheid demonstration at Wimbledon, with the courts determining that *insulting* must be given its natural meaning. This has also been applied to 'threatening and abusive'.

32 This is based on the meaning of the word 'offence' found within *The Concise Oxford Dictionary*, 8th edn, 1990. Thus the term 'racial offence' could be determined as a mixture of law and fact, based upon 'the wounding of feelings as a result of expression directed towards a group of persons in Britain defined by reference to colour, race, nationality (including citizenship) or ethnic or national origins'.

33 The issue of religious terms that may incite racial discrimination or hatred will be discussed later in this chapter.

34 *Litster v Forth Dry Dock Engineering Co. Ltd* [1989] 1 All ER 1134 – House of Lords is a leading case on the issue of a purposive construction. Essentially this derives from the requirements of the European Union and a need to interpret Directives consistently within domestic legislation.

35 This material was considered in detail in chapter 3, 'Racist Speech and Literature'.

36 This assessment is determined by applying the *natural meaning* approach advocated in *Brutus v Cozens* [1972] 2 All ER 1297 with regards to the word 'offence, threatening, abusive and insulting'. However, a statutory definition, consistent with Section 17 of the Public Order Act 1986, is applied to the word 'racial'.

37 Likewise, it is less obviously 'racially offensive'.

38 See chapter 7, 'Racial Motivation and Hostility'.

39 Examples of more extreme militant racist literature can be found in the appendices and are referred to in chapter 3, 'Racist Speech and Literature.'

40 i.e. Appendices 14 and 18.

41 Racial offence as a prerequisite.

42 The figure is limited to 20 per cent due to the problem of the prosecution proving that the words are intended, or likely, to stir up racial hatred.

43 This is self evident, since the law currently only limits the use of words that are threatening, abusive or insulting. By extending the law to also deal with racially offensive words the parameters are being extended to include words that are racially offensive. The issue of interference with freedom of expression will be discussed in the remainder of this chapter and also in the next chapter.

44   See discussion later in this chapter on the CERD Convention.

45   Eighty per cent of militant racist materials sampled could result in a criminal prosecution.

46   See 'Britain to Take 1,000 Refugees a Week', *The Times*, 5 May 1999.

47   It would certainly be offensive to a Kosovo refugee who has fled from Serbia amidst bombs etc.

48   Thereby inciting racial discrimination.

49   David Feldman, *Civil Liberties and Human Rights in England and Wales*, Clarendon, Press, 1993, chapter 1.

50   Certain aspects of racist and anti-racist protest and the Public Order Act 1986 will be considered later.

51   The Vienna Convention on the Law of Treaties defines a treaty as an international agreement concluded between states in written form and governed by international law, whether embodied in a single instrument or in two or more related instruments and whatever its particular designation (see Wade and Bradley, *Constitutional and Administrative Law*, Longman, 1993, p. 331). Under UK law such International Treaties are generally signed by ministers under Crown prerogative powers and are not, as a result, incorporated into UK law (they are not expressly incorporated via an Act of Parliament). This means that such unincorporated International Treaties cannot be directly relied upon in domestic courts (*Cheney v Conn (Inspector of Taxes)* [1968] 1 All ER 779).

52   As of 31 December 1997; source United Nations, *Multilateral Treaties Deposited with the Secretary-General*, 1998.

53   This resulted in an addition to Section 6 of the Race Relations Act 1976 (*having regard to all the circumstances racial hatred is likely to be stirred up thereby*). This was later incorporated into Part III of the Public Order Act 1986.

54   33 UN GAOR Supp No 18 UN Doc. A/30/18 (1975), para 144. See also Joanna Oyediran, 'The United Kingdom's Compliance with Article 4 of the International Convention on the Elimination of All Forms of Racial Discrimination', in Sandra Coliver (ed.), *Striking a Balance*.

55   Except in certain very limited contexts.

56   Part III of the Public Order Act 1986.

57   See chapter 1, 'Introduction – Tackling Militant Racism'.

58   For example, the vilification of Milosovic and the Serbs.

59   Ratified 20 May 1976.

60   That is assuming those responsible can be identified.

61   See Therese Murphy, 'Incitement to hatred: Lessons from Northern Ireland', in Sandra Coliver (ed.), *Striking a Balance*.

62   It is also possible it may not amount to an offence under Section 4 or 5 of the Public Order Act 1986, since any 'threatening, abusive or insulting' words need to be directed to a person rather than a group. As such, the only offence that may have been committed relates to criminal damage.

63   [1983] IRLR 209.

64   It seems unfortunate that Lord Fraser in *Mandla v Dowell Lee* should have used such terminology as apostates, which on any natural meaning of the word seems to relate to a belief often associated with religion. To this extent, his judgement can be criticised for producing religious terminology within a racial definition – thereby clouding the issue even further.

65   *CRE v Dutton* [1989] IRLR 8.

66 *Seide v Gillette Industrial Ltd* [1980] IRLR 427. This decision was reached on the basis of the shared cultural tradition of those of Jewish descent (rather than on the religion of Judaism).

67 *Dawkins v Crown Suppliers* [1993] IRLR 284. In this case the Court of Appeal determined that Rastafarians did not fulfil the criteria because there was no group history, descent (only 60 years) or language.

68 In *Malik v Bertram Personnel Group* (1990) No: 4343/90, Muslims were not considered to be protected by the direct discrimination provisions of Section 1(1)(a) of the Race Relations Act 1976, but may be able to show indirect discrimination on the basis the majority of Muslims may be coloured.

69 It is estimated there are more than 1,000 million followers of Islam across many continents, with around two million existing in the UK (Source: comments of George Galloway MP, *Hansard*, 3 February 1999, Column 887).

70 'Crawley Mosque Vandalised', *Searchlight*, April 1995; 'Anti-mosque Campaign Provokes Violence', *Searchlight*, August 1996. 'Veteran Racists behind Anti-mosque Campaign', *Searchlight*, November 1996. See also *Searchlight*, January 1998 for a report on a man being convicted in relation to an attack upon a Mosque in Leeds.

71 A prosecution for possession of material that may stir up racial hatred, would be brought via Section 23 Public Order Act 1986.

72 Problems of this nature have occurred in Hounslow over recent years (see 'College Blames Extremists for Religious Riot' in which the Hizb-Ut-Tahrir were said to have been active in a riot which involved the use of sticks and knives – *Hounslow, Feltham and Hanworth Times*, 13 January 1995).

73 For an example of this, see *Malik v Bertram Personnel Group* (1990) Industrial Tribunal case No 4343/90.

74 Commission for Racial Equality – second review of the RRA 1976 [1991] 58.

75 In the House of Commons, George Galloway MP referred to 'Islamaphobia as being the last "acceptable" form of racism, suitable even for the dinner tables of Islington and Hampstead', *Hansard*, 3 February 1999, Column 888.

76 Section 28(3) of the Crime and Disorder Act 1998 which relates to 'racial hostility' reads: 'It is immaterial for the purposes of paragraph (a) or (b) of subsection (1) whether or not the offender's hostility is also based, to any extent on the fact or presumption that any person or group of persons belongs to any religious group ...'. The Crime and Disorder Act 1998 will be discussed in chapter 7.

5 'Say No to Racism' – Part Two: A Counter-Message

In chapter 4, I considered the legal options for change. I concluded that a combination of Option 1 (incitement to racial discrimination or hatred) and Option 2 (a racial offence prerequisite in relation to prosecution) may be politically, and even legally, problematic due to the undermining of free expression. Thus, I suggested that the only realistic way that this combination could be applied is through some form of refinement of Option 2. In this chapter, I intend to consider this matter.

To look for refinement, I turn to the policy of counter-speech adopted[1] by the National Council for Civil Liberties (Liberty).[2] At its base, counter-speech or expression suggests that where racist words are used, it is important that the counter argument is put. Obviously, this is sound common sense and to a large extent the work of the Commission for Racial Equality reflects this approach.[3] Examples of the CRE's use of counter expression can be seen in the poster campaigns which demonstrate that people are equal no matter what their colour or nationality[4] and which emphasise that 'racial attacks are crimes'.[5] Further, the CRE have worked with well-known sports personalities, and sports companies, to 'say no to racism',[6] though it should be recognised that not all of the CRE advertising campaigns have been regarded as notable successes. A shock tactic campaign in 1998, which depicted powerful negative images of black and Asian people and carried a telephone number of a fake 'company' which people could ring to complain about the images, resulting in controversy. A few weeks after the introduction of the shock tactic campaign the offending posters were replaced by some that said, 'What was worse? This advert or your failure to complain?'. As a consequence of complaints made to the Advertising Standards Authority, the CRE became the first organisation within the country to be required to submit advertising campaigns, in advance, for approval.[7]

While Liberty has cited the advertising work of the CRE as an example of counter-speech,[8] they do not propose that counter-speech should be an alternative to legislation. Indeed, their proposals suggest that counter-speech should work alongside legislation. In addition, Liberty also argues that changes are needed to our current laws to deal more effectively with racism.[9]

Perhaps though, an alternative approach is to see counter-expression as part of legislation. For an example of this in practice, we can look at the government's approach to the production/distribution of cigarettes. The government has been clearly aware of the dangers to health that may exist from the smoking of cigarettes. Despite such dangers, they have not attempted to ban smoking. Indeed, since 1971 they have worked with the tobacco industry to establish an industry-wide code of conduct, resulting in government health warnings being added to the side of cigarette packets and on any tobacco advertising. Undoubtedly, when they were first introduced the health warnings were ridiculed by some, with a few children deliberately flaunting their desire to smoke.[10] However, this was just the initial reaction, over the years the warnings have chipped away at societal attitudes, helping to educate people to the dangers of smoking. Now, nearly 30 years later, there is a much greater acceptance of the need to limit smoking in public places and places of work.

Obviously, the smoking health warnings have not stopped smoking – but they have undermined support for the habit.[11] By adapting this health warning, or counter-message principle, to 'racially offensive' material the comparison and intent of influencing and educating people over a period of time is self-evident. Any legislation, requiring an anti-racist counter-message, would be directed at the publisher or distributor of the 'racially offensive' material (similar to the producer/distributor of cigarettes), with the individual free to read the material just as s/he is free to smoke. An example of the kind of message that could be required to be displayed, is given in the title of this chapter – i.e. 'Say no to racism – Warning: parts of this material could be racially offensive'. An alternative could be more general in terms, with a message that says: 'Committed to equality of opportunity – Warning: this material could be racially offensive'.

An Outline of the Legislative Approach

In establishing a counter-message health warning on tobacco packets, the government developed a voluntary code. This voluntary code worked because the tobacco industry is structured and identifiable, with consultation achieved through the Tobacco Manufacturers' Association. Despite cooperation from the tobacco industry, the government complied with European Union requirements[12] and introduced the Tobacco Products Labelling (Safety)

Regulations of 1991, which can result in the imposition of fines should there be any refusal to display a health warning.[13]

While a voluntary approach was reasonably successful with regards to tobacco, it seems inevitable that it would fail with regards to material that is 'racially offensive'. This applies because militant racists are ill-defined individuals (unlike tobacco companies who have an identifiable structure), many of who are likely to reject any form of voluntary 'anti-racist counter-message' process. It follows that, in order to enforce a counter-message process, a prohibitive and punitive approach will be necessary. Given that the proposals for reform relate to people who intentionally stir up racial hatred/discrimination, it seems appropriate, and consistent with existing legislation, to take a public order approach. Indeed, the proposal that I make is to amend Part III of the Public Order Act 1986 so as to make it a criminal offence to incite racial discrimination or hatred through the use of 'threatening, abusive, insulting or racially offensive' words. This involves extending the current law so that it tackles 'racially offensive' words[14] that are intended or are likely to stir up racial discrimination or hatred, while also providing for a counter-message – say no to racism – defence for words that are 'racially offensive'.[15]

Defining 'Racial Offence'

In the case of cigarettes, a cigarette can generally be readily identified and accordingly the need for a counter-message health warning – in accord with regulations – is self-evident. By comparison, words that are 'racially offensive' may not always be so easily recognised and the need to display a counter-message may be not so obvious.

This problem of 'identification, interpretation, and/or definition' is inevitable with laws that tackle issues associated with morality, in that what gives offence to one person – may not give offence to another. However, this problem is not new or insurmountable. In *Brutus v Cozens*,[16] the problem of defining 'insulting behaviour'[17] was discussed in a case that involved an anti-apartheid protester who blew a whistle and threw leaflets, at the Wimbledon tennis tournament. The defendant protestor was charged with undertaking insulting behaviour contrary to Section 5 of the Public Order Act 1936 and the Magistrates found, on the facts, that the defendant's behaviour had not been insulting – dismissing the case without calling on him to give evidence. On appeal by the respondent prosecutor, the Divisional Court held that insulting behaviour is 'something which affronted other people and evidenced a disrespect or contempt for their rights'. On further appeal, by the defendant Brutus, against a decision that the case should be referred back to the Justices for a rehearing, the House of Lords rejected the approach of the Divisional Court and applied an 'ordinary usage – natural meaning – methodology'.[18] In doing so Lord Reid suggested there should be no legalistic definition of insulting, just an acceptance that 'an ordinary sensible man knows an insult when he sees or hears it'.[19] This establishes that the courts should apply a natural meaning approach to words that may be 'threatening, abusive and/or insulting', and it seems that there have been no serious difficulties in the application of this principle. Accordingly, it is suggested that – for the sake of legal consistency – a combined statutory and natural meaning approach should be taken with regards to words that may be 'racially offensive'. This would mean that the word 'race' should be determined on the basis of a statutory definition,[20] with the word 'offensive' being given a natural meaning based upon fact and not law.

Inevitably, such a combined statutory and natural meaning will result in a strong element of subjectivity in establishing just what is 'racially offensive'. Thus, while an ordinary sensible man can recognise a cigarette, so he should also have the aptitude to recognise that the use of certain words can – in certain circumstances – give 'racial offence'.

The Advantages of a Counter-Message Defence

As acknowledged in the last chapter, to prosecute a person for distributing/ publishing material that stirs up discrimination/hatred, through the use of racially offensive words, could inhibit freedom of expression. It would certainly make discussion of issues associated with refugees, asylum and possibly immigration, exceedingly problematic due to an interference with freedom of expression.

The introduction of a counter-message defence will enable such discussion without an expectation of being prosecuted. Indeed, all that would be necessary to avoid prosecution, for the use of racially offensive words that stir up racial discrimination or hatred, is to display a counter-message consistent with the government aim of saying 'no to racism'.

Further, the approach shows the potential of enhancing freedom in the sense that it does not absolutely deny expression of 'racially offensive' words, but provides additional authoritative counter-message information for the receiver of the expression.[21] In this sense it provides freedom, while developing responsibility. If we take a discussion concerning refugees as an example, a 'counter-message approach'[22] facilitates open and frank debate about the issue of refugees and asylum even in circumstances of providing 'racial offence' and the probability of inciting racial discrimination.

Those opposed to racism, may be inclined to criticise the counter speech proposals on the grounds that they provide a form of legitimacy to 'racially offensive' material, making it clear to those offended that they cannot sue because of the existence of the counter-message. While there may be some merit to this argument, it is important to reflect that material which is purely 'racially offensive' is currently given legitimacy in the sense that it cannot be considered to be in breach of existing laws. Under the proposals I submit in this book, to use 'racially offensive' words, with intent or likelihood of stirring up racial discrimination/hatred, would be a criminal offence. The counter-message defence is only proposed as an inbuilt defence for 'racially offensive' material – it is not intended as a defence for material that may be 'threatening, abusive or insulting' and also 'likely' (or there exists an intent) to incite racial discrimination or hatred. As such, it is not limiting the existing law, but extending the parameters for prosecution with regards to racist material.

The Educational Value of a Counter-Message Defence

It is also clear that a counter-message approach can have some educational value. For example, many journalists could fear producing articles that related to racial attacks in case the story gave 'racial offence' and resulted in a prosecution. It follows, that one advantage of the proposed counter-message defence would be that it could provide a visible safety net from prosecution for incitement to racial discrimination – i.e. so long as the material was not also 'threatening, abusive or insulting'. It follows also, that newspaper proprietors would be required to display counter-message equal opportunities statements along with any story, within their papers, which might cause 'racial offence' and be likely to incite racial discrimination or hatred. Thus, they would be thereby sending out a message that was consistent with the government's desire to say no to racism. This may also result in readers of newspapers and journals becoming more aware of material that provides the potential for being 'racially offensive' and therefore aware of the legislation.

Clearly, this would serve to help educate the general public to a policy of saying 'no to racism'. Indeed, the philosophy behind this book proposal is one of education, with the law being used as a means of developing societal acceptance of equality of opportunity and equal treatment of all citizens irrespective of race. Sociological arguments in relation to using the law to help develop anti-racist education, as a means of societal change, will be discussed in the next chapter. For the purposes of discussion, in this chapter, it is important to note that the proposed counter-message legislation is intended to educate – possibly more so than it is intended to penalise. This can be of special value in relation to militant racist literature that is 'racially offensive', rather than 'threatening, abusive or insulting'. This applies because such racist material often 'purports to make a contribution to public education and debate'.[23] The value of the counter-message is that it helps warn the reader of the potential of racial offence, while briefly giving them an alternative viewpoint.

Other consequences may also develop from the existence of such counter-message legislation. Would the publishers of material, which may be 'racially offensive' and capable of inciting racial discrimination, be prepared to face prosecution by refusing to put within the material an equal opportunities statement? It is possible they may wish to be martyrs to their cause and distribute material that is in breach of the law, but does not contain a publisher imprint, in effect, hiding the existence of those directly responsible for publishing the material. In these circumstances it may prove difficult to prosecute the leadership of any organisation which, although benefiting from the literature, is not evidentially responsible for its publication or distribution. Should the literature display the emblem of the organisation, it is theoretically possible, on the basis of *London Borough of Merton v Edmonds and Tyndall*,[24] that the leadership of the organisation could be prosecuted. However, the prosecution of these two political activists, was in relation to the display of a BNP poster and in circumstances of them being made aware of its ongoing display by the local authority. This may suggest that the leadership of an organisation could be held criminally liable in circumstances where they have been formally notified that a leaflet being distributed, with the organisation's logo, is offensive (and should contain a counter-message), and where members of that organisation continue to distribute the leaflet without a counter-message being displayed.[25]

An Organisation's Liability for the Stirring up of Racial Discrimination/ Hatred

It is also possible that a militant racist organisation itself could be criminally prosecuted and open to a fine.[26] This view is supported by the comments of Smith and Hogan,[27] who argue that unincorporated associations could be convicted of a criminal offence. This arises as a result of the effect of the Interpretation Act 1978, which establishes that unincorporated associations are 'persons' and are liable to be convicted of any offence where the definition uses the word 'person', as is usual. It follows that an unincorporated association can be convicted as a result of the acts of superior officers who carry out the function of management and speak and act on behalf of the organisation.[28]

As Smith and Hogan argue, by analogy the same legal principles that apply to corporations should also apply to unincorporated associations. Thus, as Denning LJ said in *Boulton Engineering Co Ltd v Maile*:[29]

> A company may in many ways be likened to a human body. It has a brain and a nerve centre which controls what it does. It also has hands which hold the tools and act in accordance with directions from the centre. Some of the people in the company are mere servants and agents who are nothing more than the hands to do the work and cannot be said to represent the mind and will. Others are directors and managers who represent the directing mind and will of the company and control what it does. The state of mind of these managers is the state of mind of the company and is treated by the law as such.

Similarly, in the leading case of *Tesco Supermarkets Ltd v Nattrass*[30] it was held that the company can be criminally liable for the acts of 'the board of directors, the managing director and perhaps other senior officers of a company [who] carry out the functions of management and speak and act as the company'. Applying these principles to an unincorporated association, it seems that if it can be proved that illegal racist materials have been distributed in the name of the organisation, and with the approval of the leadership of that organisation, then both the leadership and the organisation could face prosecution.

It follows that the leadership, of such organisations, will be careful and likely try to take steps to avoid prosecution. Indeed, all the evidence of my research shows that prominent militant racist organisations generally comply with the law with regards to the open production of racist materials. There is no evidence to suggest that groups like the BNP or NF have openly defied the law with regards to their literature.

Obtaining the Views of Militant Racists

Based on the assumption that such militant racist organisations will comply with any new counter-message legislation, I decided to interview some[31] militant racists and ask how they felt members would respond to a legal requirement that an anti-racist counter-message should be displayed on material that may give racial offence. I deliberately decided to approach activists, rather than the national leadership of the parties, since I was interested in establishing if volunteer activists would readily accept and distribute literature that displayed an anti-racist message.

One criticised the proposals for a counter-message on the grounds that 'it would deny freedom of expression and try to propel words out of people's mouths'.[32] Despite such criticism, he expressed a belief that the party would comply with any new law requiring the inclusion of an equal opportunities statement within 'racially offensive' literature, his argument being that the party respected the law and always complied.

Assuming this to be the case, it is clear that much of the current party material could continue to be distributed (albeit with an anti-racist counter-message displayed). However it is possible that, as a result of this decision, there could be some internal political consequences. To illustrate, how many militant racists would be prepared to walk the streets to deliver material that expresses 'no to racism'? Obviously some will, but it must be possible that a number would resent the leadership's decision to comply with the law and display a counter-message that they have little support for. The consequences for the leadership of the racist organisation could well be that they would lose support as some of their membership rebel against compliance with the law. The activist argues that he does not believe that the party would lose support. However, he does suggest that some disillusioned activists could turn to distributing racist materials without any indication of a printer and/or publisher[33] – with some even joining forces with other, more militant, organisations. By comparison, another activist expressed a view that party activists would also be very unhappy about being required to display an anti-racist counter-message on their materials. He suggested the party would make every effort to work around the law – using the material to criticise the counter-message, while arguing their right to freedom of expression.[34]

Concern that a Counter-Message could Act as a Signpost for Racist Material

It may also be feasible that militant racists could benefit from a counter-message approach, i.e. because the message – although anti-racist – will indirectly act as a signpost for racist material. Clearly, if firm evidence exists that an anti-racist counter-message will only serve to attract people towards reading racist material, it could seriously undermine the value of such an approach.

To consider this issue, I have examined a report initiated by the government and produced by the British Broadcasting Corporation, Broadcasting Standards Commission, and the Independent Television Commission. This Joint Working Party report[35] was primarily concerned with content-warnings rather than counter-messages.[36] Its findings rejected the notion of set rules and TV censorship – preferring broadcasters to promote viewer choice and operate via a statement of common principles, based upon content-warnings with regards to TV violence.[37]

The TV coverage of the Joint Working Party report talked about consideration of concerns that certain viewers may use their remote control to channel hop – i.e. hopping between stations and selecting programmes that display a 'V' for violence symbol. However the published report, while commenting that, 'They were a very basic and a limited mechanism which may not be as effective as a specific description of problematic content', stated that the working party 'do not wish to discourage the adoption of these (rating symbol) techniques'.[38]

What is clear is that the Joint Working Party, in recommending the use of some form of content-warnings, emphatically rejected the idea of censorship through utilising a V-chip.[39] This rejection of censorship being primarily based on arguments that the V-chip is imprecise technology that has not yet been proven in the USA or Canada – with it also taking many years to introduce.[40] Noticeably, in reaching this conclusion, the Joint Working Party failed to give detailed consideration of the legal and political issues associated with freedom of expression.

Naturally, this Joint Working Party report does have some relevance to the issue of counter-messages, but it is important not to overstate that relevance. Indeed, the TV report was concerned with content-warnings, while the arguments in this book are also about counter-speech legislation. Clearly a counter-message also acts as a content-warning, in that the counter-message alerts any potential reader that the material could contain racially offensive content.[41] However, there is a subtle but significant difference, with a counter-message extending beyond the parameters of any straightforward warning message. To reiterate, the arguments in this book are not for a big 'R' to be placed on racist material with the intent of discouraging readership by a certain category of people.[42] Rather, the aim is to append to material that may be 'racially offensive', a counter-message, educative in itself, and consistent with the government's aim of saying 'no to racism'. Obviously, on reading the counter-message the reader may opt to refrain from reading the material content – but that is not the principal aim of the counter-message. Indeed, the principal aim is to educate by reaffirming into the mind of a potential reader, viewer, or listener, that racism is unacceptable within society. To this extent, a counter-message should not become a form of magnet that pulls in readership.

Applying the counter-message principle to a TV programme that may express 'racial offence', the counter-message legislation would require the broadcaster to display a 'say no to racism' message at the beginning of the programme. Therefore, it would be targeting 'racially offensive' material at its source of distribution, being proactive in the sense that it serves to educate the viewer as to the law and the societal aim of saying no to racism. To this extent, the counter-speech proposals would appear to be broadly consistent with the principles laid down by the Joint Working Party on Violence on Television. What is more, any concerns that anti-racist counter-messages may encourage racist readership would seem to be even less justified than those that may exist concerning the promotion of TV violence by the use of TV content-warnings.

Clearly there will inevitably be instances where it is not possible to warn in advance of a racially offensive comment. For example, in any chat show it is possible that a guest or audience member could unexpectedly express a view that is racially offensive and likely to stir up racial hatred/discrimination. Obviously, the person making the racially offensive statement may be liable, but so too could be the producers of the programme. In the case of the producer, assuming he were to be prosecuted, he could argue in his defence that he was not aware that the words might be racially offensive – i.e. because he was not aware that those particular words might be used. While such a defence seems logical, it could be undermined by any failure of the production team to alert the presenter of the programme (i.e. via his earpiece) of the need to make a correcting counter-message.

Consistency with the CERD Convention

In his comments, concerning the likely response of his party to counter-speech legislation, the activist criticised the proposals on the grounds that they would 'deny freedom of expression and try to propel words out of people's mouths'. This argument has a legal basis, on civil libertarian grounds, and is not reconciled by the likelihood that the party may make it clear that the counter-message statement derives from a government requirement and is not of their own volition.

Despite the charismatic appeal of this civil libertarian argument, it is weakened by the fact that in both international and UK law, there is no such thing as absolute freedom of expression. Indeed, under existing British public order laws there are restrictions on freedom of expression in situations where 'threatening, insulting or abusive' words are used that can stir up racial hatred. The United Nations propose that incitement to racial discrimination should be made unlawful by nation states. As such, the proposals for legislative change are reasonably consistent with international requirements,[43] under the United Nations CERD Convention, for dealing with incitement to racial discrimination. The counter-speech defence being designed to enable responsible discussion of racial issues. Accordingly, militant racists are free to espouse whatever views they consider fit – but if they do not temper their views in accord with the law, they may face prosecution.[44]

Possession of 'Racially Offensive' Material

Section 23 of the Public Order Act 1986 deals with the possession of racist material that is 'threatening, abusive and insulting' with 'intent or a likelihood' of stirring up racial hatred. Clearly, the application of Options 1 (incitement to racial discrimination) and 2 (a racial offence prerequisite) would mean the law is also extended with regards to the possession of 'racially offensive' material that may stir up racial discrimination/hatred.

Assuming that a counter-message – say no to racism – defence is to be introduced, the application of an amended Section 23 should not create any serious problems. In that if a person is in possession of racially offensive material[45] that stirs up racial discrimination/hatred, with a view to distribution, he is open to prosecution if that material does not display a counter-message.

Obviously, a defendant could argue that he possessed 'racially offensive' material that is likely/intended to stir up racial discrimination or hatred, but did not intend to distribute it. While this may be a reasonable argument with regards to a single item of material,[46] a person possessing a quantity of 'racially offensive' material is unlikely to succeed with this form of defence – since holding a quantity of material infers distribution. Alternatively, a person possessing material could accept he possesses but argue, since the material is not of his design or within his copyright, he is not in a position to add a counter-message to make the racially offensive material lawful. While this may seem to be an appealing argument, it is possession with a view to distribution that results in a finding of guilt, with possession of a quantity of 'racially offensive' materials likely to result in the court inferring intent to distribute.

Possibly a stronger defence for a person found in possession of a quantity of racially offensive material is that he did not realise that it was 'racially offensive' – i.e. due to the lack of a counter-message being displayed.[47] This in itself could be a viable defence in accord with Section 23(3),[48] but its success – in light of the *Brutus v Cozens*[49] 'ordinary usage – natural meaning – methodology' – would obviously depend upon the facts of the case and whether an ordinary sensible man is likely to recognise the material as being racially offensive.

Seizing 'Racially Offensive' Material

Section 24 of the Public Order Act 1986 provides powers for entry and search, with Section 19(2a) of the Police and Criminal Evidence Act 1984 enabling seizure. Clearly, the lack of a counter-message equal opportunities statement, on racist material which has indications of being 'racially offensive', should provide grounds for seizure. It may be that for first time offenders, this will result in a police reprimand being given,[50] which may well have the impact of warning them of the consequences of handling 'racially offensive' material, with the possibility that they will not re-offend. It will also mean that grounds would exist for removing the unlawful material out of public circulation, which can only be to the benefit of society generally.

Applying the Principle to Speech

So far as 'racially offensive' literature/material is concerned, the principle of establishing an equal opportunities counter-message defence is clearly viable. In order to prosecute for the stirring up of racial discrimination or hatred, four questions will need to be answered positively in relation to a person who is responsible for the material:

1   can the words used by the person be considered to be 'racially offensive' – i.e. applying an ordinary usage – natural meaning – methodology;

2   did the defendant intend the words to be racially offensive, or was he aware that they might be racially offensive;[51]

3   do the words stir up racial discrimination or hatred;

4   is there a counter-message displayed on the material that is consistent with legislative requirements of saying no racism?

The logic behind the approach is relatively straightforward, the use of a counter-message provides a defence in relation to the stirring up of racial discrimination/hatred through the use of racially offensive material. If no counter-message is displayed, and the material is considered to be racially offensive and likely to stir up racial discrimination or hatred, than any person responsible for the material is open to prosecution.

However, the application of this approach to speech may be prone to some practical difficulties because it is not so easy to see and thus establish that a counter-message has been given. Even if a counter-message is given at the beginning of a speech, it is possible that its content may be lost amidst a speech that may be littered with detail and include phrases or an overall message that is 'racially offensive'.

However, a live show or presentation could create a few problems. Firstly, the organiser of the show must apply the 'ordinary usage – natural meaning – methodology' of *Brutus v Cozens* in determining if 'racially offensive' words are to be used. Clearly, the organiser may not know in advance that racially offensive views might be expressed. Hence, he cannot be expected to give an advance counter-message warning in circumstances where he may not be aware of the likely racially offensive comment. Secondly, what if the counter-message is given in derogatory terms? For example, what if the counter-message was incorporated into one of the jokes and therefore given with possible contempt or limited sincerity? This kind of situation clearly establishes a problem, but not so much for the prosecution as for the defence. This applies because, the legal principles associated with prosecution in relation to racially offensive speech would be synonymous with those used in relation to racially offensive literature or materials – except that, due to the nature of speech it is obviously not possible to finish every sentence with a counter-message. It follows, therefore, that a counter-message would need to be given in association with the speech and could be delivered before, during, or after the performance.

In practice, the prosecution would be required to establish, beyond reasonable doubt, that: (1) the words used were 'racially offensive'; (2) the defendant was aware the words used might give racial offence; (3) an intent or likelihood of inciting racial discrimination or hatred is evident. Once the prosecution has established this aspect of the case, the burden of proof – to the extent of convincing the magistrates or jury of a viable defence – moves to the defendant. This may and could involve the introduction of a draft of the speech given – the use of witnesses from the audience, or even a tape of the proceedings. All that the defendant would need to show is that associated with the words that gave 'racial offence', and incited racial discrimination/ hatred, he expressed or displayed a view consistent with the required counter-message.

Naturally, this approach could establish a degree of a problem for the Crown Prosecution Service (and/or Attorney General) in deciding whether or not to instigate legal proceedings, since they may not have full details of any defence. However, it can be assumed that the police will primarily bring requests for prosecutions and that they will have made full and diligent enquiries before referring the case to the CPS.

If not, the CPS would be justified in returning the file with an insistence that this defence element is thoroughly examined. Certainly, if the police were present while the speech was made, or they have a number of witnesses who are prepared to give evidence of a 'racially offensive' speech, they should have no difficulty in presenting the relevant evidence before the courts.

Public Interest Issues

Under the existing Public Order legislation the Attorney General must give consent to any racial prosecution.[52] In practice, the Attorney General or the Solicitor General personally consider each and every application for prosecution submitted by the Crown Prosecution Service,[53] with grounds of public interest often playing a prominent part in his determination of whether or not to prosecute.[54] Obviously, with no details of specific cases published, it is only possible to speculate upon the public interest grounds that relate to particular cases. An illustration of the issues involved can be deduced from the famous Enoch Powell 'rivers of blood' speech that talked of a flood of immigrants undermining the British culture.[55] It may be that doubts exist over whether the words used by Powell were 'threatening, abusive or insulting', but assuming they were, would a prosecution of such a prominent Conservative[56] politician be in the public interest? An obvious danger is that a prosecution would have brought a much greater media focus upon his words, with campaigns of support and opposition possibly developing. This could have heightened community tension and even led to the incitement racial hatred. The alternative of failing to prosecute, is that it legitimises the racist view – giving racism a norm of respectability – and leads the public to understand that such expressions are legitimate free speech and not in violation of any laws.

Over the years there has been much criticism of the need for the involvement of the Attorney General, with a common argument being that the Crown Prosecution Service should be the body responsible for determining whether or not to prosecute. In particular, *Searchlight* has been critical of the role of the Attorney General, arguing that he had refused to sanction the prosecution of certain political figures in two 'watertight cases', with soundings from the CPS indicating they were 'good cases'.[57]

Should Options 1 and 2 be adopted, it is clear that people such as Enoch Powell would be free to speak of what they perceive are the undesirable consequences of a course of action, i.e. so long as they do not stir up racial discrimination/hatred through the use of words which are 'threatening, abusive and insulting'. In expressing their views, they can stir up racial discrimination/ hatred through the use of 'racially offensive' words, so long as they associate a counter-message with their speech.

Even allowing for a counter-message defence, it seems possible that many more opportunities for prosecution would develop – in the sense that incitement to racial discrimination, by giving 'racial offence', is much easier to fulfil than incitement to racial hatred by the use of 'threat, abuse or insult'. As a consequence of this, it seems likely that the public interest question would become a very live issue in what could be a significant number of cases.

Whatever the merits, or otherwise, of the Attorney General's role under the existing public order legislation, it seems the introduction of Options 1 (incitement to racial discrimination) and 2 (a racial offence prerequisite) may justify a different approach. This justification stems from the proposed movement of the legislation into the sphere of 'racially offensive' literature, and the prospect of a great deal of immigration, refugee and asylum material from political parties being open to legal scrutiny. Given the political office of the Attorney General, it is clear that conflicting interests may arise, with suggestions developing that, in making a decision on whether it is in the public interest to proceed with a prosecution, he may use the law for party political purposes. Consequently, by distancing himself from the decision-making process, he should be able to demonstrate that prosecutions stem from a politically neutral legal process. This could be achieved by the provision of guidelines being issued by the Attorney General, with the CPS given the responsibility for deciding whether or not to prosecute in accord with those guidelines. It may also be desirable for the Director of Public Prosecutions to keep the Attorney General informed of their prosecuting intentions.

The Nature of any Guidelines that may need to be Introduced

Under existing legislation, the issuing of any guidelines will be at the discretion of the Attorney General, possibly after consultation with other interested parties.[58] However it is important to recognise that the Crown Prosecution Service currently have ample and adequate experience in determining whether or not it is in the public interest to bring a prosecution – indeed, on each and every occasion that they bring a prosecution they are required to consider this issue. The CPS prosecution manual provides guidance on racial motivation cases in the following terms:

> When considering the public interest test, you must balance the factors for and against prosecution carefully and fairly. However, cases in which there is a racial motivation are almost invariably serious; prosecution will usually take place unless there are very powerful public interest factors tending against prosecution which clearly outweigh those tending in favour.

Given this public interest test applies to all racially motivated cases, it seems reasonable to argue the same criteria should apply to Part III of the Public Order Act 1986 prosecutions – essentially because by definition all such cases are inherently likely to have a racial motive. Indeed, such an approach would be consistent with the recommendation made by Sir William MacPherson, in the *Stephen Lawrence Public Inquiry Report,*[59] who argued that once the CPS has satisfied the evidential test, there should be a rebuttable presumption that the public interest should be in favour of prosecution.[60]

While this approach may suggest that there could be a relatively high number of Option 1 and 2 prosecutions,[61] this could be lessened by a proactive use of police cautions. This form of approach may be especially of value in the early application of the legislation, since it is likely to help balance the public interest question with the possibility that the accused was genuinely not fully aware of just where the boundaries to 'racial offence' and discrimination apply.

Tackling Racism on the Internet

The Internet is a global network of connected computers,[62] belonging to different individuals and organisations,[63] with over 200 million worldwide users. These organisations include governments, universities, schools, libraries,[64] large and small businesses. To help monitor the Internet in the UK there exists the Internet Watch Foundation, which is an industry led, regulatory body designed to monitor and report upon unacceptable web-based materials.[65] In contrast to such regulation, there is a Blue Ribbon Campaign for Online Free Speech[66] which seeks to enhance the freedom of an individual to display his talents on a worldwide stage.[67]

Despite such a situation, it is clear that the Internet is open to abuse. A three-year study of Internet crime found that crimes committed include paedophilia, pornography, hacking, hate, fraud and software piracy.[68] For example in Germany, an investigation into the transmission of illegal pornographic material on the Internet resulted in Compuserve, the world's leading global service provider, suspending 200 Internet services. This action being taken following the raiding of Compuserve's German office, with government officials identifying 200 services as being illegal under German Law.[69] The services was later reintroduced after Compuserve established new controls that enabled parents to restrict the access of children to pornographic sites on the Internet.[70]

One of the biggest Internet providers in Germany – Webcom – has cut off access to a website that denied the Holocaust.[71] This decision of Webcom came after prosecutors said they were considering bringing incitement charges against the company for facilitating the distribution of neo-Nazi propaganda on the Internet. This threat is reported to have failed, as students of a number of US universities made copies of the website available worldwide – on the grounds that they were upholding free speech and the First Amendment.[72]

Searchlight[73] has undertaken research into 'hate on the Internet',[74] producing evidence of full-colour web pages which show and incite skinheads to beat up blacks and even give details of how to make bombs,[75] with networks from Austria, Germany, Netherlands, Norway, and the USA – representing just a few of the countries from where militant racists operate to spread their message worldwide.

The European Union's Council of Ministers Consultative Commission on Racism and Xenophobia has set its sights on cleaning up the Internet[76] 'from the evil of its racist filth'.[77] Indeed, as Glyn Ford MEP has remarked:

> The propagation of racial hate, anti-Semitism and nazism is growing and the young are dangerously susceptible to being influenced by this propaganda because it is dressed up in Internet Technology.

The problem though, is in establishing a viable means of controlling the

Internet. Indeed, it seems that in general, there have been three approaches to this problem.

1 To prosecute those who are directly responsible for the unacceptable electronic mails or web pages appearing on the Internet.

2 To make the Internet Service Provider liable for unacceptable electronic messages that are sent via his service. The idea being that he will then clean up the airways.

3 To make use of counter-messages, so as to warn people about the content of unacceptable materials.

1   Prosecuting those who Directly Produce/Publish Unacceptable Materials

While an individual is generally free to publish material on the worldwide web, it is clear that he will be legally responsible for that publication.[78] He could still be sued for defamation[79] or held liable for the content for any pornographic materials,[80] with individuals also being liable should they download unacceptable materials.[81]

A person could be prosecuted under Section 19 of the Public Order Act 1986 for the distribution of 'threatening, abusive or insulting' material that, in all the circumstances, is likely to stir up racial hatred. On examining the BNP web-page,[82] it would seem that the literature displayed is typical of the vast majority of its material – i.e. while it is 'racially offensive', it is unlikely to be found to be 'threatening, abusive or insulting'. As such, under existing laws, BNP leaders are unlikely to face prosecution for stirring up racial hatred via the Internet.

Indeed much of the BNP material is mild, in comparison to some of the race hate web pages stemming from the USA. For example, while searching for the BNP web-page I came across a link to the USA based organisation Stormfront[83] whose publications would almost certainly be unlawful under Section 19 of the Public Order Act 1986, if published within Britain – though it seems it may be considered as acceptable under US laws.

In addition to the Stormfront website, there exists a variety of racist newsgroups which provide a specific Internet forum for militant racists to enjoy. At such locations, you can find some of the vilest forms of racial discrimination and hatred imaginable.

On this basis, it may seem rather pointless to introduce legislation that could outlaw a comparatively mild UK distributed worldwide web page, when material emanating from other countries is far more extreme and 'racially offensive'. This particularly applies when it is just as easy to obtain the information from these other countries, as it is from the UK.[84] Quite apart from the fact that any organisation could get around the legislation by operating from, say, Norway,[85] it seems a futile exercise to try to tackle such problems in isolation. Indeed, such is the extent of the problem it seems evident that only worldwide action via the United Nations could have any impact, and even then it would only be as good as its weakest link. For, if the First Amendment enables distribution in the US, it also enables distribution in the United Kingdom – it not being possible to isolate the UK from the telephone-linked network.

2   Making the Server Liable for Unacceptable Electronic Data

It is possibly because of such practical difficulties, that governments have been attempting to make the domestic based Internet Service Provider (the server) responsible for unacceptable electronic data. This approach has been taken in Germany and the United States.

In Germany, as a result of an investigation into pornographic materials, the authorities raided the German office's of the global Internet Service Provider Compuserve, eventually arresting and prosecuting Felix Somme the Managing Director of the company for the distribution of pornographic materials.[86] Again in Germany, as discussed earlier in this chapter, one of the biggest Internet providers – Webcom – responded to a threat of them being prosecuted for incitement charges in relation to neo-Nazi propaganda by cutting off the Internet access of a website that denied the Holocaust in direct defiance of a domestic law.[87]

In the USA, the Clinton administration introduced a Communications Decency Act 1996 which made the server, whether domestic or foreign, legally responsible for ensuring that a person under the age of 18 did: not have access to sexual or excretory activities or organs in terms which are 'indecent' or 'patently offensive' by 'contemporary community standards'. While this legislation is related to sexual matters, and not racist materials, it is nonetheless typical of a governmental desire to make servers responsible for electronic materials that they facilitate. Despite such, the CDA 1996 has been declared, in the case of *Janet Reno, Attorney General of the United States et al v American Civil Liberties Union et al*,[88] unconstitutional by the US Supreme

Court, on the grounds that the legislation breached the First Amendment of the US constitution. However in declaring so, the Supreme Court held that the interest of encouraging freedom of expression in a democratic society 'outweighs any theoretical but unproven benefit of censorship'. The Court accepted that users cannot accidentally walk into indecent material, with them needing to make a conscious decision to locate it and to overcome the variety of warning signs which exist – with 'almost all sexually explicit images' being 'preceded by warnings as to the content'. In this sense, the court was accepting the principle of a counter-message – in that the warning signs themselves portray a message that sexually explicit material is ahead and juveniles should not enter. Indeed without the existence of such counter-messages, it seems probable that the outcome would have been very different. This can be deduced from the majority judgement of Justice Stevens who distinguished the case of *Ginsberg*[89] because that case had involved a radio medium which 'as a matter of history' had received limited First Amendment protection because 'warnings could not adequately protect the listener from the unexpected program content'.

In 1996 the then Labour Party Women's Spokesperson Tessa Jowell MP, talked about the need for a future Labour government to introduce similar Communications Decency legislation in the UK.[90] However, as a result of a developing consensus in the European Union,[91] there seems to be a move away from making a server directly liable for electronic materials that he may facilitate. The Home Secretary in 1998 indicated that new laws were not needed since the 'National Criminal Intelligence Unit' would tackle the problem of racist sites by liaison with police in other countries, to try and get them to persuade servers to remove racist sites.[92] It seems this shift in emphasis, derives from the practical and evidential problems associated with determining *mens rea* in circumstances of 'innocent dissemination'.[93] Indeed, the very nature of computer technology makes the establishment of a server's knowledge of material content often difficult to determine. While a television broadcaster may not know in advance that a guest may express unacceptable views, he can generally make subsequent announcements – while the show is on air – to counter any comments that are considered to be unacceptable. In comparison, a server facilitates millions of words of data, to and from thousands of users, in any one second and as such a server generally has no real meaningful knowledge, which goes to *mens rea*, of the data content. To prosecute a server for unacceptable electronic data, which he facilitates, seems as nonsensical as proposing to prosecute British Telecom because someone may have been abusive over the telephone.

However, where a server is aware that its service is being used to conduct *illegal activity* and does not take action, it becomes liable to prosecution as accessory to the crime. If it cooperates in identifying the perpetrator and ceases providing the service to him or removes the illegal material concerned, it will be protected against prosecution.[94]

3 Using a Counter-Message to Warn People of Unacceptable Materials

Should the law be amended to include Options 1 (incitement to racial discrimination) and 2 (including 'offence' or 'racial offence' as a prerequisite), it seems that a great deal of the racist literature that certain parties display on the Internet could be illegal. However if the counter-message principle were to be applied, they would still be able to display such material so long as the appropriate counter-message was displayed.

The problem is that racist offensive materials produced outside of the UK – which may be more unacceptable in terms of stirring up racial discrimination or hatred – would still be displayed on computers based in the UK. By illustration, there may be no value in asking the US authorities to close down such a website, because the First Amendment prevents such an action. Likewise, there would be no point in making the receiver of the racist materials liable, since he would have no knowledge that it may be racially offensive, and in breach of the law, until he had downloaded and read it.

To make the server responsible for distributing racially offensive material without a counter-message seems doomed to failure, since it is generally an 'innocent disseminator'.[95] Accordingly, it may be necessary to take an altogether different approach, which involves tackling racially offensive materials as they enter the UK's computer airways. To use an analogy, to establish a form of customs' checkpoint at which all computer data is searched for 'racially offensive' words, with the material being stamped with a counter-message consistent with the government's aim of saying 'no to racism'. On the basis of this stamping, the material is then authorised for circulation within the UK.

A key element of this form of approach is that all 'racially offensive' materials would be allowed into the UK airways.[96] Indeed to try electronically to refuse entry to materials that convey certain racist terminology would be exceedingly difficult, since the 'cybersitter' style of computer censor technology is exceedingly limited in its search criteria, with key words the basis of excluding web-pages.[97] The obvious problem with this form of approach is that it would involve excluding web-pages because they contain offensive key words. This would result in an unacceptable form of censorship, and also a pointless exercise since I am not proposing that the law should tackle the use of 'racially offensive' words in isolation. My proposals for legislative change are only concerned with the use of 'threatening, abusive, insulting or offensive' words that stir up racial discrimination or hatred – this requires a legal analysis based upon intent or likelihood, which is far beyond the capabilities of the current 'cybersitter' style of software.

What could be done, however, is for the government to require anti-racist counter-messages to be displayed in circumstances where the web-page contains certain defined expressions or words. It is possible that this form of counter-message approach could be achieved by consensus, with the computer community responding to the prospect of legislation by introducing its own code that promotes the use of a uniform anti-racist counter-message.[98] This could be backed up with a voluntary undertaking from Internet Service Providers that they would disconnect any website that failed to conform. Despite hopes that such an approach could work, the evidence from the approach taken by the European Union with regards to its action plan on promoting safer use of the Internet, suggests that self-regulation may not be wholly successful. After over 15 months of a four-year £25m action plan, there seems to be no obvious evidence of any Euro-wide self-regulatory filtering and rating system, that is designed to tackle Internet content which incites hatred on grounds of race, sex, religion, nationality or ethnic origin.[99]

Clearly any approach built on self-regulation, is likely to be prone to difficulties, but this applies more so when there are problems due to international boundaries and differing legal requirements in each member state. For these reasons it may be more effective for the UK government, in cooperation with the European Union, to legally require software production companies, like Microsoft and Netscape, to programme all Internet browsers (intended for the UK market) so that they display a counter-message when certain conditions materialise. The alert counter-message would reflect the values of an anti-racist equal opportunity statement such as – 'Warning this site could be racially offensive – "Say no to racism"'.

This form of counter-message approach, would at least alert the potential web-page reader that the material might be 'racially offensive'. However, it must be recognised that there may be civil libertarian concerns that such an approach may lead to counter-message legislation being applied to a whole range of issues – e.g. drugs, smoking and even religious or political ideas that some societies disapprove of. There may also be some medical concern that such a counter-message approach could lead to a form of brainwashing or indoctrination, with excessive usage of messages possibly unnaturally influencing the minds of individuals. Thus any usage of counter-messages on computer and TV, needs to be used moderately and responsibly, possibly only after a detailed research study of the medical effects of repetitive messaging.

Possibly a price that society must pay for the advancement in computer technology, is that militant racists will be able to exploit its use and spread their message. Just as it is not practical to deny the use of the telephone, because it can be used to deliver threatening and/or abusive messages, so it is not practical to deny the use of the computer. For such reasons, laws are needed to deal with the worst examples of abuse. A counter-message approach to racially offensive Internet materials, certainly seems preferable to outright censorship, but detailed research may be needed to establish the most effective and safest means of achieving this aim.

Averting the Threat to Freedom of Expression

In the last chapter I acknowledged that the combination of Options 1 (incitement to racial discrimination) and 2 (a racial offence prerequisite), may threaten freedom of expression. The real test of the advantage of a counter-message defence is whether it would help avert this threat. So far as the discussion, by mainstream political parties, of issues such as refugee status goes, it is clear that it would provide a shield from any likelihood of prosecution for inciting racial discrimination by the use of 'racially offensive' words. It seems probable that all of the major political parties in the UK should have no difficulty in incorporating an equal opportunities – 'say no to racism' – statement within their literature. They may have reservations about giving an indication that their manifesto warrants such a requirement, but they could comply without any undermining of their political beliefs. As such, they could easily avert prosecution for inciting racial discrimination, i.e. so long as their material does not become either 'threatening, abusive or insulting'.

It may well be that political parties who can be described as militant racist, will be less than happy at being required to include an equal opportunities statement,[100] but the fact remains that if they choose to do so, they could avoid grounds for a prosecution for incitement to racial discrimination by the use of 'racially offensive' literature. Likewise, any militant racist citizen could avert a prosecution by the use of this simple and straightforward counter-message statement.

To this extent, the counter-message can provide a basis for averting a serious threat to freedom of expression. However, there can be no doubt that the overall impact of Options 1 and 2, even with a counter-message defence, can be argued to amount to a limited form of restriction upon freedom of expression because it may place a contradictory statement on the author's material. Whether on balance, after taking into account the benefit to the rights of the receiver, a counter-message restriction is justified, is a matter of political judgement. It can certainly be argued that it is in the public interest, in a democratic society, to root out and limit the evil of militant racism – the aim of which is to obtain support for the undermining of equality of opportunity.

Indeed, equality of opportunity must be considered as one of the cornerstones of a democratic society, in that it offers to all people a degree of understanding that men and women, no matter what their race and ethnic origin, are equal under the law. In this sense, it undermines any racist message that suggests any expressions that people belonging to certain groups, or races, are of a lesser value than those of another. To this extent, equality of opportunity enhances freedom of expression, with counter-messages helping to develop a climate that signifies that no matter what a person's race, that person's views should be given respect. In this sense, it may help liberalise individuals in their use of expression.

Compatibility with the Convention on Human Rights

While it may be practical to introduce legislation to ensure that racists display counter-messages on material and/or computer screens, it is important to reflect that any such proposals for change benefit from being consistent with the Convention on Human Rights as introduced into United Kingdom law through the Human Rights Act 1998.[101] This inevitably means considering if the proposals for change – in particular Option 1 (amending the public order laws in order to tackle 'incitement to racial discrimination and hatred') and Option 2 (adding 'racial offence' to the prerequisites for such prosecutions) – are compatible with the 'Convention rights'. To consider this point, it seems evident that it is obviously necessary to establish if the proposals may breach Article 10 of the European Convention on Human Rights.

However, before considering this issue, it is important to recognise the special position that the ECHR now holds in UK Law. As a result of the Human Rights Act 1998 the ECHR, unlike the vast majority of other international treaties, is being introduced into UK law,[102] albeit that the UK

Courts would not be directly bound by the judgements of the European Court of Human Rights.[103]

While the Human Rights Act 1998 does not give the courts power to strike down an Act of Parliament that is incompatible with the Convention rights, it does provide powers for a court to make a 'declaration of incompatibility', with the responsibility then falling upon an appropriate government minister to enable Parliament to decide if it wishes to amend legislation.[104]

However, the influence of the Human Rights Act 1998 is not just legal, but also political. This applies because the 1998 Act places a minister under a statutory duty, in relation to any Bill he places before parliament, to provide a written statement as to compatibility with the Convention on Human Rights. The political consequences of this are significant, because while the Bill could still become law if it is declared by the minister to be incompatible with human rights, it must be accepted that any such legislation will have a troublesome passage through parliament. Applying these principles to the proposals for legislative change within this book, this means that it is clearly desirable that Options 1 and 2 are not incompatible, in particular with Article 10 of the 'Convention on Human Rights'.

Article 10 states:

> (1) Everyone has the right to freedom of expression. This right shall include freedom to hold opinion and to receive opinion and impart information and ideas without interference by public authority and regardless of frontiers. This Article shall not prevent States from requiring the licensing of broadcasting, television or cinema enterprises.
> (2) The exercise of these freedoms, since it carries with it duties and responsibilities, may be subject to formalities, conditions, restrictions or penalties as are prescribed by law and are necessary in a democratic society, in the interests of national security, territorial integrity or public safety, for the prevention of disorder or crime, for the protection of health or morals, for the protection of the reputation of others, for preventing the disclosure of information received in confidence, or for maintaining the authority and impartiality of the judiciary.

The very nature of the wording of Article 10, emphasises that there is no such thing, under the ECHR, as an absolute right to freedom of expression. Indeed, the emphasis in Section 2 is that along with the exercise of the freedom are duties and responsibilities. Where there is a conflict between freedom of expression and some other interests, the Strasbourg authorities are inevitably engaged in some sort of weighing exercise to determine the priority of one over the other.[105] Despite such a position, it is clear that the European Court of Human Rights gives a high priority to the protection of expression, with the term 'expression' having been interpreted to include not merely words,[106] but relating to pictures,[107] images,[108] and actions intended to express an idea or to present information.[109] Equally, the means of protecting expression go beyond speech to print,[110] radio[111] and television broadcasting,[112] artistic expression,[113] film[114] and probably electronic information systems. In *Handyside v UK*[115] the Court said:

> Freedom of expression constitutes one of the essential freedoms of a [democratic] society, one of the main basic conditions for its progress and for the development of every man. Subject to paragraph 2 of Article 10, it is applicable not only to information or ideas that are favourably received or regarded as inoffensive but also to those that offend, shock or disturb the state or any sector of the population. Such are the demands of pluralism, tolerance and broadmindedness without which there is no 'democratic society'.

This judgement clearly gives strong emphasis to the protection of information and ideas that may be 'offensive'. As such, it displays a potential for seriously undermining the arguments presented in this book in relation to tackling material that gives 'offence'. However, it is important to note that freedom of expression is subject to enormous limitations, with the courts consistently providing protection for individuals who suffer as a result of someone's use of expressive terms that may sexually or racially discriminate.[116] It is argued therefore, that the limitations I propose in this book are not in any sense revolutionary or ground breaking, they are simply a continuance of a principle that is firmly established within domestic law. Further, through my proposals, I am not advocating legislative change with regards to material that is 'offensive' in the normal wide meaning of the word. Indeed, I have related my concerns to information that stirs up racial hatred/discrimination through the use of 'racially offensive' material. This is clearly much narrower than the term of 'offence' and can clearly be considered as being more specific due to its relationship to race. This point is especially of value when it can be shown that the protection offered, under Article 10, to militant racist expression is scant compared to that offered to expression in general.

The ECHR and Tackling Militant Racism

Indeed so far as tackling militant racism is concerned, the ECHR[117] guarantees nondiscrimination only in the exercise of a right specifically protected by the Convention.

At first glance this appears to be less than positive. However, the wording of the ECHR does provide grounds for arguing that rights such as expressed in Article 9: freedom of thought, conscience and religion; Article 10: freedom of expression; and Article 11: freedom of peaceful assembly and association; are all subject to:

- Article 14: The enjoyment of the rights and freedoms as set forth in this Convention shall be secured without discrimination on any ground such as sex, race, colour, language, religion. Political or other opinion, national or social origin, association with a national minority, property, birth or status.
- Article 17: Nothing in this convention may be interpreted as implying for any State, group or person any right to engage in any activity or perform any act aimed at the destruction of any of the rights and freedoms set forth herein or at their limitation other than is provided for in the Convention.

Thereby, the ECHR can be interpreted to provide that a person can only secure his/her right to freedom of expression, under the ECHR, if the claim displays no discrimination on grounds such as sex, race, colour, national origin etc. The potential for this is significant because it prioritises the rights of individuals and gives credence to the argument that equality (or at least the absence of discrimination) is a prerequisite to freedom of expression. No doubt as a result of this, the European Commission of Human Rights has taken a limiting approach to protecting racist expression.

For example, the Commission in the case of *X v Italy*,[118] considered claims in relation to freedom of expression,[119] association[120] and Article 14. This case concerned an issue of whether criminal law in Italy was justified in making illegal engagement in intrigue aimed at reconstructing a fascist party, as being necessary on the grounds of public safety and to protect the rights and freedoms of others. The Commission took the view that a difference in treatment, directed towards fascist ideology, had a legitimate purpose in order to protect democracy and thereby rejected the application.

In the case of *Glimmerveen and others v Netherlands*,[121] the European Commission took both the CERD Convention and Article 17 as its guide, in ruling that the Chairman of the racist Nederlandsde Volks Unie party,[122] may not invoke the provisions of Article 10 to challenge a Netherlands' Authority decision which imposed a two-year prison sentence, on the grounds of incitement to racial discrimination, for distributing literature addressed to 'Netherlanders of the white race'.

Two other cases, concerning freedom of expression and revisionism, further strengthen the restrictive approach of the Commission. In *X v Federal Republic of Germany*,[123] applicants complained about a judicial decision banning an exhibition of brochures that alleged that 'the death of Jews under the Third Reich was Zionist trickery'. The Commission held that the murder of Jews in the Second World War was 'an historic fact' established beyond doubt. Thus, in the interests of the protection of others, it did not disagree with the judgement of the domestic German court banning the exhibition on grounds of defamation. Likewise, in *T v Belgium*,[124] the author-publisher was deemed responsible for the publication of a text, written by a former leader of the Belgian Rexist movement, entitled 'Letter to the Pope concerning Auschwitz', which questioned the extermination of millions of Jews. The European Commission took the view that 'T' had not been punished for being co-author, but for having participated in the publication of a Nazi leaflet which was insulting. The Commission, therefore provided no protection under Article 10.

Clearly these declarations – which show limited or scant protection for racist expression[125] – are those of the European Commission and not of the European Court, but they do reflect consistency with the ECHR. However, a word of caution must be sounded in that proportionality[126] is always a criterion that weighs in the mind in relation to the ECHR.[127]

An indirect example of proportionality can be seen from the case of *Jersild v Denmark*,[128] which considered the conflict between the freedom of the press and the dissemination of insulting racist views. In *Jersild*, the European Court of Human Rights expressly endorsed the practice of the Commission of giving only scant protection to racist expression.[129] Indeed, this restrictive admissibility, and scant protection, approach of the Commission was effectively distinguished in *Jersild* because the press was not propagating racist views – they were in effect reporting on the activities of others that were racist.

Press Freedom and Racist Material

Jersild involved a journalist who had filmed a group of racist teenagers known as the Greenjackets, for a television news documentary. The Danish authorities were concerned by the broadcasting coverage that, *inter alia*, compared 'niggers to gorillas', and gave details of how the members of the Greenjackets had been involved in an attack upon an immigrant family. Not only were the teenagers prosecuted under Danish laws for racially insulting members of the targeted groups, the journalist was also charged and found guilty of 'aiding and abetting the dissemination of a statement which was threatening, abusive or insulting or degraded a group of persons on account of their race'.[130]

When the case reached the European Court of Human Rights it was held, by 12 votes to seven, that the Danish authorities had violated the rights of the journalist by establishing this prosecution. This decision was founded upon Article 10 of the European Convention on Human Rights, on the basis of what is necessary in a democratic society.

In upholding the journalist's appeal the European Court reiterated that, while the racist teenagers did not enjoy the protection of Article 10, freedom of expression constitutes one of the essential foundations of a democratic society and the safeguards to be afforded to the press are of particular importance. It was stressed that it is incumbent on the press to impart information and ideas of public interest, while emphasis was placed on the need to counterbalance the extremist views. The Court rejected the Danish Authority's view that the broadcast material did not contain counterbalancing material and held that, 'taken as a whole the broadcast contained a number of counterbalancing elements'.

The European Court stressed that the punishment of a journalist, for assisting in the dissemination of statements made by another person in an interview, would seriously hamper the contribution of the press to discussion of matters of public interest and should not be envisaged unless there were particularly strong reasons for doing so. It was argued that news reporting based on interviews, whether edited or not, constituted one of the most important means whereby the press was able to play the vital role of 'public watchdog'.

Amongst the dissenting judges' views, was the argument that the Danish courts had taken into account the conflicting interests between freedom of expression and its international commitments under the UN Convention on the Elimination of All Forms of Racial Discrimination (CERD). Thus, the Danish Courts had applied the correct principles of law and concluded that such outrageous racist and insulting statements could only be justified if balanced by opposing considerations that could have outweighed the wrongfulness of the statements. It was clear the dissenting members did not consider that the counterbalance provided by the journalist was adequate.[131]

There was greater emphasis placed by the dissenting members on the importance of the United Nation's CERD Convention. Judges Ryssdal, Bernhardt, Spielman and Loizou argued that the CERD Convention manifestly could not be ignored when the European Convention was being implemented – 'It is binding on Denmark. It must also guide the European Court of Human Rights in its decisions'. By comparison, the majority took the view that:

Denmark's obligations under Article 10 must be interpreted, to the extent possible, so as to be reconcilable with its obligations under the UN Convention. In this respect it is not for the Court to interpret the 'due regard' clause in Article 4 of the UN Convention, which is open to various constructions. The Court is however of the opinion that its interpretation of Article 10 of the European Convention … is compatible with Denmark's obligations under the UN Convention.

Despite these subtle differences between the majority and minority judgements, it is clear they agreed that the United Nations CERD convention cannot be ignored when the ECHR is being implemented, with it being relevant to the European Court of Human Rights in any of its decisions. Also accepted, by all of the judges, was the need for journalists to provide some form of counterbalance to racially insulting views. Indeed, the dissenting argument between the judges was not whether an absolute freedom of expression should be given to journalists, when reporting racist material, but whether there had been an adequate counterbalance provided.

To this extent, the proposed establishment of a formal counterbalancing statement should be welcomed, since it should remove any degree of uncertainty from the proceedings. If government legislation specifies the form and nature of the counter-message statement, then it should be relatively easy to determine if this condition has been met. Indeed, it would provide a clear counterbalancing statement on the face of any racist material being circulated.

A Right to Receive Expression

It is also important to recognise that Article 10 is not just concerned with the rights of the expresser. In fact, Article 10(1) specifically refers to the freedom to 'receive' information – with the European Court of Human Rights asserting, in the case of *The Sunday Times v UK*, that this extends to being 'willing' receivers of information.[132] Consequentially, it is argued that a counter-message recognises the freedom of the expresser – i.e. by enabling publication in accord with conditions – while enhancing the freedom of the receiver by alerting them to the fact that the material may contain elements that could be 'racially offensive'. Indeed, as receivers of information, a person can only exercise a right to be a 'willing' receiver if they have some form of *prima facie* or prior knowledge of the nature of the content of the material. Once they have this *prima facie* knowledge, they can then exercise a right of choice as to whether they should read or ignore such material.

In Conclusion

Over the past two chapters, I have considered the practical implications of amendments to Part III of the Public Order Act 1986. Chapter 4 outlined and considered the principal options for change. Option 1, relates to the need to tackle militant racism by changing the law so that it penalises incitement to racial discrimination as well as hatred. In addition, Option 2 proposes the inclusion of 'racial offence' as a prerequisite to prosecution.

By considering racist material, distributed in the London Borough of Hounslow, I have shown that legislative changes involving just Option 1 – incitement to racial discrimination or hatred – would have limited impact due to the evidential shield of prerequisites that require material to be 'threatening, abusive or insulting'. By comparison, also including Option 2 – 'racial offence' – as a prerequisite would certainly tackle militant racist material, but it could have potentially serious consequences in relation to the undermining of freedom of expression. Indeed, it could seriously impede open political discussion on important issues such as the status of refugees and asylum seekers thereby threatening the value of a democratic parliamentary process.

While these options, in themselves, would present a threat to the undermining of freedom of expression, it has been argued in chapter 5 that enabling an equal opportunities counter-message defence helps avoid this situation. That being said, it is acknowledged that a combination of Options 1 and 2 along with a counter-message defence could result in arguments being made that the proposals amount to form of restriction on the ideal of freedom of expression because the counter-message may contradict the author's opinion. Quite whether such a restriction is justified in the interests of limiting incitement to racial discrimination is a matter of political judgement, but grounds exist for believing that the combined proposals do not amount to a breach of the Convention on Human Rights[133] and to this extent they can be considered as compatible, and certainly not incompatible.

The advantage of tackling 'racial offence' in such a restrictive legislative manner is that the proposals show a consistency of approach between speech and literature, while also laying the foundations for enabling domestic legislators to tackle the problem of racism on the Internet – notwithstanding the practical difficulties involved. Further, these legislative options, because of the counter-message defence, display respect for freedom of expression – while also helping to undermine the fermentation of support for extreme right wing political parties who espouse 'racially offensive' views.

Possibly a strong argument for the counter-message approach is that at its core it enhances freedom of expression. It does this by recognising not just the rights of the expresser, but also of the reader or receiver. Indeed, it does not deny a person the right to publish 'racially offensive' material – it just lays down the conditions for such publication. Further, it enhances freedom of expression by alerting a potential reader to the probable content of the material and enabling then to choose whether they wish to proceed.

One worrying downside of a counter-message defence, so far as the distribution of local leaflets is concerned, is that the proposals may force militant racists to choose between legality and illegality. The racist organisation may, as seems likely, decide to comply with the law and include an equal opportunities statement within the material. By doing so they may find support for the party's ideals ebbing away, as activists within the party feel little enthusiasm for delivering a leaflet that would say no to racism. The obvious worry is that these militant racists would, as a result, turn to the extremity of attacking racial victims in their homes and in the streets. While this is an ugly thought, it is important to recognise that this form of illegality is already evident amongst some militant racists.

Notes

1   At the 1995 AGM of Liberty a motion was approved which instructed the Executive to explore the encouragement of counter-speech as an approach to problems of racism and sexism. This included possible forms of legislation that would mandate publicly-funded counter speech.
2   The National Council for Civil Liberties uses Liberty as its shortened campaigning name – see letter from Atija Lockwood of Liberty, *New Law Journal*, 9 February 1996.
3   In 1998 the CRE had an advertising budget of £250,000.
4   An example were the advertisements on the underground which demonstrated that Asian, Europeans etc. all have the same size brains – while racists do not.
5   In 1995 the CRE undertook a racial equality's poster campaign – 'Racial Attacks are Crimes'.
6   Eric Cantona and the Nike sportswear TV advertisements.
7   The Advertising Standards Agency confirmed (in a telephone call of 12 March 1999) that they had received in total 27 complaints nationally about the CRE campaign. It is understood these complaints came from members of the public and anti-racist organisations. Clearly, one complaint is undesirable, but 27 complaints is not a significant number nationwide and for these reasons it may be considered that the ASA have taken a heavy-handed response in requiring the CRE to obtain advance approval for any future advertising campaigns.
8   In a telephone conversation held 24 January 1996.
9   There are various examples of this, one such example is the motion, approved at the 1995 AGM, calling for an inclusion in the law of a formal concept of racially motivated crime.

10   I am indebted to Mrs Elisabeth Woollard, a Harrogate teacher, for this observation.

11   For example, the actress Joan Collins was on 'Good Morning TV' reporting on the 1999 Oscar ceremonies and remarked that 'You are not allowed to smoke at any of the parties – it is politically incorrect'.

12   It seems the need for an EU regulatory approach was more about enforcing a common standard across all members states, than it was about obtaining the cooperation of the tobacco companies to display a counter message.

13   The British government has indicated that they intend to introduce legislation to prohibit newspaper, magazine and billboard advertising by tobacco companies. This challenge ruled on by the ECJ in 2001 (see 'Smoking Adverts to be Stubbed out Early', *The Times*, 18 June 1999).

14   In the last chapter, I argued that words that are 'racially offensive' could be determined on the basis of a combined statutory and natural meaning approach. This would mean that the racial element is determined in accord with the definition of a 'racial group' in Section 17 of the Public Order Act 1986 and 'offence or offensive' determined in accord with the principles laid down in *Brutus v Cozens* [1972] 1 All ER 1297. This would result in words that are threatening, abusive, insulting or offensive all being determined as a matter of fact and not law.

15   It is suggested that a new Section 18(5a) be created which states: 'A person who attaches to racially offensive words or material a warning and anti-racist counter message, which is consistent with saying no to racism, is not guilty of an offence under this section'.

16   [1972] 1 All ER 1297. This case was also discussed in chapters 3 and 4.

17   The same legal principles apply to words that are 'threatening or abusive', though it is clear that a greater degree of objectivity may exist in determining if the words used were threatening or abusive.

18   In applying this definition a person using insulting words must take the audience as he finds them. See *Jordan v Burgoyne* [1963] 2 All ER 225 and the discussion in chapter 3 of this book.

19   See comments of Lord Reid in *Brutus v Cozens* [1972] 1 All ER 1297.

20   This definition of race is synonymous with the definitions of a 'racial group' applied under Section 17 of the Public Order Act 1986, Section 3 of the Race Relations Act 1976 and Section 28(4) of the Crime and Disorder Act 1998.

21   This issue will be discussed more fully when consideration is given to Article 10 of the Convention on Human Rights.

22   By which I mean the display of a counter message on material what is racially offensive and is likely to stir up racial discrimination or hatred.

23   See comments of Roy Jenkins (Home Secretary). Paragraph 126, 'Racial Discrimination', White Paper presented to Parliament, September 1975, HMSO, 1976.

24   Case number CO/1772/92 Divisional Court. For a discussion of this case see chapter 3 and the section 'Racist Graffiti and Fly Posting'. It should be noted that a key element that established guilt in this case was the fact that the two defendants knew that the poster was being displayed and took no action to rectify the situation.

25   Clearly this kind of case would be determined on the facts and dependent upon proof of distribution by persons belonging to or associated with the organisation. Also at issue may be what steps the leadership of the organisation may have personally taken to stop the distribution of the offensive material. Any person who tried to set up or frame another, by duplicating the logo, could be charged with perverting the course of justice.

26   I do not intend to discuss the civil or criminal liability of unincorporated associations in detail since it may take me outside the parameters of my book. I raise the point by way of illustration and would add that this subject is a book in its own right, with limited substantive case law in this area.

27   *Criminal Law*, 6th edn, Butterworths, 1988, p. 176.

28   This comes from the comments of Lord Reid in *Tesco Supermarkets Ltd v Nattrass* [1972] 1 AC 153. While this case was in relation to a corporation, by analogy the same principles should apply to unincorporated associations.

29   [1982] RTR 260, [1982] Crim LR 510.

30   [1972] AC 153.

31   This approach was preferred to a formal questionnaire since the likelihood was that they would ignore such requests or present a party line.

32   This aspect of his criticism will be discussed later in this chapter (see the section 'Consistency with the CERD Convention').

33   The inference is that those producing such non-attributable racist materials – because they cannot be readily identified – will feel free to be more openly threatening, abusive or insulting.

34   This undoubtedly is true, but after the first few leaflets or publications such an approach will inevitably die down.

35   'Violence and the Viewer', Report of the Joint Working Party on Violence on Television, 1998.

36   The distinction between the two being that a content warning is designed to warn the reader of material content with a view to parents excluding certain vulnerable sections of society – i.e. children. In comparison, a counter-message is more educational in content – in that its primary purpose is to remind and educate the public of a societal goal. Obviously, a counter-message may also be a warning in that it enables people to choose whether or not to view (or read) the content knowing that it may contain material that is offensive. However, its primary purpose is not the exclusion of certain sections of society.

37   The report of the Joint Working Party rejected the notion that identical rules can be established to cover all service providers and agreed upon a statement of common principles or guidelines. This statement utilising the 9 pm family viewing watershed and recognising the value of on-air announcements and warnings (working towards a new initiative utilising teletext page numbers) prior to programming and during any TV break.

38   See 'Violence and the Viewer', p. 23.

39   The V-chip is a computer chip that can be inserted into the television thereby enabling parents to prevent children from watching certain unacceptable TV programmes.

40   For example, the report points out that on average people replace their television sets once every 10 years and even then they often give the old TV set (with no V-chip installed) to their children for their bedrooms. They also argued that this could result in children whose viewing is unsupervised, or whose families cannot afford the latest technology, will be put at risk if, with the excuse of the V-chip behind them, broadcasters are encouraged to relax the standards on which they rely. The V-chip would therefore be an inadequate 'quick fix' solution that would not protect the most vulnerable viewers.

41   It could even say such as part of the agreed counter-message.

42   In the case of TV violence the primary purpose is to protect children – enabling parents to opt to prevent children from watching a programme that displays violence.

43   For a discussion of this area see chapter 4.

44 This same principle could be said to apply to tobacco companies with regards to tobacco advertising.

45 That is applying a natural meaning to the words.

46 He could have received one and simply had an intent to read it. Hence, he has no intent to distribute.

47 This should be a complete defence if say he had sought advice from the Commission for Racial Equality and they had advised that they did not consider it was racially offensive. In such circumstances, a defendant could easily establish that he was not aware that the material could be racially offensive.

48 The existing Section 23(3) provides for a defence for the accused to show that he did not suspect, and had no reason to suspect, that it was threatening, abusive, insulting. Under the proposals for reform, it follows that this would be amended to provide a defence for the accused to show that he did not suspect, and had no reason to suspect, that it was threatening, abusive, insulting and/or racially offensive.

49 [1972] 1 All ER 1297. This case was discussed earlier in this chapter under the heading 'Defining Racial Offence' and was also discussed in chapters 3 and 4.

50 Possibly, for a specified introductory period a reprimand and/or warning as per Section 65 of per the Crime and Disorder Act 1998 should be given. In theory a reprimand is the first step, a warning the second and prosecution the third. However, these are only applicable if the offender has no previous convictions (see Leng, Taylor and Wasik, *Blackstone's Guide to the Crime and Disorder Act 1998*, p. 82). The advantage of applying a reprimand approach is that it would allow people to get used to the new legislation.

51 This is consistent with Section 18(5) as currently applies to words that are threatening, abusive or insulting and stir up racial hatred.

52 Section 27(1) of the Public Order Act 1986.

53 This was confirmed in writing to Cllr Jagdish Sharma, Deputy Leader of Hounslow Council, in correspondence from the Attorney General's Legal Secretariat (17 August 1993).

54 See comments of Sir Ivan Lawrence QC, Chairman of the Home Affairs Committee: see Home Affairs Committee, *Racial Attacks and Harassment*, Third Report, Session 1993–94, paragraph 417.

55 This speech of Enoch Powell was made on the 20 April 1968, a date that marked the anniversary of Hitler's birth. See 'When the Tiber Failed to Foam', *Searchlight*, June 1997, http://www.s-light.demon.co.uk/stories/powell.htm. Also see Robert Shephard, *Enoch Powell: A biography*, Pimlico, 1997.

56 At the time of the speech he was a Conservative MP.

57 See Home Affairs Committee, *Racial Attacks and Harassment*, Third Report, Session 1993–94, paragraph 416.

58 In order to extend neutrality, the guidelines could be agreed, in Parliament, with the Leadership of the Opposition. One suggestion for such guidelines are those considered later in this section which apply to racially motivated crime.

59 Recommendation 33.

60 The Home Secretary accepted this recommendation in the *Stephen Lawrence Inquiry: Home Secretary's Action Plan*, 23 March 1999.

61 That is relative to the number of prosecutions that occur under the existing Part III of the Public Order Act 1986.

62 The roots of the Internet go back to 1969 when the Advanced Research Project Agency (ARPA) in the United States commissioned work on the 'ARPAnet', an experimental

wide area computer network designed to withstand the effects of a nuclear strike. By 1971 there were 23 hosts on the network, by 1981 it had reached 800 and in 1996 the number of hosts reached 9.4 million, with an estimated 200 million worldwide users by 1999. (This is an estimated figure based upon the comments of Justice Stevens in the USA Supreme Court decision in *Janet Reno, Attorney General of the United States, et al., Appellants v American Liberties Union et al.* – case No 96–511. Although, a press report in October 1998 suggested that the Internet usage was thought to be much higher – with an estimated 1,000 million people signed up for the Internet: see Adam Barnard, 'Cafe Society? It's a piece of cake', *The Times*, 7 October 1998.)

63 For an insight into some of the difficulties of applying the law to the Internet see: Edwards and Waelde, *Law and The Internet*, Hart Publishing, 1997.

64 'Millennium plea for Libraries', *The Guardian*, 21 March 1996 gives news of a £45m lottery fund bid, to the Millennium Commission, so all public libraries can be connected to the Internet. Hounslow Council's main library already provides the Internet service to the public. Students at schools and universities can also often make use of the Internet service 'for study purposes'.

65 The Internet Watch Foundation was set up in 1996 after discussion between Internet Service Providers and the Police. It was reported, by the Home Office Minister Kate Hoey, that the Internet Watch Foundation established 453 actionable reports of illegal material on the Internet between December 1996 and August 1998. Almost 90 per cent of these were child pornographic material. See 'IWF says Porn is Increasing', *Practical Internet*, Issue 26, 1999.

66 http://www.eff.org/blueribbon.html (March 1996).

67 The freedom the Internet gives to the individual is clear to see, with him not dependent upon an editor or publisher to obtain recognition.

68 See http://news.bbc.co.uk/hi/english/sci/tech/newsid_375000/375156.stm – a report on Project Trawler by Internet correspondent Chris Nuttall (25 June 1999). See also http://www.ncis.co.uk/newpage1.htm for the report: 'Project Trawler: Crime of the Information Highway' published by the National Criminal Intelligence Service (http://www.ncis.co.uk/newpage1.htm, 26 June 1999).

69 *The Times*, 29 December 1995.

70 'Attempt to Block Zundel Fails', *Searchlight*, March 1996. This pornographic parental control can be found by searching for 'CyberPatrol' on the Internet (http://cybernet.co.nz/cyberpatrol/wwelcome.html, March 1996). For a review of various commercial software/Internet censorship controls, such as 'Cybersitter' and 'Net Nanny', see 'Sensible Censorship', *PC Advisor*, June 1996. See also 'Software Stops Pupils seeing Net Porn', *The Times*, 13 January 1999. See also Gervase Webb and Mark Hughes-Norman, 'Porn: the darker side of the Internet', *Evening Standard*, 12 April 1999.

71 Under German law it is illegal to deny the Holocaust.

72 See 'Attempt to block Zundel Fails', *Searchlight*, March 1996.

73 London-based international anti-Fascist organisation.

74 Article written by Louise Bernstein, *Searchlight*, March 1996.

75 There was no direct instruction to bomb certain people, but the inference was evident via the site linkage.

76 However, the Council of the European Union has opted to undertake a self-regulatory approach with industry users being encouraged to develop and implement adequate systems of self-regulation. For details see European Union, 'The European Union adopts Action

Plan on Promoting Safer use of the Internet', 21 December 1998, http://www2.echo.lu/
iap/pressrel.html. See also the 'Proposal for a European Parliament and Council Directive
on Certain Legal Aspects of Electronic Commerce in the Internal Market'. The EU proposes
to encourage 'quality licensing' by developing an exemption from legal liability for Internet
Service Providers who play a passive role and act as a mere conduit of information from
third parties. However, to be eligible for a form of EU quality licence it is clear that ISP's
will need to comply with 'ethical' codes of conduct drawn up by professional associations:
http://www2.echo.lu/iap/pressrel.html.

77 Glyn Ford MEP, 'EC targets racism on the Internet', *Searchlight*, March 1996.

78 A stark example of this comes from the USA case where anti-abortion activists were
found guilty of inciting violence and fined $107.9m for posting a 'wanted' list of doctors'
names. See 'Free Speech Anger over Nurembourg Files Ban', *Practical Internet*, Issue
26, 1999.

79 See the Defamation Act 1996.

80 For example in the UK child pornography is dealt with under the Protection of Children
Act 1978 and Section 160 of the Criminal Justice Act 1988. These acts were amended by
the Criminal Justice and Public Order Act 1994 so as to make it easier for the courts to
deal with computer data.

81 For example, a pop star was arrested and charged with a variety of sexual offences after he
took his computer in for repair to Computer World and they allegedly found child
pornographic materials on his hard drive. It is alleged that a number of indecent pseudo
images (digitally produced computer photographs) of children under the age of 16 had
been downloaded from the Internet. Subsequently he was also charged in relation to other
offences concerning sexual assault on two girls between 1975 and 1981, http://www.nme.
com/newswire/199980811132751news.html.

82 http://ngwwmall.co/frontier/bnp/, March 1996.

83 Stormfront is a white supremacist organisation.

84 By using search tools it is easy to locate almost any website – no matter where it was
published – by just the click of a mouse.

85 At one stage, in 1994 the BNP sent messages from Norway to British bulletin boards
announcing that it had banned cross-membership with a violent terror organisation.

86 This applied notwithstanding the fact that the operation was effectively run from computers
in the USA and not Germany. For a translated case note see http://www.cyber-rights.org/
isps/somm-dec.htm.

87 See brief report earlier in this chapter and 'Attempt to Block Zundel Fails', *Searchlight*,
March 1996.

88 Case No 96–511 decided 26 June 1997.

89 *Ginsberg v New York*, 390 US 629, 633 (1968).

90 Mike McCormack, 'Natural Porn Killers', *.net*, April 1996.

91 The 'Proposal for a European Parliament and Council Directive On Certain legal Aspects
of Electronic Commerce In the Internal Market' proposes to encourage 'quality licensing'
by developing an exemption from liability for Internet Service Providers who play a passive
role and act as a mere conduit of information from third parties. In return for this exemption
servers will need to comply with certain ethical codes of conduct drawn up by professional
bodies. See also Decision No/98/EC of the European Parliament and of the Council' which
adopts an action plan on promoting safer use of the Internet by combating illegal and
harmful content on global networks. This four-year £25m action plan takes an industry

self-regulation and content-monitoring approach to child pornography or content which incites hatred on grounds of race, sex religion, nationality or ethnic origin.

92   'Action Promised over Internet Racism', *The Times*, 16 September 1998.

93   What is termed as an 'innocent dissemination' defence originated in common law and was effectively built into Section 1 of the Defamation Act 1996. The defence applies in circumstances where the defendant was: '(a) not the author, editor or publisher of the statement complained of; (b) he took reasonable care in relation to its publication; and (c) he did not know, and had no reason to believe, that what he did caused or contributed to the publication of a defamatory statement'. In the case of *Godfrey v Demon Internet Ltd* (http://www.courtservice.gov.uk/godfrey2.htm [26 March 1999]) Mr Justice Morland – in a pre-trial judgement – rejected an 'innocent dissemination' defence, because the server had not responded to a request by the plaintiff to remove a newsgroup posting that was defamatory.

94   Source: '15th UK Periodic Report to the UN Committee on the Elimination of All forms of Racial Discrimination relating to the period up to 31 March 1999', Home Office Equality Unit, 1999.

95   This aspect was discussed earlier in this chapter.

96   Albeit with an anti-racist counter-message being associated with the web page.

97   In the USA, former Vice-President Gore has given his personal support to a business funded website that encourages parents to use 'CyberSitter', and other software applications, which prevent the computer from displaying web pages that display certain words. This could mean the word 'gay' is allowed, but not 'gay rights', 'gay community' or 'lesbian'. Likewise, 'sex' by itself is OK, but not 'sexual', 'safe sex' or 'have sex'. Also banned are words like 'naughty', 'violence' and 'fairy'. See *CyberSitter: Where do we want you to go today?*, available from the website of Cyberights and Cyber-liberties, http://www.leeds.ac.uk/law/pgs/yaman/cybersit.htm (23 March 1999).

98   The US computer community responded to concerns about legislation by introducing warnings on all sites that contain sexually explicit materials. Indeed, the existence of such warnings was a key deciding factor in the Supreme Court in the case of *Janet Reno, Attorney General of the United States et al v American Civil Liberties Union et al* (see above in this chapter).

99   See Decision No/98/EC of the European Parliament and of the Council which promotes safer use of the Internet by combating illegal and harmful content on global networks. This action plan commenced 1 January 1998 and also tackles child pornography.

100   The BNP website (http://www.bnp.net/ 20 September 1997) carried a slogan 'Fighting anti-white racism'. This cannot be considered to be a statement consistent with equal opportunities since it reflects opposition to only anti-white racism.

101   The term 'Convention' as per the Human Rights Act 1998 means the Convention for the Protection of Human Rights and Fundamental Freedoms agreed by the Council of Europe at Rome on the 4 November 1950.

102   The Human Rights Act 1998 was given Royal Assent on 9 November 1998 and came into force on 2 October 2000. The HRA 1998 gives statutory force to a general presumption that all legislation (past or future) is intended to be compatible with the ECHR. It requires the courts to interpret all other laws so as to conform to it. Most importantly, it requires public authorities to act in compliance with the Convention unless they are prevented from doing so by statute. Failure to do so is unlawful. This provides an applicant with a right to rely upon the Convention in any case that involves a public authority. A public authority is to be widely interpreted and will include courts and tribunals, government

departments, local authorities, the police, prisons and NHS trusts. Indeed, paragraph 2.2 of the White Paper explains that it will also include, to the extent that they are exercising public functions, companies which were responsible for areas of activity which were previously in the public sector – such as privatised utilities (Philip Leach, 'Incorporating Human Rights – the Process Begins', *NLJ* [1997] 1595).

103 A domestic court or tribunal is not directly bound by the decisions of the European Court of Human Rights. Though section 2(1)(a) of the Human Rights Act 1998 makes clear, that the court must 'take into account' any judgement, decision, declaration or advisory opinion of the European Court of Human Rights. Further, Section 2(1)(b) and (c) extends this to opinions and decisions of the Commission.

104 While an accelerated process is provided, it is at the discretion of the relevant Minister to choose to take it. See Geoffrey Bindman, 'Protection from Discrimination', *NLJ* [1998] 1617.

105 See *Chorherr v Austria* A 266-B para 32 (1993) where the government of Austria justified its interference with expression by reference to its positive duties to protect the right of assembly under Article 11.

106 Freedom of expression includes the negative freedom not to speak as well as the more usual freedom to speak. See the reliance of the Commission in *K v Austria* A 255-B (1993) Com Rep paras 45, 49.

107 *Muller v Switzerland* A 133 (1988).

108 *Chorherr v Austria* A 266-B (1993).

109 *Stevens v UK* No 11674/85, 46 DR 245 (1986).

110 *Handyside v UK* A 24 (1976).

111 *Groppera Radio AG v Switzerland* A 173 (1990).

112 *Autronic v Switzerland* A 178 (1983).

113 *Muller v Switzerland* A 133 (1988).

114 *Otto-Preminger-Institut v Austria* A 295-A (1994).

115 A 24 para 49 (1976).

116 In the UK through the Sex Discrimination Act 1975 and the Race Relations Act 1976. It is also worth noting that freedom of expression is likewise limited by the laws concerning defamation.

117 On which the Human Rights Act 1998 is based.

118 Case No 6741/74.

119 Article 10.

120 Article 11.

121 8348 and 8406/78.

122 The political party supported the idea that it is in the general interests of the state for its population to be ethnically homogeneous.

123 9235/81.

124 9777/82.

125 See Harris, Boyle and Warbrick, *Law of the European Convention on Human Rights*, p. 374 for a discussion on the scant protection offered to racist expression.

126 'Proportionality' was referred to in *Handyside v UK* (1976) 1 EHRR 737 as being 'proportionate to the legitimate aim pursued'. In the case of *Dudgeon v UK* (1981) 4 EHRR 149 the court considered whether a law which made buggery between consenting gay men a criminal offence found against the UK government stating: 'On the issue of proportionality the Court considers that such justifications as there are for retaining the law in force unamended [the UK government argued that the law was needed to protect

vulnerable members of society] are outweighed by the detrimental effects which the very existence of the legislative provisions can have on the life of a person of homosexual orientation like the applicant'.

127 See Turk and Joinet, *The Right to Freedom of Opinion and Expression*, ch. 6; Sandra Coliver (ed.), *Striking a Balance*. See also John Wadham and Helen Mountfield, *Blackstone's Guide to the Human Rights Act 1998*, p. 13.

128 A 298 para 37 (1994).

129 A 298 para 35 (1994).

130 As per Article 266(b) of the Penal Code.

131 Mrs Jane Liddy in a sole dissenting judgement argued that there was no counterbalancing material.

132 See *Sunday Times v UK* A 230 paras 65–66 (1979) in which the Court said that there was a right to express opinions and there was an independent right of a willing hearer to hear such opinions. The *Sunday Times* case was concerned with the freedom of the newspaper to publish articles about the merits of pending litigation. The government argued that to publish created 'trial by newspaper' and that it was, therefore necessary to restrain publication in order to maintain public confidence in the courts. The majority rejected this argument for a variety of reasons including that the UK court had not given proper weight to the right of freedom of expression that the litigation was dormant, and that there was substantial public interest in the case. Thereby, they recognised and respected the right to hear opinions.

133 This argument is consistent with the interpretation of the ECHR that suggests that a complainant can expect only scant protection if he wishes to claim freedom of expression for the purposes of expressing a racist opinion. It is also consistent with the European Court of Human Rights decision in *Jersild v Denmark*, where the ECHR accepted a need for a counterbalance approach.

6   A Counter-Message – Education and the General Will

I have consistently argued that the law should be used to tackle militant racism. In particular, I argued that the existing law on stirring up racial hatred is inadequate because it only tackles material that is 'threatening, abusive or insulting' – with it failing to deal with material that is 'racially offensive' and intended to or likely to stir up racial hatred/discrimination. As outlined in the chapter 5, my solution to this problem is to add 'racial offence' to the prerequisites necessary to bring a prosecution for stirring up racial hatred.[1] In addition, I have argued that this proposed law should provide for a counter-message defence. That is, an applicable defence in circumstances where the 'racially offensive' material[2] also clearly displays a counter-message consistent with the legislative intent of equality through racial tolerance.[3] It is, therefore, only if citizens reject the rule of law, by deliberately refusing to display a 'say no to racism' counter-message, that criminal punishment would be appropriate.

The traditional philosophical justification for introducing criminal laws that limit the freedom of individuals, stem from J.S. Mill and his 'harm principle'. With his essay 'On Liberty' presenting the argument in the following words:

> The only purpose for which power can be rightly exercised over any member of a civilised community against his will is to prevent harm to others. His own good, either physical or moral, is not a sufficient warrant.[4]

This harm principle is intent on giving political priority to individual freedom from coercion. However, it has two central weaknesses. The first is that it provides no means of measuring harm and providing justice consistent with that measurement. Hence, as remarked by Wilson, society criminalises theft because it is a violation of that which one is entitled to keep – thus a worker stealing a packet of cigarettes can face criminal charges. By comparison, society does not criminalise a failure to reward an employee in accord with his or her value. This applies despite the fact that financial exploitation may produce a sense of inferiority and injustice – also providing harm by preventing the exploited worker from finding satisfactory accommodation and enjoying a meaningful life. Indeed, all such harms may be far more damaging to the individual than the theft of a packet of cigarettes.[5]

The second weakness stems from the first, in that because there is no objective way of measuring harm there is no real method of determining the level of harm that is necessary to justify the undermining of certain freedoms that may be regarded as fundamental. For example, 'racially offensive' material can produce harm to both an individual and society as a whole.[6] The problem with this simple interpretation is that harm is like a piece of elastic – on face value it seems limited in length, but it can at times be stretched sometimes beyond understanding. Thus, our political leaders could use the argument of harm to justify almost any legislation they see as being in the public good – even if this legislation may undermine an important freedom like freedom of expression. To this end, in seeking to establish a philosophical justification for counter-message legislation, I will endeavour to look beyond the harm principle and try to find a philosophical justification beyond that of the subjective values determined by our political leaders. I do this because I consider that the harm principle has been met, with strong arguments existing for saying that racist material has the potential to do harm to society and individuals within society. As such, the government can claim justification for legislation that tackles militant racism. However, what I want to examine is the philosophical basis for the government restricting freedom of expression in the interests of promoting equality of opportunity and establishing people's freedom from racial discrimination.

Indeed, I will start from the premise that a counter-message approach is not just about tackling potential racial harm within society, but also about establishing an educational role for legislation. This chapter will consider how this applies from a sociological and jurisprudential perspective. I will then go on to consider the relevance of philosophers such as Sumner, Rousseau, and Rawls.

Legislation and Education

Lester and Bindman insist that 'legislation and education are not incompatible'.[7] In particular, they concurred with the first annual report of the Race Relations

Board in April 1967 summarising the role of anti-racist legislation as follows:

1   a law is an unequivocal declaration of public policy;

2   a law gives support to those who do not wish to discriminate, but who feel compelled to do so by social pressure;

3   a law gives protection and redress to minority groups;

4   a law thus provides for the peaceful and orderly adjustment of grievance and the release of tensions;

5   a law reduces prejudice by discouraging the behaviour in which prejudice finds expression.

As remarked by Cotterrell,[8] several of these purposes go well beyond the use of law to redress grievances or to control behaviour. Although these may not give a green light to the arguments for counter-message legislation – they do signify the importance of the educative function of law, i.e. to change ideas by influencing behaviour.

While the educative function of law was behind the Race Relations Act of 1968 – by 1975 the government was acknowledging both the success and the limitations of such an approach. In a White Paper presented to Parliament in 1975 the Home Secretary (Roy Jenkins) stated:

> ... during the previous decade, probably largely as a result of Section 6, there has been a decided change in the style of racist propaganda. It has tended to be less blatantly bigoted, to disclaim any intention of stirring up racial hatred, and to purport to make a contribution to public education and debate.
>
> The more apparently rational and moderate is the message, the greater its probable impact on public opinion.[9]

What this clearly signifies is that the government recognised that, in the name of public education and debate, racist propaganda was being distributed. Despite the probable success of its impact on public opinion, it was felt that '... it is not justifiable in a democratic society to interfere with freedom of expression except where it is necessary for the prevention of disorder or for the protection of other basic freedoms'.

The problem with this governmental approach is that it leaves a massive hole in its anti-racist defences. While the Race Relations Act 1976 can deal with individual acts of discrimination and offences by corporations, the Public Order Act 1976 may deal with criminal acts of stirring up racial hatred where 'threat, abuse, or insult' exists. However, the problem of dealing with 'racially offensive' material, which may stir up racial hatred, has been largely ducked. The best that can be said, is that the work of tackling 'racially offensive' material (which purports to make a contribution to public education and debate) has been left to the efforts of the Commission for Racial Equality. While the CRE do a worthwhile job by advertising within newspapers and on television, they have budget considerations and the impact is limited because the anti-racist message is not directly related to the racist message in time, place, or person. It follows that a person may read or hear a racist and not an anti-racist message, or vice versa.

In comparison, the principal aim of the counter-speech proposal is to require a form of public advertisement, displaying a commitment to equality through racial tolerance in situations where 'racially offensive' material is published or distributed. This counter-message legislation operates as educative legislation in a number of ways:

1   the counter-message visibly demonstrates to the reader that the law is committed to equality through racial tolerance and that society does not find racism, and/or racist behaviour, acceptable;

2   it signifies to the reader the type of comments that are 'racially offensive' and may be unacceptable within society;

3   perhaps more importantly, it requires the speaker, author, and/or publisher, to examine the content of their material and to ask themselves if they could be overstepping the tolerance levels of society by expressing views that give 'racial offence';

4   it tends to discredit the contrary racist statement in the material to which it is appended.

1   A Demonstration of the Law

The first report of the Race Relations Board in April 1967 echoed these aims by specifying that the role of anti-racist legislation is to provide an unequivocal declaration of public policy. In particular, this involved saying no to racial discrimination and yes to racial tolerance.

However, it is important to reflect that simply passing anti-racist legislation may not be enough. Indeed, Jowell has referred to some laws as being simply 'dead letters' and conspicuous symbolic gestures designed to reassure the mass public, making them quiescent, while conferring the real benefits on small organised groups.[10] Clearly, it cannot be realistically argued that the Race Relations Acts have been dead letters, with many successful applicants at Employment Tribunals and some constructive work from the Commission for Racial Equality. Though, with just a token number of prosecutions under Part III of the Public Order Act 1986, and the buffer of the Attorney General before prosecutions can be instigated, it can be argued that the criminal arm of dealing with racism is essentially symbolic and 'almost a dead letter' law. I prefer the term 'almost a dead letter law', because the common usage of dead letter law refers to a law that has become obsolete by long disuse[11] – it would be a misnomer to give this tag to Part III of the Public Order Act 1986 given its recent introduction and occasional use.

Obviously, a counter-message would also be symbolic, in the sense that it displays the public policy argument of being opposed to racism – acting as an ongoing, and possibly daily, reminder of the public policy goal. The purpose of the counter-message being to provide an alternative to the intolerant message of 'racial offence'. As such, it needs to be placed, as a symbolic demonstration of the law, where acts of 'racial offence' may display its ugly intolerance. This could be in newspapers, on Internet pages, in publications of political parties and extremist organisations, even on television or at cinemas.

Any counter-message needs to be consistent with the ideals of existing laws on race discrimination.[12] Thus, in a few words, it needs to warn of material content, while saying 'no to racism' and reflecting 'equality through racial tolerance'. By this, I mean an acceptance and respect for the rights and cultures of peoples from other races so long as their customs and practices do not directly conflict with our domestic laws.

2 Signifying the Type of Comments that may be 'Racially Offensive'

Clearly, the existence of a counter-message and warning displayed on a leaflet, publication, computer or TV screen, will signify that somewhere within the material may be a statement that can give 'racial offence'. Thus, to a limited extent, it should help educate the reader to the type of comments and material that possesses the potential for giving 'racial offence'. In addition, it operates as a warning, alerting people to the likely content and giving them the opportunity to choose not to read the material. In this sense, this should help develop freedom, since freedom is not just about the rights of the author to express his views, but also the audience to receive.[13] A counter-message can give a reader the opportunity to exercise his or her freedom by turning away before s/he reads the offending material. In an important way, a counter-message can enhance freedoms.

This statement, however, assumes that the reader can rely upon the author/ publisher in his use of the counter-message. Indeed, it is possible the material may not be 'racially offensive', but that the author has erred on the side of caution so that he would not fall foul of the law. There is also the possibility that the material may be 'racially offensive' and it does not display a counter-message.[14] To this extent, it is important for the reader to regard a counter-message as being no more than an indication of the type of material that may give 'racial offence'. Indeed, the very nature of a reader examining material – while looking out for a 'racially offensive' passage – must itself be of some educational and intellectual value.

It must also be the case that a reader could examine some material and take the view that it is 'racially offensive', where no counter-message has been displayed. To help deal with this, it must be of importance to provide a channel for complaint. One possible solution to this problem, would be to enable a complainant to make representation to the Commission for Racial Equality and/or the Police about the offending material. With the CRE, as well as the Police, being given powers to issue warnings and refer cases to the Crown Prosecution Service requesting prosecution. In effect, the proposed mechanism is that it should be an offence[15] to publish/distribute 'racially offensive' material that is intended to, or likely in all the circumstances to, stir up racial hatred or discrimination. A defence against this Public Order offence should be that the material displays a counter-message consistent with society's general will of saying: 'no to racism'.

3   *Requiring the Author/Publisher to Examine the Content of Material for Racism*

While some authors of 'racially offensive' material may have intent to be intolerant, it may be that an author or distributor of the material has genuine doubt as to what is 'racially offensive'.[16] It was suggested in the last chapter that the term 'racial' has an easily recognisable and accepted statutory meaning, with 'offence' holding its own natural meaning that it is widely recognised within society, with the dictionary providing an adequate reference on what may be considered appropriate. Indeed, this form of ordinary usage – natural meaning – methodology[17] is preferential to a statutory definition of 'offence', which can often result in the tautology of law and even reliance upon natural meanings to clarify further.[18]

In any cases of genuine doubt about what is, or may be considered to be, 'racially offensive' the author/publisher could seek assistance from the Commission for Racial Equality, which could advise as to whether the material should carry a counter-message defence.[19] At any rate, it should be relatively easy to err on the side of caution and display a counter-message where any doubt as to the possibility of 'racial offence' may exist.

Clearly, this process of effectively requiring authors and publishers of material to examine content for any area that may possibly give 'racial offence', has significant potential for being of educational value. It may be that they could edit the material so that it no longer gives 'racial offence', or that they consider it is essential to include the material without editing. It could also be that an author, or publisher, does not genuinely recognise that their material is 'racially offensive'. For example, a person writing a historical publication about Jews could inadvertently cause 'racial offence' by questioning certain aspects of the holocaust. This could mean that the *actus reus* of an offence of publishing 'racially offensive' material – without a counter-message – has been established, but it is possible that guilt would not be determined due to a lack of intent or *mens rea*. However, in such circumstances, it may be that a caution, or warning, that any future occurrence could result in prosecution would prove worthwhile. This too would establish an educational process, and could be determined by the Commission for Racial Equality working with the police to help educate authors and publishers.

4   It Tends to Discredit the Contrary Racist Statements in the Material to which it is Appended

In the process of (a) demonstrating the law, and (b) signifying the type of comments that may be 'racially offensive', a counter-message also tends to discredit the contrary racist statement in the material to which it is appended. It does this by the symbolic action of displaying the official state line and by appealing to the conscience of the reader – expressing what is to be considered to be right – while contrasting it with what may be considered to be wrong.

While this combination of a demonstration of the law and the tendency of their material to be discredited by the existence of the counter-message, may encourage authors to change the style – and possibly content – of their writing, this should not necessarily be the intent behind the counter-message proposals.

Indeed, the priority intent should be to enable free expression while requiring a counter-message to be displayed. What is intended is to educate readers and authors that certain material may be 'racially offensive' and that this could lead to the stirring up of racial discrimination or hatred. If, as a result of the realisation of the impact of their words, authors choose to edit their own material, that would be their own choice. In one sense, this would prove the value of the educational process of the legislation, since authors or publishers, on reflection, would be choosing the road of tolerance and equality of opportunity rather than the giving of 'racial offence'.

Establishing a Sociological Basis for using the Law to Educate

This book is concerned with using the law to promote racial tolerance. In a sense, this involves the state trying to educate people to accept a policy of racial tolerance. In contrast with this, the American sociologist William Graham Sumner argues that 'stateways cannot change folkways'. Should his sociological argument be correct – using the law to educate people within society could well prove to be futile. This section seeks to examine this issue.

In his classic work *Folkways*[20] Sumner argued that the first task of man is to survive. This was achieved for early man by trial and error, with the ability to distinguish pleasure and pain the only physical power that was to be assumed. This experience of pleasure and pain provided the test of success; if a man felt pain he would avoid a repeat, if he felt pleasure, the process was worth repeating.

As a result of man being a pack animal and tending to struggle for survival in groups, men tended to learn from each other's experience and come to similar conclusions as to what was likely to produce pleasure and pain. Consequently, over time, a common approach became a custom from which instincts developed. In this way *Folkways* arose, with these being the group ways of doing things and solving problems. For Sumner 'the life of human beings in all ages and stages of culture is primarily controlled by a vast mass of folkways handed down from the earliest existence of the races.

The basic concept of Sumner's theory is that law derives from folkways.[21] In particular, he argues, 'Stateways cannot change folkways' – essentially because folkways derive from instincts handed down from primitive man. This view has been criticised by progressive sociologists such as Morison and Friedman, both of whom have described the classic work of Sumner as being conservative and essentially codifying existing mores. Both Morison and Friedman convincingly argue that the law can change society, with Morison citing the decade of Thatcherism as an example of how the law was used to change the folkways of society.[22]

Further examples of this are the laws on sex and race discrimination, which have had at least some influence on the way organisations treat their staff and customers. This in turn has had an impact upon individuals who have used the laws to help pursue their rights. There are also other less obvious societal changes. For example, the changing of the property laws earlier this century enabled women to own property in their own right. This, combined with women being given the vote, has helped develop a century in which women's role within society has been significantly transformed.

All of these are clear examples of law being used to help develop social change within society, albeit that the change may develop in ways not fully appreciated by those who draw up the legislation. Perhaps an obvious example of this is the introduction of the Beveridge Report.[23] Legislators could not have imagined the medical and technological developments that have helped push up the costs of the welfare state. Likewise, those who responded to women suffragettes' demands for the vote are unlikely to have envisaged the electorate and the Conservative Party putting into Downing Street a woman Prime Minister.

Not only do the above examples signify that Sumner may be wrong when he argues stateways cannot change folkways – there could also be problems, in a multi-cultural society, with any reliance upon Sumner's concept of folkways. This could particularly apply when the mores or customs of one race, conflict with those from another. Given such a conflict, whose folkways would take priority? Sumner suggests an evolutionary solution. The problem with this is that it would take generations for mores and customs to adapt and change. With the application of the old adage 'When in Rome do as the Romans do', it seems obvious there would be little change, with indigenous mores generally prevailing.

An illustration of this point can be seen from the way that folkways have developed into the law of blasphemy. The domestic courts in *The Satanic Verses* case,[24] have interpreted the law on blasphemy as applying exclusively to Christianity, thereby denying access to Muslims wishing to protect Islam. While such a decision is justified on legal grounds, it says little for the values of our society that the religious ideals of the state – based upon folkways of the past – are given priority over the mores of people who have settled in the UK from other continents. While the court may have been sympathetic to the ideals and mores of the Islamic faith – they were bound by existing law which was built upon the foundations of indigenous folkways.[25]

Clearly, where folkways of different cultures conflict, tolerance may be a more desirable outcome. Indeed, applying Sumner's theory of pain and pleasure we should recognise that the causes of pain and pleasure also change. Thus, pain and pleasure should not be seen as an absolute barrier to change. Further, man, in following an instinct and desire to avoid pain, would likely accept tolerance if it meant that his folkways remained reasonably consistent. To this extent, Sumner's theory could be stronger if it were to accept that where folkways conflict, tolerance and understanding might become an overriding more. However, making the theory of Sumner stronger would not make it right. It is abundantly clear that his theory is flawed, because our own experiences tell us that government action can help change the way that society responds to certain issues.

Changing Folkways

Another critic of Sumner's folkways theory is William Evan. He has argued[26] that Sumner's conception of the law assumes that the law is passive rather than an active social force, which gradually emerges into a formal or codified state only after it has taken root in the behaviour of members of society. For Sumner, whenever an effort is made to enact a law in contradiction to existing folkways and mores, conflicts arise which result in the eventual undoing of the law.

However, Evan explains the contrary view, arguing that law is not merely a reflection of existing customs, morals or codes, but also a potentially independent social force that can influence behaviour or beliefs. He argues that these opposing views of the function of law suggest a hypothetical continuum of the amount of potential resistance to the enactment of a new law. Where there is likely to be a zero resistance to a new law, one would obviously question the need for it, since complete agreement between the behaviour required by the law and the existing customs or mores, apparently exists. In this situation, there would be no need to codify the mores into law. At the other extreme, where there is likely to be 100 per cent resistance to a law, one would expect the law to be totally ineffective because nobody would enforce it. According to Evan, no law would ever emerge if these two extremes always existed. Between the ends of Evan's continuum there are two important thresholds. He concedes that the point at which a new law provokes the majority of citizens to violate it so as to nullify it, is not known.

Evan argues that whenever a law is enacted in the face of appreciable resistance, it is somewhere in the middle of his hypothetical continuum, with the legal system involved in an educational as well as a social control function. If the educational task is not accomplished, a situation arises in which individuals are obliged to obey a law with the threat of punishment, while not having any belief or respect for that particular law. This produces forced compliance and a situation in which any resulting tensions may lead to disobedience of the law – i.e. depending on the nature of the sanctions and the consistency and efficiency of enforcement.

William Evan, writing in light of American experience with race relations' law, suggests seven necessary conditions for the law to perform an educational function:

1   the source of law is perceived to be authoritative and prestigious;

2   the rationale behind the new law is articulated in terms of legal, as well as historical and cultural continuity and compatibility;

3   pragmatic models for compliance are identified;[27]

4   a conscious use of the element of time in legislative action. He suggests the shorter the transition time the easier the adaptation to the change required by law. Reduction of delay minimising the chances for organised, or unorganised, resistance to change;[28]

5   the enforcement agents are themselves committed to the behaviour required by the law;

6   positive, as well as negative, sanctions are employed to buttress the law;[29]

7   effective protection is provided for the rights of those persons who would suffer from evasion or violation of the law.

On the basis of the argument of William Evan, it can be seen that the law is involved in a continual process of education. This must apply because citizens are not born with a complete knowledge of the law, but acquire this knowledge through interaction with other humans, through reading, the media and their general experiences of life. The establishment of new laws will almost certainly result in some formal announcement, with individuals within society becoming aware – through newspapers, television, and discussion – that to do X in future could result in a punishment or a finding of liability. In introducing new legislation, the government are seeking to form and mould public opinion, to persuade the public to accept and respect the law, with punishment only necessary for a minority of the citizens who may break the law.

One criticism of Evan's theory. It is that it does not differentiate between the purpose and the method of the application of the law. For example, if society agrees with the purpose of eradicating racial discrimination, but not with the method of restricting a person's freedom of speech, it is possible that his hypothetical continuum would display a false reading. Likewise, a person may have reservations about the method applied but accept the legislative approach, because of his moral support for the purpose.

Clearly, the use of the law as an educational tool would help overcome any reservations as to method and/or purpose. Possibly a good example of the law as an educative force, can be found in the law relating to indirect race discrimination. The law is not only a symbol of public policy – it also educates various people and professionals in different ways. In applying the 'but for' test, of *James v Eastleigh Borough Council*,[30] it can be relatively straight-forward to determine direct discrimination on grounds of race or sex, in the sense that 'but for' the fact that Mr James was male, he could have swum free of charge in his local baths. However, indirect discrimination law can be much more complex with the law seeking a requirement or condition which is applied to persons not of the same racial group – which is such that the proportion of persons of that racial group who can comply with it, is considerably smaller than the proportion of persons not of that racial group who can comply with it.[31] Even if this aspect is proven on the balance of probability, the employer may still be able to justify his action – with the employee needing to show that it is to his detriment because he cannot comply. In the case of a schoolboy being refused admission to a school because he wore a turban, this amounted to race discrimination because the boy could not comply with the ban while remaining consistent with the customs and cultural conditions of that racial group.[32] Not only was it necessary to show that a ban on turbans indirectly discriminated against Sikhs, it was also necessary for the Lords to determine that Sikhs are an ethnic group and covered by the legislation. What is more, the Lords became embroiled in the question of religion, rejecting a defence of justification that the ban was necessary because the Head wished to run a Christian School and the turban conflicted with the school's uniform since it was an outward manifestation of a non-Christian faith.[33]

With complex issues and laws such as this, it is necessary not just to educate the public to respect the principle of nondiscrimination, but also to educate those directly involved in its process as to the ways and means the law applies and may be breached. This clearly involves an educational function of both method and purpose. It is also about modifying the customs and practices of organisations, so that they can comply with the law. In this sense it brings about changes in society – by its very act of educating and requiring compliance with the principle of equality of opportunity and racial tolerance.

In relation to Sumner's theory, it can be argued that stateways have prioritised conflicting mores. Applying the traditional concept of folkways to employment law, the law provides for freedom of contract – which means the employer can choose to employ whom he wishes. The discrimination laws do not deny the employer that freedom, but the law does impose parameters for refusal – a breach of which may result in the employer having to pay compensation. Thus, the employer can refuse to employ a person for a whole range of reasons (e.g. they do not have the appropriate qualifications, a dislike of their interview technique, or possibly their scruffy dress style).[34] However, the employer may be liable should he refuse to employ someone because of his or her race or sex. Indeed, the law is such that a tribunal may be entitled to draw an inference from the primary facts, 'while bearing in mind the difficulties which face a person who complains of unlawful discrimination and the fact that it is for the complainant to prove his or her case [i.e. on the balance of probability]'.[35] What the legislator is doing here is embodying folkways into law, while prioritising any conflicting mores. He is putting the will of society (opposition to discrimination) over and above the particular will of an individual employer. While the law is pursuing a government policy of promoting equal rights it is also, in a sense, using the law as a form of government health warning – penalising those who breach the rules and thereby alerting society to the dangers of discrimination.

This also takes us back to the discussion on international covenants,[36] when it was argued that within the ECHR is the principle that equality takes precedence over freedom of expression. Likewise, in applying UK discrimination laws, stateways have determined, on public policy grounds, that freedom from discrimination takes higher precedence over the freedom to discriminate and/or freedom of contract. This can suggest conflict with Sumner's folkways theory because it appears that the government, in applying these laws, has used the law to bring about societal change. However, after close examination it can be recognised that the government has only prioritised conflicting mores so as to conform to a societal goal.

Rousseau – Society and the General Will

It can also be argued that the concept of an anti-racist counter-message is not about changing society, but about reaffirming to individuals, within society, certain moral and legal principles that are widely accepted and respected.[37] For example, suppose the law requires an author to display a counter-message on material that may give 'racial offence'. If the author (who is sympathetic to racism) rationally decides to recognise the morality behind the law, and displays a counter-message, this should not be considered as societal change. This is self evident, because it is not society that may be changing but the individual author – albeit that the author is one of many and together they may form society. Perhaps, as argued by Rousseau, in these circumstances choice and freedom would be taking on a moral sense.[38] The individual author (possibly) surrendering his private will for his perception of what is the general will of society. Indeed, the idea of the counter-message is not to change society, but to prick the conscience of an individual reader, or author, and remind them of a recognised societal goal. To remind individuals of a 'general will' which recognises equality through racial tolerance.

Certainly the idea of forcing an individual author of racist material to be free – that is to suppress his private writing in the wider interests of racial tolerance and the perceived general will of society – can be prone to civil libertarian objections.[39] However, the idea of forcing him to take a step towards freedom, by putting on his racist material a counter-message, is a compromise solution. The author would be recognising the general will of society, as displayed by the anti-racist legislation, albeit he would be continuing with expressing his private will. In this sense, assuming that racial tolerance accurately reflects the general will of society, he would be going some way towards freeing himself from the chains of his inner passions. As Rousseau has argued: man can be distinguished from other animals by his freedom of will. He is not a being determined by instincts; he can choose, accept and reject – while being aware of the consciousness of his liberty.[40]

The problem with Rousseau's concept of a 'general will', is in recognition of just what is the 'general will'. Is it just another way of describing public opinion,[41] or is it more profound than that? Rousseau argues that the 'general will' is recognised from one's inner self and that it is not simple majoritarianism, since laws can only be properly instituted if the citizens possess the virtue to suppress their private will.[42] This suggests that a 'general will' must be more profound than public opinion – since that itself is no more than a reflection of a majority view on a particular subject. Despite such comment, it is clear that a general will cannot exist which is contrary to public opinion – simply because a general will can only will what all would conceivably will.

Is There a Difference between a General Will and Public Opinion?

To discuss this issue further, I intend to provide an illustration by reference to the Public Inquiry concerning Heathrow Airport.[43] Indeed, there are many objections to the plans for a fifth airport terminal. For example, the Director of Kew Gardens, Professor Sir Ghillean Prance, has placed formal objections because he considers the expansion could bring noise that would 'shatter the gardens' peace and tranquillity'.[44] Such an objection can be best described as a particular will being expressed. It is particular because it relates to the sole interest desires of an individual or organisation. Likewise, many residents have signed petitions about aircraft noise that have been submitted to the Public Inquiry. All of these objections are particular in the sense that they reflect individual concerns about aircraft, noise, safety etc. However collectively, they may also reflect a public opinion. Naturally the Airport Authority which submitted the development plan, has its own particular interest, as do the Trade Unions who support the application in the interests of employment.

It is the job of the Inspector at the Public Inquiry to consider the plans and any objections, making recommendations to the Minister of State in the general interests of the wider community.[45] It is essential to the public inquiry process, that he does not have a particular interest – he must be impartial, balancing conflicting opinions and making an objective assessment of the general needs. It seems obvious that the Inspector will not find a general will already existing – simply because there exists deep-rooted conflicting particular wills if not public opinions, on the subject. He may make efforts to bring the parties together by making recommendations that seek to enable a terminal to be built, while also providing some environmental protection for the community. Despite such efforts, it is certainly possible that one side of the debate will be upset by any outcome – with even a vow to protest and disrupt construction should the plans be approved. All of this would clearly suggest that there is a split in public opinion – with sections of the community being for and others against the proposals.

Despite such deep-rooted objections and split public opinions, it is just possible that out of such bedlam, an outcome synonymous with a 'general will' could develop. This is possible where after an open and public scrutiny of conflicting opinions, an impartial adjudicator reaches an outcome that seeks compromise and which is given legislative authority through a perceived and accepted democratic process. Once this happens, the people could see the outcome as authoritative and the issue becomes one of respect for law and order and the general will of society.[46]

Seen in this way, it suggests than an almost essential ingredient of establishing what Rousseau terms a 'general will' could be legislative authority. Once legislative approval is obtained, any individuals or groups acting outside of the scope of the decision, by using unlawful or illegal means, are likely to be seen as acting outside of law and order and against the general will of society. This implies that the 'general will' is as much about respect for a democratic process, as it is for the actual decision that has been made.[47]

Central to the concept of Rousseau's general will is equality – in that all citizens have an equal say and an equal vote in the process. Going back to the contemporary illustration of the Public Inquiry, an essential element is a Public Inquiry Inspector who displays complete and utter impartiality. Indeed, it is essential that all people, going through the public inquiry process, must be treated equally. Should preferential treatment be seen to be given to one side – i.e. without valid justification – it is probable that it would undermine the whole process and invalidate the perceived neutrality of the outcome[48] – thereby resulting in widespread resistance to any resulting legislation. This perception of equality may not be as extreme as that proposed by Rousseau (since he proposed that every man should give himself, with all his rights and property, to the community with a social contract existing between the individual and an artificial person (the state) which has a will like a natural person – obtaining legitimacy from the general will of the people) but it is of the same importance. Indeed, the perception of equality displays synonymity in that all men, no matter what their property rights and interests, bow to the authority of the Public Inspector. Thus complying with the social contract theory of Rousseau.

Rousseau and the State of Nature

Rousseau develops his concept of equality from a *state of nature*. For him, a state of nature goes back to a time prior to civil society – i.e. to find man as he is, naturally. Rousseau differs from philosophers such as Hobbes who see man, in the state of nature, as a beast naturally hostile to every other member of his species.[49] For Rousseau, man – in a state of nature – cannot be in such inevitable conflict because he lives alone with little knowledge of other men and only the simplest needs of the sort that are easily satisfied. He is not frightened of death, because he cannot conceive it – he only avoids pain.[50]

According to Rousseau, this animal-man has only two fundamental passions, a desire to preserve himself and a certain pity or sympathy for the sufferings of others of his kind. This latter passion preventing him from being brutal to other men, so long as it does not conflict with his own preservation. He has no morality, because this has not developed. Whatever he does, he does for pleasure, and since he does no harm, he demonstrates a certain goodness.

In his state of nature man lives independently. If men have differences in strength, they have little meaning because the individuals have no contact with each other. From this natural state can be derived no right of one man to rule another. One man can never enslave another, because men have no need of one another. Likewise, man cannot discriminate against others – because he has little knowledge of, or need for, the existence of others – because men all have equal worth. As remarked by Bloom, 'considered in this way it may be said that all men are by nature equal'.[51] Rousseau's state of nature, is a state of equality and independence.

It is only through the development of civilisation, that political society and laws become necessary. Rousseau argues that the founder of political society and the man who brought the greatest evils to mankind, was the first who said: 'This land belongs to me'. This cultivation of the soil being the source of private property, and the basis for Rousseau's claim that, 'Man was born free, and everywhere he is in chains ...'.

Thus, from the works of Rousseau, it can be argued that man is born free and that men, by nature, are equal. Applying these principles to this book, it can be argued that the equality described by Rousseau is one of actual equality in terms of economic values and rights and privileges. By comparison, equality through racial tolerance is not economic equilibrium, but equal treatment so far as rights, privileges, and immunities are concerned. Obviously, this may be politically less radical than a concept of equality based upon economic values, but it can be considered as a synonym of the concept of equality referred to in Rousseau's state of nature.

Criticisms of Rousseau's Theory

Rousseau's theory is more collective than individual. His view that private property is unnatural, always a source of inequality and the root of power within society, has been described by Bloom as 'not wholly unlike [Karl] Marx'.[52] Not surprisingly therefore, in a predominantly capitalist society, Rousseau's philosophy has found a number of critics. Since this book is not principally concerned with political philosophy, I do not intend to give a detailed analysis of his work, or to examine in depth the views of his critics. Instead, I have given an outline of his basic theory and intend to examine four central criticisms relevant to this book. These being:

1 that the philosophy of Rousseau is vague, justifies dictatorship, and is not readily adaptable to contemporary society;

2 that Rousseau's desire to force an individual to be free can be seen to be anti-libertarian;[53]

3 concern about Rousseau's reliance upon a 'social contract';

4 Rousseau develops a notion of freedom and equality from his state of nature – i.e. without any consideration of the need for justice.

In looking at the last of these I will also give consideration to the arguments for 'a theory of justice' as developed by John Rawls.

1   Rousseau's 'General Will' – is Vague, Justifies Dictatorship and is not Adaptable?

Rousseau's philosophy is often considered as vague, due to a problem of differentiating a 'general will' from a 'particular will'. This issue of vagueness will be considered shortly, but it is fundamental to the problem of Rousseau's philosophy because it leads to a second central criticism – which is that Rousseau justifies dictatorship. The dictatorship argument stemming from the theoretical circumstances of a leader claiming that his 'particular will' is in fact a 'general will' – thereby using his powers to enforce his will on society.

On face value this criticism that Rousseau justifies dictatorship seems appealing, but such criticism can easily be challenged due to Rousseau's rejection of dictatorship in no uncertain terms. Indeed, he argues that the death of a government occurs when particular wills substitute themselves for the general will, with this leading to either anarchy or tyranny – anarchy when individuals go off each in their own direction, and tyranny when the private will of a man or group directs the government.[54]

This inevitably indicates that the perception of Rousseau justifying dictatorship, relates to the central issue and problem associated with Rousseau – how can you distinguish a general will from a particular will?[55] In dealing with this question, I intend to give a few illustrations, which lead to the argument that in terms of government of a political society the philosophy of Rousseau may be limited. It can work in a localised community, but it does not seem to be readily adaptable to a large political structure such as a national government.

In a localised community, it is possible to involve all members in determining certain moral and political objectives. Thus, it may be possible to have even an unwritten understanding about certain moral principles that are generally accepted within the community. One classic example exists from my days of living at college. You knew, from your inner self, that the general will within the college was respect for women's rights. The very idea of having a few pints and taking a sexy blue movie back to your student room for some friends to watch, would be totally alien to that community. There were no signs that said – 'no blue movies'. But you knew, without the existence of such signs, that to undertake such an act could offend the moral principles of the community and result in you being condemned by all within that localised community. In effect, you were indirectly and internally pressurised to accept an unwritten public morality and reject any selfish particular will.

The fact that there was no direct legislative authority for the blue movie restrictions does not mean that it is inconsistent with there being a general will. This applies because the blue movie restriction is synonymous with openly debated rules of the college and Student Union that demand respect for women's rights. However, while such deep-rooted moral support for women's rights may exist within the small college community, these high 'no blue movie' morals are not generally so firmly established outside that narrow community. This comes from the fact that within the small confines of the college you can develop, from the general meetings which involve the active participation of students, an understanding of the moral principles that weld together the community. This is possible because all of the students can participate, and often do participate, in moral and political debates. By comparison, a great deal of contemporary society is developed not within small community environments but in large highly populated communities that are modelled on the principles of a representative democracy. Within such large communities you need detailed legislation to spell out the parameters – you cannot expect the morality associated with legislation to be consistent in all corners of the land. It is possible to gauge public opinion – via polls – on specific issues, but there is no real method of determining if such support is reflective of a societal trend or from a deep felt desire embedded within the heart and soul of the people. As such, specific and detailed legislation is required to establish legitimacy for a general will to develop.

The obvious problem with this argument is that a government could abuse the democratic process (and that of the general will) by pushing through legislation which reflects particular interests and then use the law and order argument to demand popular support. Indeed, over the years there have been examples of this, with the issue of poll tax a prime example – with the result that popular resistance resulted in a repeal of the legislation. In general, critical to such legislative climb-downs is popular resistance on grounds of a perception of unjust or unequal treatment.[56] However, this must be regarded as a questionable safeguard given that people in general may be regarded as law-abiding and not prepared to challenge the state.

To summarise with regards to point one: as a model towards an idealistic society the theory of Rousseau may have a useful purpose – but his concept of the 'general will' seems vague and can be open to abuse. This essentially being due to the difficulty of determining just what is the general will of society – with a danger that politicians will seek to exploit the theory of a 'general will' so as to advance their own particular policy or will.[57] The safeguard that the people will rebel against unjust laws that are produced from particular wills must be questionable – particularly in a society where strong policing enforces law and order.

That being said, there are many laws within society that do demand popular respect and reflect a general will. For example, 'thou shall not steal' would appear to be reflective of the general will of society. Obviously, there are individuals who steal and show disregard for the principles of law and order – but society sees these individuals as pursuing their own particular interests and forces them to be free. The force in this instance being via a criminal justice system which punishes theft.[58]

2   Forcing an Individual to be Free

This also leads to the question of an apparent inconsistency in the philosophy of Rousseau with regard to his claim that society can be justified in forcing an individual to be free. The very concept of forcing an individual seems antithetical to his claim that man is by nature free and equal. However, as the last illustration concerning theft demonstrates, there is no such thing as absolute freedom in our contemporary society – the law being littered with examples where an individual's freedom is restricted for the good of society. A further example, discussed already in this book, is the way that public order law punishes people who display racial hatred by the use of 'threatening, abusive or insulting' words.

Such restrictive laws apply because the ideal of absolute freedom within a civilised society is essentially a fantasy – a pipe dream. It seems only possible in a theoretical state of nature where we live a lone independent life – and where there are no obligations, no masters, no servants, and where resources are plentiful and available to all. In the reality of a civilised society we are never totally free from the period immediately after our birth. As a baby, we have parents that we depend upon to survive. As children we have rules – respect your elders, conform to society etc. As an adult we have rules, regulations, laws, a need to show respect for your boss, your bank manager etc. We are continually fighting for our freedom, but are often prepared to compromise in the wider interests of society and out of respect for others and their freedom. Rousseau is simply recognising this conflict and suggesting that we ourselves take steps to limit our particular selfish freedoms in the wider interests of the general will of society. This, in itself, enhances the freedom of society. We (in our mind) force ourselves to be free – just as society may also force us to be free.

Rousseau's theory may be unpopular to some, because his statement 'forcing an individual to be free' challenges the absolute concept of freedom sometimes argued for within society. But at its simple core, this statement does little more than urge an individual to recognise that along with freedom there is responsibility. He urges an individual to accept a 'general will' which deep down he recognises as being correct. Once the individual faces up to this reality, he becomes a free person within himself – escaping from the chains of his selfish interest.

3   Reliance on the Social Contract Theory

Rousseau's theory centres upon man having certain rational and intuitive desires – based upon freedom and equality. In order to achieve his desires, within a political and civilised society, man enters into a social contract with Rousseau's theory of the general will central to this contract.

As Kymlicka observes[59] there are a number of reasons why social contract theories are thought to be weak. Central to these is that social contract theories seem to rely upon implausible assumptions. They ask us to imagine a state of nature before there was political authority – with each person on their own and with no higher authority. The question is what kind of contract would such individuals agree upon concerning the establishment of political authority. Different theorists have used this technique – Hobbes, Locke, Kant, Rousseau, Rawls, and come up with different answers. But they have all faced the same criticism – namely there never was such a state of nature or such a contract. Hence neither citizens nor government are bound by it.

We can counter this criticism by saying that it is not a formal contract of modern contemporary standards – it derives from a theoretical state of nature and is merely a hypothetical contract. But as Dworkin says 'a hypothetical agreement is not simply a pale form of an actual contract, it is no contract at all'.[60]

Dworkin does, though, note that there is another way to interpret social contract arguments. We should think of the contract not as an agreement, hypothetical or otherwise, but as a device for teasing out the implications of certain moral premises concerning people's moral equality. We invoke the state of nature not to work out the historical origins of society, or the historical obligations of government and individuals, but to model the idea of the moral equality of individuals.[61] As Rousseau said, 'man is born free and yet everywhere he is in chains'. The idea of a state of nature does not, therefore, represent an anthropological claim about the pre-social existence of human beings, but a moral claim about the absence of natural subordination amongst human beings.

This Dworkin analysis is also of value because it helps rationalise the relevance of Rousseau's theory to the present day. On present day analysis, the claim of Rousseau that man is born free and equal seems a complete nonsense – i.e. because we can all recognise that some men were born into a wealthy and/or royal family, while others were born into squalor. However, by seeing Rousseau's state of nature and social contract theory as a device for teasing out the implications of certain moral premises, it helps us to rationalise the morality of the value of our laws and the community they serve. If we view the 'contract' as a device for debating the values or otherwise of certain moral premises, it is of value to this book. It is of value since this enables us to establish a theoretical and analytically jurisprudential consideration of the moral equality of individuals. This is central to the analysis within this book, since the debate concerning an anti-racist counter-message is, likewise, directly concerned with the concept of freedom and equality.

4   Equality and Justice?

Rousseau was highly critical of justice in a political society. He argued that justice, as it can be seen in nations, consists of maintaining the privileges of those in positions of power, all known states being full of inequalities of birth, wealth and honour. These inequalities can perhaps be justified in terms of the preservation of the regime, but that does not make them more tolerable for those who do not enjoy them. Rousseau considered that laws institute and protect those differences of rank.

Rousseau saw such inequality as an outcome of a politicised society. He considered that if there are natural inequalities, those existing in the nations do not reflect them, since they are the results of human deeds and chance. Since he considered civil society as not being natural, he sought to go back, prior to the existence of a civilised political society, to a state of nature – i.e. to find man, as he is naturally, a primitive man existing alone before civil society existed.

One problem with this approach is that this means that his concept of equality is established before any concept of justice is necessary. Indeed, it is only when resources are scarce that justice in terms of equal treatment becomes necessary. If man had no need for justice – on what basis can it be argued that it is possible to have developed a rational need for equality?

This is indeed a valid concern that goes to the route of using a state of nature as a means of determining philosophical arguments. But it is a little like the chicken and egg argument. Which came first the chicken or the egg? Rousseau suggests that man, in his origins, lived in a state of nature before society developed. As such, following the analogy, let us assume that a hen finds herself in a state of nature. She is, to her knowledge, the very first hen – before she had laid an egg and before other hens became commonplace.

Clearly, as the first hen in this state of nature she was independent having plenty of food and absolute freedom. Accordingly, she would certainly be equal to any other hens she may accidentally come across (or that may drift into the nature reserve). It is only when the eggs arrive, and more hens follow, that it becomes necessary to share food etc. Thus, justice only really becomes necessary when the hens start fighting due to an insufficient food supply. Indeed, it is only then that the hens recognise the need for justice based upon equal treatment – with it being fundamental to a system of justice that the hens are treated equally, for without such equal treatment they would recognise that to survive they must fight for their food. As such, they intuitively yearn for what existed in the state of nature – independence based upon a clear and unequivocal notion of equality.

Due to evolutionary change man, like the hen, will never be able to return to the ideal of the state of nature. While he intuitively yearns for the ideal of absolute freedom and equality, he rationally recognises that the second best option is to share the available resources equally. In this way he has some hope of guaranteeing his own freedom and survival.

In a sense, as this analogy demonstrates, the issue of whether the egg or the hen came first is a diversion from the essential issue. For the species to survive there must be secondary hens – to produce secondary hens, an egg needs to be laid. Likewise to establish justice, the foundation of equality needs to be laid so that man can recognise the value of that justice. Without a system based upon equal treatment there can be no justice.

Absolute freedom, compatible with that found within a state of nature, is the ideal. Fundamental to this is that man is equal – neither dominating another, nor dominated by another. Should another dominate him, he does not have and cannot have absolute freedom. To this end, interlined within the concept of absolute freedom, is the concept of equality. Justice only becoming necessary once that man moves from his idealistic state of nature to a civilised political society.

Rawls – A Theory of Justice

John Rawls in 1971[62] argued that political theory was caught between two extremes – utilitarianism on one side and an incoherent jumble of ideas based upon intuition on the other. He argued that such intuition is an unsatisfying alternative to utilitarianism since 'intuitionism' provides no real principles that underlie or give structure to the jumble of ideas.

Rawls describes intuitionist theories as having two features:

> first they consist of a plurality of first principles which may conflict to give contrary directives in particular types of cases; and second, they include no explicit method, no priority rules, for weighing these principles against one another: we are simply to strike balance by intuition, by what seems to us most nearly right. Or if there are priority rules, these are thought to be more or less trivial and of no substance in reaching a judgement.[63]

This can, indirectly, be seen as a criticism of Rousseau since his philosophy lacks a determining methodology and consequently seems to be based upon intuition. Indeed, Rousseau's method for determining moral conflicts rests with his solution that every man gives himself entirely to the community with all of his rights and property. The deposit is being made with the whole, not with the individual. In this way no one puts himself into the hands of another, nor reserves any rights by which he can claim to judge his own conduct. Hence there is no source of conflict between individual and the state, because the individual has contracted to accept the law as the absolute standard of his acts. The social contract forms an artificial person, the state, which has a will like the natural person; what appears necessary or desirable to that person is willed by it and what is willed by the whole is the law. Law is the product of the *general will*. Each individual participates in legislation, but law is general, and the individual as legislator must make laws that can conceivably be applied to all members of the community. He makes his will into law but now, as opposed to what he did in a state of nature, he must generalise his will. As legislator he can only will what all could will; as citizen he obeys what he himself willed as legislator.

This solution of Rousseau, seems to expect man intuitively to know what is the correct course. He provides general guidance, which puts communal interests based upon equality before individual desires, but Rousseau gives us no real method of distinguishing a 'general will' from a 'particular will', other than the individual recognising from deep down the general will of society. Nor does Rousseau deal with a problem of conflict between a perceived 'general will' relevant to one area, conflicting with that of another. For example, I have argued that treating people as equals reflects a general will of society. However, I would also concede that a 'general will' exists which recognises freedom of expression – with this being an essential ingredient in a modern democratic society. What Rousseau's theory does not do, is provide a method of enabling us to determine which is the priority 'general will' should there be a conflict between two.

In contrast, Rawls seeks to produce a theory that provides principles for determining justice – albeit that it is a snapshot based upon the needs of society at that time. He does this by tying the idea of justice to an equal share of social goods, but he adds an important twist. He argues that you treat people as equals not by removing all inequalities, but only by those that disadvantage someone. If certain inequalities benefit everyone, by drawing out socially useful talents and energies, then they will be acceptable to everyone. If giving someone else more money than I have (to do a specific job) promotes my interests, then equal concern for my interests suggests that we allow, rather than prohibit, that inequality.

This in itself is clearly a limited theory of justice – since it provides no formula for determining the value of the task or goods being produced for the benefit of society. It does suggest that I may well accept that a doctor is paid more than me because his work benefits society – since I may also benefit from his work – but it provides no means of determining what is a socially useful talent and what is not socially useful?

Rawls, while accepting that inequality may exist, rejects the usual pure market forces argument and suggests that we need a system of priority to sort out disadvantages in liberty and opportunity. He produces two principles that he orders lexically:

> *First principle* – Each person is to have an equal right to the most extensive total system of equal basic liberties compatible with a similar system of liberty for all.
> *Second principle* – Social and economic inequalities are to be arranged so that they are both:
> (a) to the benefit of the least advantaged, and
> (b) attached to offices and positions open to all under conditions of fair equal opportunity.

> *First Priority Rule* (The priority of liberty) – The principles of justice are to be ranked in lexical order and therefore liberty can be restricted only for the sake of liberty.
> *Second Priority Rule* (The priority of justice over efficiency and welfare) – The second principle of justice is lexically prior to the principle of efficiency and to that of maximising the sum of advantages; and fair opportunity is prior to the difference principle.[64]

These principles form the 'special conception' of justice, and they seek to provide the systematic guidance that intuitionism could not give us. According to these principles, some social goods are more important than others, and so cannot be sacrificed for improvement in those other goods. Equal liberties take precedence over equal opportunity – which takes precedence over equal resources. Within each category Rawls' basic idea remains – inequality is only allowed if it benefits the least well off.[65]

This lexical formula of Rawls is however subject to modification in light of his 'difference principle', which is conceived from behind a theoretical 'veil of ignorance'. The basic idea of this 'veil of ignorance' is that we do not know what position we will occupy within society, or what goals we will have – but there are certain things we will want to enable us to lead a good life. Indeed, as humans we all share a desire for a good life. Thus, certain things are needed – what Rawls calls primary goods – in order to pursue this basic desire. There are two kinds of primary goods:

1 *social primary goods* – goods that are directly distributed by social institutions, like income and wealth, opportunities and powers, rights and liberties;

2   *natural primary goods* – goods like health, intelligence, vigour, imagination, and natural talents that are affected by institutions but are not directly distributed by them.

According to Rawls, when choosing principles of justice, from behind the veil of ignorance, people seek to ensure that they will have the best possible access to those primary goods distributed to social institutions. The theory suggests because nobody knows of their existence beyond the veil of ignorance, they will put themselves into the shoes of everyone in society and decide in the wider interests of the community, or everyone in society.

It is also clear that the ideal of equality of opportunity that Rawls talks about, is very different to that which prevails in our market forces society of today. Within our contemporary society economic distribution is founded upon a concept of an 'equality of opportunity' that is market orientated. Inequalities of income and prestige (etc.) are assumed to be justified if, and only if, there is fair competition in the awarding of the offices and positions that yield those benefits. It is acceptable to pay someone a £100,000 salary when the national average is £20,000, if there was fair opportunity – so long as no one is disadvantaged by their race, sex or social background. Such an unequal income is considered just, regardless of whether the less well off benefit from that inequality.[66] Rawls would not accept such a pure market forces argument. A Rawlsian society may pay people more than the average, but only if it benefits all members of society to do so. Under his 'difference principle', people only have a claim to a greater share of resources, if they can show that it benefits those who have lesser shares.

In this book there has been a central conflict throughout – i.e. a conflict between the right of an individual who may wish the liberty to express racist views and those who may be offended, or suffer, as a result of those views. Certainly, it could be argued that such racist views do harm to society, hence on purely J.S. Mill 'harm principle' grounds there exists a justification to restrain such liberty. This book has so far argued that a 'general will' has developed that rejects racism and promotes treating people as equals, with a variety of international treaties reflecting this will. Rawls is of value to this book because he provides a formula for prioritising our liberties. This must be of value, since in this book we have a conflict between two essential liberties – i.e. 'freedom of expression' and that of 'equality'. The question facing us being: 'Should a racist be entitled to use his freedom of speech to undermine the concept of equality for others?'

Rousseau would seek to limit those who express a 'particular will' inconsistent with a 'general will'. Thus, if the 'general will' says that people should be treated as equals – then a particular selfish racist will is unacceptable and should be restrained. This approach of Rousseau I call 'intuitive', because man recognises from within his inner self, the general will of treating people as equals and, as such, he should put that general will before any particular selfish will he may possess. The problem with the Rousseau approach, is that you cannot, as an individual, be certain that your interpretation of the general will is one hundred per cent accurate. You may deep down believe that you have recognised the general will, but there is a danger that you could be confusing your particular will with the general will. As such, because it is intuitive, it is not possible to prove its existence.

Rawls, however, provides a much more ordered route. His lexical approach inevitably means that priority is given to liberties that serve the wider community rather than the individual or the narrow community. Indeed, Rawls' theory emphatically accepts that the approach to freedom should be based upon the concept of equality – with inequality only acceptable if it benefits the least well off. This implies that Rawls accepts that you could restrict freedom if a person, by using his freedom, was undermining or disenfranchising another person's freedom. Thus, if freedom of expression for white (or black) racists means that they will use that freedom to undermine the freedom of others – society would be justified in limiting the freedom of those racists – i.e. so as to benefit the freedoms of those who may be unequal.

Rawls argues that justice needs to be founded upon equality and/or his idea of equality of opportunity that follows a 'difference principle'. In contrast, Rousseau advocates a 'general will' theory that is intuitively linked to core principles of freedom and equality emanating from his state of nature. Central to both philosophies is a social contract theory – a cornerstone of which is again freedom and equality. If we take Dworkin's suggestion that we can view this hypothetical social contract as a device for teasing out the implications of certain moral premises concerning people's moral equality, we can see the philosophical value of the exercise. However, for this exercise to become of real value to this book we need to establish that contemporary society does intuitively accept the principle of equality.

The Concept of Equality in Contemporary Law

The concept of equality in contemporary law can be found in the United

Nations Declaration of Human Rights. Under Article 1 it emphasises: 'All human beings are born free and equal in dignity and rights'.

The very concept of a principle of equality can also be found within the common law. For example, Dicey has argued[67] that the Rule of Law requires formal equality,[68] thus prohibiting laws from being enforced unequally. Although, as Jowell suggested, this does not require substantive equality, since it does not prohibit unequal laws being enacted by Parliament.[69]

Jowell also argues, citing Dworkin,[70] that the notion of equal worth is a fundamental precept of our constitution, with his argument being based upon the principle that the concept of equality requires government not to treat people unequally without justification. Just like free speech, this is a principle that derives from the very nature of democracy itself, because basic to democracy is the requirement that every citizen has an equal vote, and therefore an equal opportunity to influence the composition of government.

Further, while the UK does not have a written constitution, it is clear that the principle of equal treatment can be found in the directly effective Treaty of Rome[71] – i.e. in relation to discrimination on the grounds of nationality,[72] and in pay on the grounds of sex.[73] It is also clear, from the case of Nold,[74] that the European Court of Justice cannot uphold measures that are incompatible with fundamental rights and subsequent cases have accepted that the European Convention on Human Rights has a special significance in this respect. The Maastricht Treaty states that the 'Union shall respect fundamental rights, as guaranteed by the European Convention … are general principles of law'.[75] Since Article 14 of the ECHR outlaws discrimination on a number of grounds including sex, race colour, language, and religion, it follows that in cases where Community law is directly effective, equality of this kind – i.e. preventing discrimination without objective justification – may be the general will, or at least a fundamental will,[76] within Europe. While this may suggest a hesitant formulation by cross-reference, it is important to reflect that most European nations have also shown a commitment to the European Convention on Human Rights by incorporating it into their domestic laws. The UK government are signatories and also legislated to incorporate the ECHR into domestic law.[77]

To this extent, it can be seen that the concept of equality under the law, within its differing guises of formal equality, substantive equality, equal treatment, equal worth, and equal opportunity, is well founded within our contemporary European laws. Applying Jowell's argument that its apparent violation will provoke strong questioning, and require rational justification, it suggests that a concept of equality holds a place within the heart and soul of individuals within society. The principle of equality may be abused and/or breached by a particular will, but such abuse is likely to be questioned from within. This may indeed equate to the argument that a concept of equality, under the law, typifies the general will of society. It is certainly fundamental to our legal system. This does not mean that equality exists within society, or that the laws on equal treatment have always been respected. It does, however, suggest that in applying Rousseau's theory, man may be claiming his freedom within the restraints of a developed political society.

Possibly the strongest argument against the concept of equality through racial tolerance reflecting the general will of society, is that for century after century, society has not recognised the value of anti-discrimination laws. Indeed, it is only in the latter half of this century that man has introduced laws that tackle inequality.

An obvious explanation for man's recognition of the value of laws that reflect racial tolerance, can be found in the way that society responded after the Second World War. In the aftermath of the horrific ugliness of a war – which produced Nazi concentration camps and came to a conclusion through the use of an atomic bomb – the United Nations[78] developed a Universal Declaration of Human Rights, taking this further in 1965 with the CERD Convention. The self-evident purpose of these conventions was to try and limit the potential for national and international conflicts by dealing with its source – racial intolerance. As remarked by Schwelb[79] and Partsch,[80] the revival of anti-Semitism and apartheid also contributed towards the decision to establish the CERD convention in the 1960s.

Thus, in order to prevent racial disagreements developing into war – and the possible destruction of mankind via nuclear weapons – man has concluded that limiting racial intolerance is important, since he cannot survive as a ravenous beast in a society of conflict. In almost Hobbesian fashion, he has concluded that a social contract is better than a death through conflict. In doing this, man is seeking characteristics found within the state of nature depicted by Rousseau – i.e. developing a society built upon a state of equality and freedom.[81] Thus, the aim being, perhaps subconsciously, to free himself from the chains of any particular racist will and move towards his own inner freedom. These inner freedoms only being possible when he can live free of fear of violence from other men. Thus the general will of society is evidenced in man's desire for survival, through recognition of a social contract which typifies equality through racial tolerance.

An Overall Analysis

A great deal of this book has taken a positivist approach, in that I have sought to observe what really exists within the data of experience. I have also sought to look behind what really exists in order to find a philosophical basis for changing the law so that those who produce 'racially offensive' material, which can stir up racial hatred or discrimination, may not continue to be immune from the rigours of the law. The proposals for counter-speech involve using the law to educate society as to the values of the 'social contract' that our political leaders (in keeping with the general will) have determined are of importance – i.e. a commitment to equality through racial tolerance.

In conflict with this ideal, Sumner argues that stateways cannot change folkways. Logically, this theory is flawed given that the state regularly introduces legislation that impinges upon the traditional folkways of society.[82] Sumner's theory has justifiably been criticised, by Morison and Friedman, for being conservative and codifying existing mores. An illustration of this is that, in a multi-cultural society, an over-reliance on existing mores can result in disagreement due to the desire of people to follow the mores of their race – despite a possible conflict with mores from another race. While the outcome may be that indigenous mores will prevail, it is possible this will add to any conflicts between the races.

However, I do accept Sumner's premise that certain elements existing within society cannot be changed by stateways. I believe this is limited to folkways that are, and remain to be, consistent with the general will evident within society. Accordingly, I would argue that a general will of society can be determined from Rousseau's argument that all men are by nature equal, with society signing up, via the United Nations, to a social contract that promotes racial tolerance and accepts that human beings are born free and equal in dignity and rights. It follows, from this argument, that man will rationally recognise laws that relate to, or are synonymous with, this ideal. Should any individual reject this general will within society, he will recognise from his inner self the counter arguments, and thus society may be justified in forcing him to be free – i.e. to recognise his own conscience from within.

Clearly the concept of using force may appear, at first instance, to be anti-libertarian. However, the force, in this instance, is not a means of denying the individual the freedom to explore and examine racist views and thoughts. Rather, it is to enhance the freedom of others by giving them a choice as to whether or not they wish to read material that is 'racially offensive' and in conflict with the general will evident within society. This counter speech proposal should not conflict with the concept of the freedom of the individual as espoused by John Stuart Mill – since it enhances the freedom of the reader, without denying the freedom of the publisher/distributor to express his views. Thus, arguments for counter-speech legislation are centred upon the freedom of the individual within a democracy – i.e. accepting the rights and entitlements of others.

The net result of counter-speech legislation is that, by its application, it will perform an educational function. Indeed, William Evan has argued that in various forms the law is always involved in a continual process of education, with his hypothetical continuum suggesting if the educational task is not accomplished, a situation arises in which individuals are obliged to obey a law at the threat of punishment – while not believing in it. This situation should not arise with a law which conforms in principle to the general will. However, a government committed to the ideals of democracy, and equality of opportunity through racial tolerance, needs to do more than simply pass legislation – it needs to continue the educational process so that its laws become recognised and accepted within society.

The Counter-Message Proposals – Sex and Religion

In theory, if the anti-racist counter-message proposals are applicable for tackling militant racism, the approach could equally be applied to other areas – such as sex or religion. For example, any material that gives sexual offence, and is intended/likely to stir up hatred, could be subject to the same requirements – i.e. it provides grounds for a criminal offence unless an appropriate counter-message is displayed alongside.

This approach would appear to be consistent with the combined 'general will/social contract' theory advanced in this chapter. That is, with the UN Declaration on Human Rights, insisting that all human beings are born free and equal in dignity and rights[83] – without distinction of any kind such as, *inter alia*, race, sex and religion.[84] However, I would argue, so far as the UK is concerned, society is more troubled by issues of race. Evidence of this comes from the fact that Parliament has legislated to tackle race and sex discrimination in civil terms,[85] but it is only for race and religion (religion in Northern Ireland only) that a criminal offence[86] has been determined for incitement to hatred. Obviously, this decision of Parliament reflects a political judgement based upon priorities. But this seems a reasonably sound judgement, given that there is no firm evidence of incitement to sexual hatred[87] to justify criminal legislation. Likewise, so far as England and Wales are concerned, there is no firm evidence of organised religious hatred.[88] While in Northern Ireland, despite *prima facie* evidence of religious hatred, there has not been one single prosecution, under public order legislation, for incitement to religious hatred.[89]

Clearly, this book has primarily examined the criminal law and ways of tackling militant racism. It has not been directly concerned with discrimination law and civil remedies. Also, I have only commented upon religion in a comparative sense and when it is possible that a racially based criterion is evident within religious issues. The fact remains that it seems possible to apply counter-message legislation for religiously offensive material that is intended/likely to stir up hatred or discrimination. However, this issue is outside the scope of this book, which remains limited to tackling militant racism.

Conclusion

Anti-racist counter-message legislation suggests an educational role for the law. In this chapter I have examined this issue from a sociological and jurisprudential perspective, looking at the relevance of philosophers such as Sumner, Rousseau and Rawls.

The conclusion I have drawn from this examination is that the United Nations declaration that 'all human beings are born free and equal in dignity and rights' has an almost umbilical link with Rousseau and his state of nature, in which: 'man is born free and by nature is equal'. From this analysis, I have argued that 'equality through racial tolerance' reflects the 'general will' of society – with man recognising from his inner-self the value of this ideal. Indeed, there exists significant evidence to support this 'general will' philosophical theory – with a principle of equality well founded within the laws of Europe and the UK, albeit that it exists in the various guises of formal equality, substantive equality, equal treatment, equal worth and equality of opportunity. As remarked by Jowell, any apparent violation will provoke strong questioning and require rational justification.

Given the existence of such a fundamental or general will within our society, it seems reasonable to argue that the state should take action to educate people as to the value of such laws and help remind them of this general will. By introducing counter-message legislation the state would be attacking any racist particular wills, when and where they may arise – appending to racist material, a message consistent with the general will of society. In this way, they will be inviting citizens to reject, and possibly turn away from, 'racially offensive' material that stirs up racial discrimination or hatred and is inconsistent with the ideals of society. As argued, this would not deny the individual author the right to publish his material and pursue his own particular will. Though, by requiring him to display a counter-message, it would help him realise his own freedom through his acknowledgement of the general will.

Additional support for the principle of freedom based upon equality can be found in the contemporary works of John Rawls. Like Rousseau, he advocates principles of equality based upon a social contract theory. However, unlike Rousseau, his theory accepts inequality – but only in circumstances where the aim is to benefit the least well off in society. The specific advantage of the Rawlsian approach, is that it provides a methodology for determining any conflicts that may arrive between competing ideals – with the 'lexical priority' used by Rawls being emphatically based upon each person having an equal right to an extensive system of equal basic liberties (i.e. compatible with a similar system of liberty for all).

Central to both the philosophies of Rousseau and Rawls is a social contract theory – a cornerstone of which is again freedom and equality. Taking Dworkin's suggestion that we can view this hypothetical social contract as a device for teasing out the implications of certain moral premises concerning people's moral equality, we can see the philosophical value of the contract theory. The arguments put forward for anti-racist counter-speech legislation can be seen as consistent with the philosophical ideals of Rousseau, with Rawls providing a mechanism for prioritising conflicts that may arise between rights to freedom of expression and freedom from discrimination.

Indeed, a Rawlsian would apply lexical methodology and conclude that an individual should not exercise his freedom at the expense of the freedom of others within the community. Likewise, the arguments for counter-speech legislation are centred upon the freedom of the individual within society – i.e. accepting the rights and entitlements of others. Should an individual put his own private and particular racist will first – society can be justified in forcing him to be free.

Notes

1   Under Part III of the Public Order Act 1986 the current three prerequisites are that the words, or behaviour, used must be 'threatening, abusive or insulting' – with an intent/ likelihood of stirring up racial hatred. For a discussion on the need for racial discrimination to be included with the stirring up of racial hatred see chapter 4.

2   The counter-message defence should only apply to 'racially offensive' material. The current law concerning the stirring up of racial hatred through the use of 'threatening, abusive or insulting' words should remain. Indeed, as previously argued, this area of law should be strengthened by also making it an offence to stir up racial discrimination.

3   In simple terminology this means saying 'no to racism'. However, the term 'equality through racial tolerance' will be more fully defined later in this chapter, but for present purposes it can be understood as an acceptance and respect for the rights and cultures of people from other races.

4   J.S. Mill, 'On Liberty', in Stefan Collini (ed.), *On Liberty and Other Writings*, Cambridge University Press, 1989.

5   See William Wilson, *Criminal Law: Doctrine and Theory*, Longman Law Series, 1998, pp. 31–4.

6   It can do harm to the individual by upsetting or frightening him/her or making him/her feel inferior or threatened. Likewise, it can do harm to society because it may undermine community relations and possibly lead to friction within society.

7   *Race and Law*, Penguin Books, 1972, p. 86.

8   *The Sociology of Law*, Butterworths, 1992, p. 53.

9   *Racial Discrimination*, presented to Parliament September 1975, HMSO, 1976, para. 126.

10   See comment of Jeffrey Jowell on Friedman's 'General Theory of Social Change', in *Law and Social Change*, 1973, Osgoode Law School.

11   See *Black's Law Dictionary*, Centennial Edition, 1991.

12   Principally the Race Relations Act 1976 and Part III of the Public Order Act 1986.

13   Article 10 of the European Convention on Human Rights stresses that freedom of expression includes freedom to hold opinions and to receive and impart information and ideas.

14   This is discussed below. In such circumstances the reader should have a right of complaint to the CRE. They could then have, and be able to use, powers of prosecution where it is considered appropriate.

15   It is suggested a proven offence should be subject to the same penalties for distributing 'threatening, abusive or insulting' material likely to stir up racial hatred – see Section 27 Public Order Act 1986. Of course the Courts would have discretion as to the appropriate sentencing in the usual manner.

16   See chapter 5, 'Say No to Racism', for a more detailed consideration of these issues.

17   See the comments of Lord Reid in *Brutus v Cozens* [1972] 1 All ER 1297 and the discussion in chapter 5.

18   A classic illustration of this is Section 1(b) of the Race Relations Act 1976, where despite statutory definitions, within the legislation, the courts have been moved to rely upon natural or other defined meanings for certain phrases. For example 'racial grounds' is defined in statute as colour, race nationality, ethnic, or national origins. Despite such, the *House of Lords, Mandla v Dowell Lee* [1983] IRLR 209, in interpreting the statute in relation to the word 'ethnic', did not feel happy with the dictionary definition. As such, they produced their own essential characteristics that a group needs to meet. Critical to these is the first that requires a *long shared history*. This helped establish that Sikhs are an ethnic group, also Jews, but in *Crown Suppliers (PSA) v Dawkins* [1993] ICR 517 it was decided that Rastafarians, with a shared history going back just 60 years, are not.

19   Indeed, it seems probable that any person committing the *actus reus* of distributing 'racially offensive' material, without a counter-message, should be able to establish that the *mens rea* element has not been fulfilled on the basis of CRE approval.

20   W.G. Sumner, *Folkways*, Boston, The Athenaeum Press, 1907.
21   For a summary of Sumner's theory see *The Sociology of Law*, Butterworths, 1992, pp. 18–20.
22   J. Morison, 'How to Change Things with Rules', in Livingstone and Morison (eds), *Law Society and Change*, Dartmouth Publishing Co., 1990.
23   *The Beveridge Report*, a blueprint for a social security and welfare state, was published in 1942.
24   See *R v Chief Metropolitan Stipendiary Magistrate, ex parte Choudhary* [1991] 1 All ER 306, [1990] 3 WLR 986, Queen's Bench Divisional Court. Also Commission for Racial Equality and the Inter Faith Network of the United Kingdom, *Law, Blasphemy and the Multi-Faith Society*, report of a seminar, CRE September 1989.
25   Thus, in Sumner's terms, reflective of the abiding nature of folkways.
26   William M. Evan, 'Law as an Instrument of Social Change' (1965), in *The Sociology of Law: A social-structural perspective*, New York Free Press, 1980.
27   This can be achieved by drawing a comparison with other communities.
28   Cotterrell, *The Sociology of Law*, Butterworths, 1992, p. 60, has criticised this aspect of Evan's theory arguing that this is not always a necessary condition. He cites the Equal Pay Act 1970 as an example of complex legislation that works better if organisations are given more time to plan change.
29   An example is the use of tax incentives to help encourage the learning and adoption of a new behaviour or attitude.
30   [1990] IRLR 298.
31   For the exact wording of the legislation see Section 1(1)(b) of the Race Relations Act 1976.
32   This is another example of the mores of one racial group conflicting with the mores of the indigenous group. However, in this instance the mores of the Sikh group took precedence because the ban on the turban was not justifiable (Lord Fraser).
33   *Mandla v Dowell Lee* [[1983] IRLR 209.
34   There can be situations in which a dress code may breach the law – e.g. rejecting a person because their dress is evidently related to their race or sex may amount to discrimination – i.e. unless this can be justified as objectively necessary.
35   Neil LJ – Court of Appeal in *King v Great Britain China Centre* [1991] IRLR 513.
36   See chapter 5 and the section 'Compatibility with the Convention on Human Rights'.
37   It seems possible that even racist perpetrators may recognise that racism is unacceptable, with them often denying that they are racist. For an example of this, see Rae Sibbitt (Home Office Study 176) and the comments of a woman who had been identified by the local authority and the police as being racist. Speaking in relation to services provided by the local authority the woman said: 'All these coloured families come over to our country and take all our benefits ... Don't get me wrong – I'm not a racist. I've got friends who are coloured. I like the girl upstairs – X. You know who I can't stand? The Asians – they stink they do, but there aren't any around here' (Rae Sibbitt, *The Perpetrators of Racial Harassment and Racial Violence*, Home Office Study 176, 1997). This kind of inconsistency could be reflective of an inner conscience alerting her into recognising that racism is generally regarded as unacceptable within society.
38   See Allan Bloom, 'Jean-Jacques Rousseau', in Strauss and Cropsey (eds), *History of Political Philosophy*, p. 569.
39   It can be said to interfere with freedom of expression.

40   See Bloom, *op. cit.*, in Strauss and Cropsey (eds), *History of Political Philosophy*, p. 564.

41   This must be relevant in relation to racism because often those carrying out acts of racism believe that those in their peer group share concerns about foreigners taking jobs etc. To this extent, perpetrators may reject the political correctness of the state because they feel that at grass roots level there is deep down support for their racist attitude.

42   See Bloom, *op. cit.*, in Strauss and Cropsey (eds), *History of Political Philosophy*, p. 570.

43   Obviously this is a contemporary illustration in a form of society that may be different to that envisaged by Rousseau. However, by relating popular expression to either a particular or general will it serves as an applicable illustration.

44   'Kew Gardens Fights to Block Terminal 5', *Evening Standard*, 11 June 1998.

45   The Frank's Committee Report Cmnd 218 (1957) paragraph 293 argued that 'the ideal would be for the Minister himself to hold the enquiry and thus hear the evidence at first hand, but since this is clearly out of the question the next best course is for one of his own Offices, who can be kept in touch with the developments in policy, to perform this function'.

46   This can imply a form of dictatorship, in that if all laws are synonymous with the 'general will' then citizens must follow the will of the state. This issue of Rousseau's theory advocating a form of dictatorship will be discussed later in this chapter.

47   Albeit that Rousseau's perception of democracy differs from the representative form of democracy we experience – in that he sees legislation as coming direct from the people with the fullest participatory democratic process possible (i.e. with citizens voting in the interests of the community rather than their own self-interest).

48   The Poll Tax is a classic example of legislative authority being given to a proposal despite public opinion being against. However, what really helped undermine the poll tax legislation was the fact that a millionaire could be expected top pay the same tax as his poverty stricken neighbour. While this suggested some level of equal treatment – the perception was that those with higher incomes should pay more due to them having so much more disposable income.

49   Thomas Hobbes, *Leviathan*, introduced and abridged by John Plamenatz, Fontana Paperbacks, 1963.

50   *Jean-Jacques Rousseau – The Social Contract and Discourses*, translated by G.D.H. Cole, Everyman's Library, 1913.

51   See Bloom, *op. cit.*, in Strauss and Cropsey (eds), *History of Political Philosophy*, p. 564.

52   *Ibid.*, in Strauss and Cropsey (eds), *History of Political Philosophy*, p. 577.

53   'Libertarian' in this sense refers to a form of liberalism that believes in freeing people not merely from the constraints of traditional political institutions, but also from the inner constraint imposed by their mistaken attribution of power to ineffectual things (see Roger Scruton, *A Dictionary of Political Thought*, Pan Books, 1982).

54   For confirmation of this argument see Bloom, *op. cit.*, in Strauss and Cropsey (eds), *History of Political Philosophy*, p. 562.

55   An examination of this issue often comes across as circular, in that what is perceived to be a 'general will' could in fact be a 'particular will', that is being pursued as a 'general will' and demanding the authoritative support of a 'general will'.

56   In the case of the Poll Tax, the Thatcher government claimed that they were establishing equality by requiring every taxpayer to pay the same amount. However, this argument was seen as unjust because of the vast inequality of disposable income that existed. The argument being that a millionaire should pay the same sum as a poverty stricken pensioner was rejected on grounds of inequality of outcome – with the millionaire having much more disposable income than the pensioner.

57   There is also a danger that in a tyrannical society a despotic leader could impose his particular will by saying: 'I know this is the general will of society'.

58   Coupled with this exclusion punishment is generally a desire for a convicted criminal to return to society (after serving his time) as a free person all the wiser for his experience.

59   *An Introduction to Contemporary Political Philosophy*, Oxford University Press, 1997, pp. 58–76.

60   *Taking Rights Seriously*, Duckworth, 1977, p. 151.

61   See Kymlicka, *Introduction to Contemporary Political Philosophy*, Oxford University Press, p. 60.

62   John Rawls, *A Theory of Justice*, Oxford University Press, 1971.

63   *Ibid.*, p. 34.

64   *Ibid.*, pp. 302–3.

65   See Kymlicka, *op. cit.*, p. 54.

66   See Kymlicka, *op. cit.*, pp. 55–8.

67   *The Law of the Constitution*, 10th edn, Macmillan, London, 1959.

68   'Formal equality' means that no person is exempt from the enforcement of the law, rich and poor, revenue official and individual taxpayer, are all within the equal reach of the arm of the law (Professor Jeffrey Jowell, 'Is Equality a Constitutional Principle?', *Current Legal Problems*, 1994, p. 4).

69   *Ibid.*, p.1. By illustration, he suggests that the rule of law may constrain racially biased enforcement of laws, but could not inhibit apartheid-style laws from being enacted by Parliament.

70   Ronald Dworkin, 'Equality, Democracy and the Constitution' [1990] *Alberta L. Rev*, 324.

71   Now see *The Treaty on European Union 1993* (the Maastricht Treaty).

72   Article 7.

73   Article 119. Note that Bayefsky has also said that nondiscrimination and equality are simply different ways of saying the same thing [1990] 11 HRLJ 1.

74   *Nold v Commission Case* 4/73 [1974] ECR 491.

75   Article F(2).

76   For a fuller consideration of the argument that Article 14 is a fundamental aspect of the ECHR see chapter 5 and the section 'Compatibility with the Convention on Human Rights'.

77   Human Rights Act 1998. For a summary of its proposals see Philip Leach (Legal Officer of Liberty), 'Incorporating Human Rights – The Process Begins', [1997] *NLJ* 1595. See also in this book, chapter 5, and the section 'Compatibility with the Convention on Human Rights'.

78   See chapter 4 of this book, 'The CERD Convention'.

79   Schwelb, 'The International Convention on the Elimination of All Forms of Racial Discrimination', [1966] *Int and Comp Law Quarterly*, 996, 997.

80   Partsch, 'Racial Speech and Human Rights', in Sandra Coliver (ed.), *Striking a Balance*.

81   This equates to Rousseau's state of nature.

82   Illustrations of this were given earlier in this chapter and included reference to the Sex and Race Discrimination legislation, with particular reference to changes in property laws which have enabled women to become more emancipated as property owners.

83   Article 1.

84   Article 2.

85   Race Relations Act 1976 and Sex Discrimination Act 1975.

86   Part III of the Public Order Act 1986 and Prevention of Incitement to Racial Hatred (Northern Ireland) Act 1970 as amended by Public Order (Northern Ireland) Order 1981 and Public Order (Northern Ireland) Order 1987.

87   There is plenty of evidence of sexual discrimination stemming from decisions of many industrial tribunals – but this is of discrimination – not sexual hatred. However, there is evidence of hatred towards people who are gay or lesbian, particularly from the far right groups. Ironically discrimination, on the basis of sexual orientation, does not amount to sexual discrimination as a result of a Court of Appeal decision in the case of *R v MOD ex parte Smith and Grady* [1996] IRLR 100. Though, this approach would appear to run counter to the logic applied in *P v S and Cornwall County Council* C-13/94, where the ECJ held that dismissal on grounds of transsexuality was contrary to the Equal Treatment Directive 76/207 – i.e. amounting to discrimination on grounds of sex. Gay rights campaigner Peter Tatchell ('Equal Rights for All', *NLJ* [1997] 233) has called for the establishment of a new Equal Rights Act that would provide 'equal treatment for all' irrespective of people's race, sex, class, religion, age, political opinion, disability, HIV status, gender identity or sexual orientation. Noticeably, this did not include a call for provisions to tackle homophobic hatred.

88   That is unless you include the IRA acts of terrorism as indicative of religious hatred. To tackle this there exists the Prevention of Terrorism (Temporary Provisions) Act 1989. Issues of terrorism are outside the parameters of this book.

89   For a discussion on this topic see Therese Murphy, 'Incitement to Hatred: Lessons from Northern Ireland', in Sandra Coliver (ed.), *Striking a Balance*.

7 Racial Motivation and Hostility

> Punishment has a point to it. Punishment is deserved by those who break obligatory norms of conduct ...[1]

These words of William Wilson relate to a criminal's liability for being found guilty of committing a criminal offence. In this chapter I will examine the possibility of the law further penalising a criminal, because in breaking the rules[2] of society his/her conduct displays inconsistency with the obligatory norm concerning racism. In other words, I will consider whether it is appropriate that a person should be given a longer sentence for his crime because of the racism associated with the offence. In order to consider this issue I will first explain the general rule that motive does not normally affect liability, going on to consider its relevance in relation to sentencing. This will lead to my examination of the government's proposals to introduce some new additional offences that will tackle any racial motivation/hostility while a crime is being committed. I will also consider if the government could and should have taken a different approach, based upon ignoring motive and applying a race discrimination – 'but for the race of the victim' – approach.

A General Rule – 'Motive Usually does not Affect Liability'

A general rule of criminal law is that motive has usually no effect upon criminal liability.[3] For example, if I steal some bread to feed the poor, the motive is irrelevant. I have stolen, fulfilling the *actus reus* while displaying the necessary *mens rea*. Accordingly, I should be found guilty.

This long established general rule emphasises that the law, in determining guilt, is simply concerned with the act of the offence.[4] It matters little, so far as criminal liability is concerned, whether Mohammed is hit over the head because he is a Spurs supporter or because he is black. The act (or *actus reus*) of hitting him is sufficient, together with the intent (or *mens rea*).

Smith and Hogan,[5] while agreeing with this general rule, point out that in some exceptional cases motive is an element of an offence. For example, in the case of blackmail, contrary to Section 21 of the Theft Act 1968, the motive of the accused may be relevant in ascertaining whether his demand was unwarranted.[6] Likewise, as evidence motive is always relevant – since proof of a motive to commit a crime can make it more likely that D (the defendant) in fact did commit it. Smith and Hogan also point out that motive is important when the question of punishment is at issue – with the law giving a judge discretion in sentencing. Logically, a defendant whose motive is benign, could expect a more favourable sentence than one in which the motive suggests that the defendant acted out of pure greed – with little regard for the victim's welfare.

Racial Motive and Sentencing

The approach of considering a racist motive in sentencing, can be described as being consistent with the traditional approach. In determining sentence a judge, or magistrate, is generally always influenced by facts within a case that may indicate aggravating or mitigating circumstances. These features can result in the courts either taking a tough or more lenient approach to sentencing. For example, a common assault on an elderly and vulnerable person is considered more harshly than say an attack on a football fan. Likewise, attacks on certain categories of workers, such as traffic wardens, are dealt with harshly, since it is in the public interest to indicate the unacceptability of such attacks.

In his evidence to the Home Affairs Select Committee in 1994[7] the then Home Secretary, Michael Howard remarked:

> When it comes to passing sentence, the court can take all relevant factors into account. I would have little doubt that in an appropriate case the fact that an offence was racially-motivated would be or could be relevant and therefore could be taken into account by the court and could, if they thought it appropriate, lead to a graver sentence being passed. I think it is preferable to leave the discretion with the court, rather than make it depend upon the commission of a particular offence. After all, if there is a racial element in the offence, that is something which would have to be proved to the standard of the criminal burden of proof – beyond reasonable doubt. Whereas if the court is satisfied – without being satisfied to that same extent – that racial motivation was a factor, it could take it into account in sentencing.

These words of the Home Secretary show a rejection of allowing a jury to determine a racial element. It can also be inferred from the comments of the Home Secretary, that he has faith in the judiciary to use their expertise and discretion to analyse the evidence and impose a harsher sentence where they are satisfied that a racial motive is evident. This statement, of the then Home Secretary, also accepts that a person, found guilty of an offence, could spend a period in jail for a racial element of a crime that has not been proved beyond reasonable doubt. Possibly this is understandable to an extent, because judges in passing sentence, are always likely to be influenced by unproven perceptions. A particular judge may consider that the evidence suggests a particularly vicious attack and pass sentence appropriately. Whereas, a different judge may take a slightly different view of the viciousness of the attack – being more lenient in sentence.

Case Law – A Racial Element

The case of *R v Rankin and Irvine* [1993] 14 Cr.App.R.(S).636 is an example of the courts imposing a graver sentence because of racial motivation. Both Rankin and Irvine were serving police officers convicted of assault occasioning actual bodily harm on a taxi driver.

The two police officers were amongst a group of off-duty police officers attending a stag night celebration. They approached a cab and asked the fare which was quoted. They then asked how much more it would be to take five in the cab, rather than four. The cab driver said it would cost more because he was not supposed to take five and that he would be in trouble with the police if they found him. At which point, one or other of the group announced that they were police officers. The cab driver then asked, if that was so, why were they seeking to persuade him to do something which was contrary to the law.

From that an altercation developed and Irvine proceeded to subject the cab driver to verbal abuse, calling him repeatedly 'a black bastard' or 'a spade bastard'. He also head-butted the cab driver twice and kicked him.

At that stage, one of the group of police officers tried to bring the incident to the end by taking the cab driver away from where he was being assaulted. Despite a lull in the attack, Irvine, joined by Rankin, proceeded to follow the cab driver and renew the attack. They subjected him to further punching and kicking.

At trial they pleaded not guilty, but a jury found them guilty and they were sentenced to two years' imprisonment. They appealed against sentence. At the appeal, the Lord Chief Justice, Lord Taylor of Gosforth, remarked that putting all the mitigating factors that one can in favour of the appellants, namely their good records and their home circumstances, there remained a number of aggravating factors which the learned judge had to take into account.

First, cab drivers are recognised as vulnerable to attack and sentence should reflect their vulnerability. Secondly, 'there were the unfortunate racist overtones in this case. It is perfectly clear that this attack was conducted to an accompaniment of racist remarks, and it may well have received a good deal of impetus from that sort of motivation. That too is something which this Court would wish to recognise in the level of sentencing'. Thirdly, there was the renewal of the attack, and fourthly, a lack of contrition shown. Bearing in mind all those matters, it was held the judge was right to impose the sentence that he did.

In another case, *R v Clarke* [1992] 13 Cr.App.R.(S).640, the appellant was sitting on the steps of a block of flats when Mr Patel passed him. The appellant butted Mr Patel in the forehead for no apparent reason, called him a 'Paki' and punched him in the mouth.

At appeal against a sentence of two years' imprisonment, Hutchinson J held: 'that the learned recorder sentencing him plainly and rightly took the view that the seriousness of this assault was considerably aggravated by the racialist remarks ... from which it might be deduced that there was a racial motive in what he had done'. The Appeal Judge also acknowledged that counsel for the appellant had realistically accepted that this certainly was an 'aggravating factor and that it is a factor which distinguishes the case from a number of other authorities helpfully referred to in his advice where considerably lower sentences were imposed'. However, sentence was reduced to 12 months in light of the rapid recovery of the victim, with it not being the gravest of attacks.

Both these cases show that the Home Secretary is correct when he says that the Judge will take into account racial motive in sentencing. Indeed, in both cases it is evident that the racial motive is being punished. In *Rankin and Irvine*, Lord Taylor made reference to 'that sort of motivation' saying, 'That too is something which the Court would wish to recognise in the level of sentencing'. Likewise, in Clarke, Hutchinson J 'deduced that there was a racial motive', which was recognised as an aggravating factor in sentencing.

However, in neither of these cases was there direct objective evidence of racial motive. There was certainly evidence of the use of racialist words, but the use of words itself may not be conclusive as to racial motive. Indeed, the words may be used as just another means with which to hurt the victim.

In the case of *Clarke*, it was clear that a racial motive was *deduced* from the racialist remarks. But, to what standard is the deduction established? Beyond reasonable doubt? On the balance of probability? Or just inferred, from an absence of an alternative explanation from the accused?

Likewise, in *Rankin and Irvine*, even if you can establish a racial motive from the words 'black bastard' and 'spade bastard', these words were only used by Irvine. Despite the fact that Rankin did not make such verbally racist comments, he was sentenced, along with Irvine, to the same two years imprisonment. Surely, if the racist words influenced the judge to infer a racial motive – only Irvine expressed them. This clearly suggests that the racist brush of Irvine may also have tarred Rankin – with Rankin being guilty because he took part in an attack which was itself racist. While this may seem logical in terms of consistency of sentencing, it must be the case that two assailants, although both working together in committing an offence, may actually have different motives. For example, the motive of Irvine can be described as clearly racist due to the language he used – whereas the motive of Rankin could be racist (due to his participation) but perhaps of a lesser degree? If sentencing is to reflect motive in any accurate sense, it should surely result in differing sentences where the evidence more clearly infers a racial motive.

There may also be other issues in establishing the possession of a racist motive while carrying out a violent attack. Assuming a defendant has a racist motive and this is deduced from his use of racist words, what about the issue of freedom of expression? This especially applies given that it may be much more difficult to determine a racial motive if the attacker is silent. In the USA the Supreme Court has recognised that so-called 'fighting words', 'are no essential part of an exposition of ideas, and are of such slight social value as a step to truth that any benefit that may be derived from them is clearly outweighed by the social interest in order and morality'.[8]

It is submitted that the cases of *Clarke* or *Rankin and Irvine* both fail to give a clear indication of what constitutes evidence of racial motivation. If anything, they suggest racial motive may be inferred in the absence of any viable alternative motivation.

The Ribbans Approach

The case of *R v Ribbans, Duggan and Ridley*[9] does provide evidence of racially motivated crime from the facts of the case. This case involved Mr Harris (black) and Miss Woodward (white) driving into a garage, on their way home from France, to buy some soft drinks. The three defendants by chance were in a van behind them. When Miss Woodward went to the kiosk they started throwing some chips towards her, shouting abuse.

As she returned to the car, the van drove away briefly only to stop outside the garage exit. The three defendants got out and ran towards the Cortina of Mr Harris and Miss Woodward, kicking at the door and punching at the passenger window. At which point, Mr Harris got out of the car and said, 'What's the problem?'.

The answer was, ''Cause you're black.' Ribbans challenged Mr Harris to a fight. Mr. Harris was grabbed from behind and attacked. Miss Woodward saw a shiny object, probably a screwdriver, pulled from the jacket of Ribbans. Duggan joined in the attack, with video evidence appearing to show he too pulled out a screwdriver.

Ridley left the general attack and got into Mr Harris' Cortina. He drove it into the kiosk and then reversed it over the legs of Mr Harris as he lay on the ground.

On being taken to hospital, it was established that Mr Harris had been stabbed and suffered a significant level of injuries. He had a fractured skull and probable permanent disability to his leg. There was significant forensic evidence available and also video footage of the attack from the kiosk security camera. At the flat of one of the defendants, there were racist stickers on the wall and a metal cross and chain inscribed with swastikas.

The judge, at first instance, took into account the past violent record of all of the defendants and the fact that they were all on bail at the time of the attack. They pleaded guilty to a charge of grievous bodily harm and the judge imposed a five-year sentence for Ridley and three years for each of the others. The Attorney General appealed against the sentence on the grounds that this was unduly lenient.[10] This was accepted by the Appeal Court, with the following words of the Lord Chief Justice, Lord Taylor of Gosforth:

> We are of the view that the sentences were in each case unduly lenient. This was not just a simple case of causing grievous bodily harm with intent of the kind which so often come before the court, where there is a brief encounter between one offender and a victim. This was a joint attack by three men on an innocent man. It was racist in motive; it was protracted, and the effects were grave …
>
> It cannot be too strongly emphasised by this court that where there is a racial element in an offence of violence, that is a gravely aggravating feature. There is no specific offence of racial violence, although it has been suggested that there should be one.

> We take the view that it is perfectly proper for the court to deal with any offence of violence which has a proven racial element in it, in a way which makes clear that the aspect invests the offence with added gravity and therefore must be regarded as an aggravating feature.

The difficulty in analysing this case is not in determining a racist motive, since the words used by the defendants at the time of the attack indicate a racial motive.[11] Rather, it is in analysing the words of Lord Taylor in the Appeal Court. He accepts evidence of a racist motive, but then says: 'Where there is a racial element in an offence of violence, that is a gravely aggravating feature'. Clearly, he is referring to facts that help establish the offence. Obviously a racial element must be part of the basic offence or assault – i.e. it cannot be independent to the offence. But, what exactly does he consider to be a racial element? Is it a racial motive? Is it the fact that the victim is black, and the assailants are white? Is it the use of racist language, and/or racial abuse?

Problems in Relation to the Standard of Proof

The case of *R v Leaney*[12] provides a classic example of the difficulties that can develop. Leaney, had been drinking a can of lager in Brighton. It seems that Mr Ibrahim, a Sudanese student, had a 'collision or brushing of shoulders', resulting in Leaney cutting his lip on the can. Leaney, behaved aggressively, 'swearing at three black students and abusing them'. A fight ensued down a side street and Mr Ibrahim was fatally stabbed by Leaney, with a knife he had bought earlier. At the trial neither the prosecution or any witness described the murder as racial.[13] However, on sentencing the trial judge, Judge Gower, told Leaney:

> I am satisfied that this was a killing perpetrated because you took exception, as you saw it, to three black men in your path, one of whom brushed against you; and I have no doubt that there was an element of racialism in what you did.
>
> I accept that you are full of remorse for what you did, but that cannot excuse your conduct ... Your conduct in this case ... considered in the light of your past record, convinces me that you are a continuing danger to the public, and my recommendation is that you be detained for not less than 20 years.

On appeal, Anthony Hacking QC, appearing for the appellant, submitted that the trial judge was unjustified on the merits in finding a racialist motive and was in any event unjustified in recommending such a lengthy minimum period.

In the Court of Appeal, Lord Taylor acknowledged:

> It is true that the fracas culminating in the fatal stabbing was between white and black men and there were some remarks made and terms used which could have indicated a racialist element in the hostility, but the prosecution did not describe the murder as racial at any stage of the trial, nor does it seem that any witness did so. It was not specifically put to the appellant in cross-examination by the Crown that this was a racialist murder. Certainly there was not the overt and single-minded racialist motive in this case that was, for example, present in the case of *Ribbans, Duggan and Ridley*. We consider: that even if there was a racial element in the case and even allowing for the appellant's record, a minimum sentence of 20 years was inappropriate ... and excessive.

By reading *Leaney* in conjunction with the case of *Ribbans* we can establish that swearing at and abusing people of a different race, culminating in a violent attack, is not in itself sufficient to determine a racial element. It may help indicate a motive, but it is evidence of a specific racialist motive that is critical.

The case of *Leaney* emphasises the importance of giving the accused an opportunity to deny any racial motive. However, none of the cases lay down any standard as to which evidence of a racial motive should be proven.

Criticism of this Approach

The Home Affairs Committee have been critical of this type of judicial approach – arguing that they do not consider it right for a judge to impose a significantly higher sentence for a racially-motivated assault unless there is evidence of sufficient weight for a court to be satisfied beyond reasonable doubt. There is no doubt that *Leaney* gives considerable weight to their argument.

Perhaps, behind the criticism of the Home Affairs Committee, there is concern for justice being seen to be done. It is reasonable for the judge to determine sentence on the basis of objective factors, like the judgement of the jury, the vulnerability of the victim, the element of violence used, his past record and any mitigating factors.[14] All of these can be objectively assessed, both at first instance and in any appeal. However, in the case of motive (i.e. in the absence of the defendant providing one), it is likely to be determined by purely subjective factors borne out of inference.

Balanced against this argument must be the need to ensure that the courts are indeed punishing aggravated features, such as racial motive. This concern stems from the fact that a court can only punish racial motive if it is being brought to its attention. It seems that both the police and the Crown Prosecution

Service work to the same ACPO definition with regards to identifying a racial incident.[15] This wide and all-encompassing approach being:

> Any incident in which it appears to the reporting officer or investigating officer that the complaint involves an element of racial motivation or any incident which includes an allegation of racial motivation made by any person.

This definition has been used by the police forces of England and Wales since 1986 and concern has been expressed that it is too subjective.[16] Despite such criticisms, it has the advantage that it is not dependent on the investigating officer for determination that the incident may be racial, with it taking into account the opinion of victims etc. Another key feature is that it provides a form of uniformity of approach across the police and the CPS. Although, it seems that the police and the CPS can differ significantly on what falls into this ACPO definition. For example, the CPS Racial Incident Monitoring Scheme for the year ending 31 March 1998, signifies that out of 1,506 cases identified by the CPS and police as involving a racial element only 37 per cent (557) were identified by the police. This means that in an alarming 63 per cent (949 cases), the racial element was exclusively identified by the CPS,[17] with regional variations showing that in CPS area Wales, the police identified 57 per cent of the cases – while in CPS area Northwest, the police identified racial motivation in only 15 per cent of the cases.

Out of the 1,506 cases where defendants were charged, a total of 182 were either dropped or discontinued at court.[18] Admissible evidence of racial motivation was presented to the courts in 85.25 per cent (981 cases) of the 1,151 cases which were prosecuted within the time span. However, the CPS also highlight that in cases in which there is no evidence of racial motivation, there may be brought before the court background information to enable it to draw an 'inference' that a case is racially motivated. Although this is not direct evidence of racial motivation the CPS claim it will 'consist of factors which it is proper to refer to in presenting the case so the court may make a judgement on whether the case might be racially motivated and in which it would therefore be proper to impose an increase in sentence'. It seems this form of evidence varies from case to case, but an example is that of a defendant facing a charge of criminal damage for throwing a brick through a shop window. The shop exists in a parade of shops, but is the only one owned by an Asian shopkeeper (who may have had past experience of such attacks on his property).

The CPS point out that out of a total of 1,324 cases prosecuted during the year, some 1,102 resulted in findings of guilt, with the court signifying an increase in sentence due to racial motivation in only 27 per cent of cases. This suggests, at best, out of a total of around 13,000[19] police-reported racial incidents, less than 2.3 per cent have resulted in increased sentences for racial motivation.[20]

It is possible that the judge or magistrates may have given tougher sentences on the basis of the evidence of racial motivation, but declined to give an indication they have done so – so as to limit the chances of a successful appeal. It is for such reasons, that the interpretation put on the CPS data should not be regarded as anything more than an indication of the problem. What the data does do, is to confirm that only a small percentage of racial incidents, reported to the police, result in criminals receiving an enhanced sentence for the racial motivation associated with the crime.

However, it may also be the case that the courts in these 1,102 cases did attempt to comply with the directions of Lord Justice Taylor, in *Ribbans*, but did not consider the weight of evidence was sufficient to justify an enhanced sentence in 73 per cent of the cases. This approach could well be justified in light of the further comments of Lord Justice Taylor, in *R v Leaney*, where the lack of an 'overt and single-minded racialist motive' (as was present in the case of *Ribbans*), led to an enhanced sentence being reduced on appeal.

What this may signify is that the Crown Prosecution Service need to do more than simply bring to the attention of the court any indication(s) of a racist motive. In order to obtain a graver sentence, the prosecution, where appropriate, may need to make persuasive efforts to convince the courts that the defendant displayed an overt and single-minded racialist motive.

Legislative Change

Following the election of a Labour government, in May 1997, the new Home Secretary, Jack Straw MP, set the wheels in motion for the implementation of a General Election manifesto commitment to tackle racial harassment and violence. It seems that any previous reservations of the Home Office, about tackling racial motivation were swept aside. The new government clearly wished to 'send a strong message to society at large that such [racist] crime is unacceptable and that it will be dealt with very seriously by the police and the courts'.[21] In this sense, the government is intent on giving a symbolic message that says 'any crime motivated by racial hostility is unacceptable and will be dealt with harshly by the courts'.

The Government Approach – Tackling Crime Motivated by Racial Hostility

The government approach to tackling crime motivated by, or displaying, racial hostility can be found in the Crime and Disorder Act 1998 which contains a declaratory measure to make it clear that a court should treat a racial element to any crime, as an aggravating factor in sentencing[22] – stating how this has been taken into account. Thus, in effect, giving statutory expression to the law as it stands following the *Ribbans* judgement.

In many ways, the legislation is a principled acceptance of the recommendations put forward by the Home Affairs Select Committee in 1994 – who argued for racist crime to be tackled through the use of enhanced sentencing where a racial motive is proven. However, what is unique about the crime and disorder legislation, is that the government is seeking to tackle not just racial motive, but essentially racial hostility. In effect, the legislation enables the courts to consider charges for racially-aggravated assaults, racially-aggravated public order offences and racially-aggravated harassment. Further, these racial charges will be in addition to the primary offences[23] – so the courts will first have to determine if the basic offence has been proven – and then decide if[24] –

(a) at the time of committing the offence, or immediately before or after doing so, the offender demonstrates towards the victim of the offence hostility based on the victim's membership of or association with a racial group;[25] or

(b) the offence is motivated (wholly or partly) by hostility towards members of a racial group based on their membership of that group.

Further, it is immaterial whether or not the offender's hostility is also based to any extent on the fact or presumption that any person or group of persons belong to a religious group.[26] Thus, it will not be possible to establish an arguably strong defence by claiming: 'I was not being racially hostile – I was attacking him because he is a Muslim'.

Assuming a jury determines guilt of a racial offence, then a much higher sentencing tariff level applies (Table 7.1) than exists for the basic offence itself. This Crime and Disorder Act 1998 is clearly intent on penalising racist crime, with Section 82 requiring a court, in considering the seriousness of any offence (other than under sections 29 to 32 of the Act), to treat racial aggravation as an aggravating factor that increases the seriousness of the

Table 7.1　Sentencing changes

Existing offence	Maximum penalty	Maximum penalty for racial equivalent
Common assault	6 months and/or Level 5 fine (£5,000)	2 years imprisonment and/or unlimited fine
Assault – actual bodily harm	5 years imprisonment	7 years imprisonment
Malicious wounding	5 years imprisonment	7 years imprisonment
Section 4 POA 1986 provocation of violence	6 months and/or Level 5 fine (£5,000)	2 years imprisonment and/or a fine
Section 4a POA intent harassment	6 months and/or Level 5 fine (£5,000)	2 years imprisonment and/or a fine
Section 5 POA harass/ alarm/distress	Level 3 fine – (£1,000)	Level 4 fine – (£2,500)
Section 2 Harassment Act 1997 – harassment	6 months and/or Level 5 fine (£5,000)	2 years and/or Level 5 fine (£5000)
Section 4 Harassment Act 1997 – fear violence	5 years imprisonment	7 years imprisonment
Section 1(1) Criminal Damage Act 1971	Summary 6 months and/ or maximum fine – indictment – 10 years imprisonment	Summary 6 months and/or statutory maximum fine – indictment 14 years imprisonment

offence. Though presumably this should not apply – on grounds of double jeopardy – to sections 18 to 23 of the Public Order Act 1986 which are offences that already deal with racial aggravation, in the form of stirring up racial hatred.[27]

For the Crime and Disorder Act 1998 to succeed, it is important that two major issues are fulfilled: (1) the crime needs to be correctly identified as being influenced by either racial hostility or motivation; (2) any race charges being pursued – with the case being dealt with in the appropriate court.

The key to the first of these rests with the investigative stage of the crime. To this extent, the ACPO definition discussed earlier in the chapter is in need of amendment. It needs to be amended because the current definition seeks to find racial motivation – thereby failing to require a police officer to establish racial hostility.[28] However, simply changing the wording may not be enough, with it being self-evident that police training is also of great importance. Not only should police officers benefit from training to help them to identify racial hostility and/or motivation, they would also benefit from training in relation to the form filling procedures for the labelling of crime referral forms to the Crown Prosecution Service. If the referral forms are clearly and accurately marked up displaying racial hostility and/or motive – together with any evidence to help substantiate – this must surely help the CPS when it comes to pursuing racial charges.

Secondly, once those racial charges have been laid, it is obviously vital that the case is heard in the appropriate court. Given the level of sentencing, this must mean that the vast majority of cases will need to be heard – often by jury[29] – in the Crown Court.[30] Thus, in any 'pleas for venue' it is important that the Magistrates refer the case to the Crown Court – even if the case is one of racial criminal damage, which does not normally justify reference to the Crown Court.[31]

Role of the Jury

What is interesting about the new offences, created to tackle racial violence and hostility, is that the issue of determining racial motivation/hostility is, in general, being removed from the judge. If a defendant pleads guilty to, or is found guilty of, a racial offence the judge would be statutorily bound to use his discretion to impose a suitable sentence in keeping with the new harsher sentence policy. Obviously, the judge will have a large element of discretion, but given the obligation to penalise racial crime it seems likely that any sentence imposed could be expected to exceed that which is generally available for the basic offence. Thus, if a person is found guilty of a racial common assault/s he should be given a tougher sentence than for common assault.

The question of whether a defendant is guilty or innocent of a racial criminal offence, will be left to a jury to determine beyond reasonable doubt. They will need to be satisfied that (a) that he has the *actus reus* and *mens rea* for the basic offence. If they are satisfied that the defendant is guilty of the basic offence, they will need to consider (b) – the alternative more serious verdict that at, or around the time of the basic offence, the offender demonstrated racial hostility, or that the motivation for the offence was racial hostility.

It follows that a consequence of this decision is that the judge will in effect be bound by the decision of the jury. If the jury determine, from the facts before the court, that racial motive and/or hostility was present, he will have the responsibility of passing sentence in accord with the decision of the jury.

Because most cases would be determined on the facts, it seems unlikely it will be easy to establish grounds for appeal.[32] Terms, such as 'racial hostility', will be left to the jury to determine on the basis of a natural meaning, with ordinary everyday dictionary definitions applicable.

However, such findings of guilt, on the basis of fact, does not mean the jury would always obtain the absolutely correct result. Indeed, there are dangers that a jury – faced with a lack of objective evidence as to racial motive and hostility – may infer guilt from the scarcity of evidence available. As such, the directions to the jury would need to be carefully worded with a clear instruction from the judge that proof beyond reasonable doubt is necessary. Indeed, unless this is fully understood by the jury, miscarriages of justice could well become a feature of this legislation.

Racial Motivation and Hostility – an Easier Threshold to Fulfil than Ribbans

It seems clear that Section 28 of the Crime and Disorder Act establishes a threshold that is easier for the prosecution to fulfil than existed under the terms of *Ribbans*. To make this point, I refer back to the case *R v Leaney*, which was discussed earlier in this chapter and involved the defendant stabbing a Sudanese student after swearing at black students and abusing them – with a 20-year sentence being imposed for murder. At the appeal against sentence, Lord Justice Taylor acknowledged grounds because, *inter alia*, 'there was not the overt and single-minded racialist motive in this case that was, for example, present in the case of *Ribbans*, *Duggan* and *Ridley*'.

Should *Leaney* have been dealt with under the terms of the Crime and Disorder Act 1998 it seems probable that the appeal against sentence would not have succeeded on these grounds.[33] This applies because Section 28 produces a threshold that is easier for the prosecution to fulfil than existed under the terms of *Ribbans*. Indeed, Section 82 statutorily requires the judge, even in a murder trial, to regard racial motivation and/or hostility as an aggravating feature in sentencing and to state in open court that the offence was so aggravated. This applies whether the offence is motivated *partly or wholly* by hostility towards members of a racial group based upon their membership of that group.[34] Thus, there is no longer a need for evidence of 'overt and single-minded racism'.[35] Even if the judge is not convinced that the offence is partly motivated by racial hostility, it seems highly likely that the facts, as produced in *Leaney*, would result in a finding that, at the time of the offence (or immediately before or after doing so), the defendant demonstrated racial hostility towards the victim based on the victim's membership of, or association with members of, a racial group.[36]

Difference between Racial Motivation and Hostility

This also indicates that persons who may be found not to possess a racial motive could be found guilty of demonstrating racial hostility. The case of *R v Cole (and others)*[37] provides an example of the kind of threshold situation that may arise. What is also interesting about this case, is that it also indicates that while a person may not possess racial motivation, he could still be found guilty of demonstrating racial hostility.[38]

In *Cole* the victim (Mr Kagwi) was asked to leave a public house after it was alleged that he had blown down the neck of a woman. Outside the public house, later that evening, the defendant Ms Cole made abusive remarks to her companions, proceeding to assault Mr Kagwi by throwing beer over him and smashing a glass on the side of his head. The victim was rendered unconscious and further blows caused him to lose the sight of one of his eyes. When people tried to help the victim Ms Cole again used abusive remarks. Hare[39] cites this case as an example of a situation where there is no necessary relationship between making racist comments and having a racial motivation for the assault. Presumably his comments are based upon the assumption that the words used, although racially discriminatory, are not conclusive as to a racial motivation for the attack – with an alternative explanation being that the assault was due to Mr Kagwi's conduct of blowing down the neck of a woman. While that may be the case so far as racial motivation is concerned, the racist words used, at the time of the attack, demonstrate racial hostility towards the victim.

Thus, if *Cole* had been tried under the terms of Section 28 of the Crime and Disorder Act, it seems probable that a jury might fail to establish racial motivation,[40] but find that racial hostility was evident at the time of the attack.[41] In these circumstances, the defendant would be given an enhanced sentence due to racial motivation and/or hostility – with there being no difference between racial motivation and hostility for the purposes of sentencing. It is obviously possible that in sentencing, the Judge might wish to take into account the fact that the defendant had been found guilty due to the existence of an easier threshold for racial hostility than exists for motivation. However, parliament has specifically decided not to differentiate and a Judge may have limited powers in this area – with any perceived policy of giving such leniency being open to challenge in the appeal courts.

Problems with Defining Racial Motivation

This analysis of *Cole*, emphasises that the approach to determining hostility is distinctive from that concerning motivation. In determining hostility the legislation requires the jury to determine, from the facts within the case, guilt or innocence by applying an objective assessment of what happened at the time of, or immediately before or after committing the offence. If the defendant demonstrated racial hostility – the jury should find him guilty. In other words they look at the nature of the attack and consider objective evidence like words used etc. From these objective factors, it is expected that the jury would infer, or determine, racial hostility.

In comparison, a requirement under Section 28(b) for the jury to determine if the offence is motivated (wholly or partly) by hostility towards members of a racial group, based on their membership of that group, is much more difficult to establish. The only objective element within this, is a person being a member of a racial group[42] – the issue of motivation is essentially subjective (unless the defendant admits a racial motive), with the jury in effect drawing inferences from the facts available.

In the USA, the courts have had problems in determining racial motivation. Only three states, Nebraska, Utah and Wyoming, do not possess some form of bias crime law.[43] Over 35 states already have *hate crime* legislation or *penalty-enhancing* statutes, where racial motive is a factor. However, this existence of anti-racist legislation has been more of an indication of the US' opposition to racial violence, than of a means of prosecuting such offenders. There have been only a handful of successful prosecutions – with many failing to surmount the significant hurdle of a breach of the First Amendment.[44] Such has been the US failure of this racial motivation legislation, academics[45] have argued that the burden of proof needs changing – so that racial motive is assumed, unless the defence prove otherwise. Understandably, this presumption of a racial motive has been criticised as failing to fulfil due process principles, with a guilty mind being assumed.[46]

Indeed, such proposals, and arguments, have developed because of the considerable problems that exist with regards to the proving of racial motive beyond reasonable doubt. This stems from the fact that it is purely a mental element, with any possible evidence at best circumstantial. To consider this point, I will examine the US case of *Wisconsin v Mitchell*.[47]

Mitchell had been to the cinema to see the movie *Mississippi Burning*, which contains several scenes in which white racists assault black victims. Mitchell, a black person, on leaving the cinema, remarked to some fellow youths: 'Do you feel hyped up to move on some white people?' Seeing a white teenager nearby, he said, 'You all want to fuck somebody up? There goes a white boy; go get him'. The teenage victim was comatose for four days, suffering brain damage. Mitchell was convicted of an aggravated offence carrying a two-year sentence. However, the jury also found racial motivation in the victim's selection of the teenage target. Thus, in accord with the hate crime sentence-enhancement provisions, for racially motivated crime, this was increased to four years.

On appeal, the Wisconsin Supreme Court concluded that the hate crime statute contravened the First Amendment, with pure thought being determined to be speech. Since free speech is protected, under the First Amendment, it followed that so must be thought. In effect, the majority concluded that the process of selection was not conduct, but that of speech.

On reaching the United States Supreme Court, it was unanimously held that a defendant's motive was one such factor that could either aggravate or mitigate the crime. Accordingly, it was accepted that appropriately drafted hate crimes do not violate the First Amendment rights of defendants – essentially because they are laws designed to deal with violent conduct. While this could not be stretched to encompass 'abstract beliefs', the court should be able to differentiate between *motive* and *abstract beliefs.*

Why not Tackle Racial Discrimination and Ignore Motivation?

Instead of tackling racial motive – and all the problems that ensue – the government could have taken a more stable, tried and tested approach. They could have simply introduced a two-tier level of jury determination in relation to criminal offences involving people of different races. The first task of the jury being to determine if the basic offence has been committed beyond reasonable doubt and, if established, for them then to consider if the offence would have been committed 'but for' the race or nationality of the victim or intended victim.[48]

I will demonstrate the role and approach of the law by way of example:

- *Suppose Tom finds Muhammad in bed with his wife and punches him saying:*
  'Take that you black bastard'

A jury would first have to establish that an assault has occurred. That is, they would need to establish beyond reasonable doubt that Tom committed the *actus reus* of common assault while possessing the necessary *mens rea* – or intent – for the offence. Having established such guilt the jury could then be required to consider whether, *but for* the race of the victim, or intended victim, the assault would not have occurred. The motivation for the attack can clearly be seen as stemming from jealousy, rather than being racial. However, the facts also show racial hostility was demonstrated at the time of the attack – so in theory a jury should find Tom guilty of the new offence of demonstrating racial hostility, resulting in an enhanced sentence. This outcome may be considered as being exceedingly harsh on Tom – since he is being treated, and penalised, as a racist criminal when the facts suggest that he was not motivated by race – but by jealousy.

This result reflects the swinging pendulum problem of the government's new anti-racist legislation. On the one hand motivation of racial hostility can be difficult to establish due to the opportunity of an accused to provide another explanation as to motive – thereby increasing the likelihood that he will be acquitted of a more serious race charge. While on the other hand – in the case of demonstrating racial hostility – the net is cast so wide that people who are not motivated by racism – but are essentially expressing a racist view so as to further hurt the victim – can and will be caught.

In comparison, if the government had taken the tried and tested 'but for' the race of the victim approach, the jury would have more discretion as to the overall circumstances of the case. In the example of Tom saying, 'Take that you black bastard', the jury could recognise the racial hostility – but conclude that Tom would have punched any man he found in bed with his wife. As such, the jury would be entitled to conclude that the assault was due to jealousy and have occurred irrespective of the race of the victim. Thus, on the facts, the jury could decide that Tom is not guilty of the racial element associated with the criminal assault.

This 'but for' proposal – which I will call the 'but for the race of the victim' approach – stems from the method taken by the judiciary in establishing direct discrimination in racial or sexual discrimination cases. The case of *James v Eastleigh Borough Council*[49] is applicable and involves a husband and wife, both aged 61, deciding to go for a swim in the baths of Eastleigh Borough Council. On entering the baths Mrs James was allowed in free because she had reached pension age of 60 for women, but Mr James was required to pay 75p admission because, although the same age as his wife, he was below the pension age of 65 for men. The House of Lords considered that 'but for' the fact that Mr James was a man he could swim free of charge in the baths – with the authority applying a criterion which was gender based and therefore potentially unlawful. In this case, the charitable motive of the local authority was considered irrelevant to the finding of direct discrimination. Indeed, the court was not concerned with the motive, just with the existence of discrimination.

Obviously, in any racial criminal case, if the defendant indicates that he acted according to the victim's race, colour, or nationality, it may be reasonably straightforward for the jury to determine guilt beyond reasonable doubt of a racially discriminatory offence. However, assuming that the defendant does not admit the assault was conducted because of the race of the victim, it may be necessary for the jury to infer guilt from the primary facts. This 'inference' approach is taken in civil law cases with Neil LJ, in *King v Great Britain China Centre*,[50] providing the following summary in relation to establishing direct discrimination:

(1) It is for the applicant who complains of racial discrimination to make out his or her case. Thus if the applicant does not prove the case on the balance of probability he or she will fail.

(2) It is important to bear in mind that it is unusual to find direct evidence of racial discrimination. Few employees will be prepared to admit such discrimination even to themselves. In some cases the discrimination will not be ill-intentional but merely based on an assumption 'he or she would not have fitted in'.

(3) The outcome of the case will therefore usually depend on what inferences it is proper to draw from the primary facts found by the Tribunal. These inferences can include, in appropriate cases, any inferences that it is just and equitable to draw in accordance with Section 65(2)(b) of the 1976 Act from an evasive or equivocal reply to a questionnaire.

(4) Though there will be some cases where, for example, the non-selection of the applicant for a post or promotion is clearly not on racial grounds, a finding of discrimination and a finding of a difference in race will often point to the possibility of racial discrimination. In such circumstances the Tribunal will look to the employer for an explanation. If no explanation is then put forward or if the Tribunal considers the explanation to be inadequate or unsatisfactory it will be legitimate for the Tribunal to infer that the discrimination was on racial grounds. This is not a matter of law but, as May LJ put it in Noone, 'almost common sense'.

(5) It is unnecessary and unhelpful to introduce the concept of a shifting evidential burden of proof.

At the conclusion of all the evidence the Tribunal should make findings as to the primary facts and draw such inferences as they feel proper from those facts. They should then reach a conclusion on the balance of probabilities, bearing in mind both the difficulties which face a person who complains of unlawful discrimination and the fact that it is for the complainant to prove his or her case.

This raises essentially two issues. One, the differing standards of proof between civil and criminal cases and, two, the relevance of the drawing of inferences in relation to criminal cases.

1 Differing Standards of Proof between Civil and Criminal Cases

Denning J, in *Miller v Minister of Pensions*,[51] spoke of the degree of cogency which the evidence on a criminal charge must reach before the accused can be convicted. He said:

> That degree is well settled. It need not reach certainty, but it must carry a high degree of probability. Proof beyond reasonable doubt does not mean proof beyond a shadow of doubt. The law would fail to protect the community if it admitted fanciful possibilities to deflect the course of justice. If the evidence is so strong against a man to leave only a remote possibility in his favour, which can be dismissed with the sentence 'of course it is possible but not in the least probable' the case is proved beyond reasonable doubt, but nothing short of that will suffice.

While referring to the degree of cogency which evidence must carry in relation to civil cases, Lord Denning said:

> That degree is well settled. It must carry a reasonable degree of probability, but not as high as is required in a criminal case. If the evidence is such that the tribunal can say 'we think it more probable than not', the burden is discharged, but if the probabilities are equal it is not.

While this is accepted law, it is clear that at times the distinction has been questioned. For example, Lord Goddard, in *R v Hepworth and Fearnley*,[52] once confessed that he had difficulty in understanding how there are or can be two standards. Hilberry J, in *R v Martagh and Kennedy*[53] is reported to have said:

> I personally have never seen the difference between the onus of proof in a civil and criminal case. If a thing is proved, it is proved, but I am not entitled to that view.

Despite there being a practical distinction between civil and criminal levels of proof, there exists some evidence to suggest that even within the limits of such evidential proof cogency there are circumstances where the courts consider that some decisions are more serious than others. This can result in prosecutors having a higher hurdle to surmount on the more serious criminal charges or those carrying graver consequences. Some evidence of this can be found in the comments of Denning LJ, from the case of *Bater v Bater*:[54]

> It is of course true that by our law a higher standard of proof is required in criminal cases than in civil cases. But this is subject to the qualification that there is no absolute standard in either case. In criminal cases the charge must be proved beyond reasonable doubt, but there may be degrees of proof within that standard ... So also in civil cases the case must be proved by a preponderance of probability, but there may also be degrees of probability within that standard. The degree depends upon the subject matter. A civil court, when considering a charge of fraud, will naturally require for itself a higher degree of probability than that which it would require when asking if negligence is established. It does not adopt so high a degree as a criminal court, even when it is considering a charge of a criminal nature; but still it does require a degree of probability which is commensurate with the occasion.

What this confusingly indicates is that, in practice, there may be no fixed criteria in relation to a standard of proof in either civil or criminal cases. Indeed, it suggests that – in practice – even in criminal cases the courts may display a degree of flexibility in determining guilt beyond reasonable doubt. That does not mean that the courts will willingly determine guilt beyond reasonable doubt when the standard has not been met, but rather that they may spend more time considering the issues in cases that involve longer prison sentences. Thereby, the burden of proof may become more difficult to establish because it will be tested more fully.

Inevitably this may mean that a jury will naturally be cautious when they determine issues like racial motivation – or whether 'but for the race or nationality of the victim', or intended victim, the offence would not have been committed. However, this is surely correct given that longer prison sentences will almost inevitably follow such a finding of guilt.

2   *The Relevance of the Drawing of Inferences in Relation to Criminal Cases*

As indicated, from the *China Centre* case, it is appropriate for the civil courts to draw inferences from the primary facts of any discrimination law case. Even in criminal cases it can be appropriate to draw inferences from primary facts and any failure, on behalf of the accused, to give a credible explanation can result in a finding of guilt. For example, if someone who is charged with burglary was found in the hall of a house without permission, it is incumbent on him as a matter of common sense, though not as a matter of law, to give a satisfactory explanation of his presence, and, if that is not forthcoming, the jury will be justified in inferring the requisite guilty intent.[55]

It clearly follows, that in theory a jury, which has first established that a criminal offence has occurred, should after due consideration be able to determine whether that offence has been influenced by race. Irrespective of which approach the jury is required to take (i.e. 'motivated by racial hostility', 'a demonstration of racial hostility', or a 'but for the race or nationality of the victim' approach), they may need to draw inferences from the primary facts within the case – but this is something that is already an accepted practice in criminal cases. As such, there would appear to be no logical reason why the 'but for the race of the victim' test, could not be applied in cases involving criminal assault or harassment, with longer sentences being applied should this element be proven.

It seems that the Home Office legislators when drawing up legislation to tackle racist crime, did consider this as an option. However, it is possible there are those in the Home Office who seem to have doubts about making what amounts to crime conducted with – or through – racial discrimination a criminal offence. Instead, they opted for introducing longer sentences for crimes that display racial hostility or are motivated by racial hostility. The only justification for this approach seems to be a political desire to avoid 'racial discrimination' becoming a criminal offence, with the government believing that tackling racial hostility is preferable because 'hostility' has a direct relationship to 'conduct'. In other words, the government wishes to be seen as tackling racial conduct as opposed to racial thought.

However, this argument, although initially attractive, is easily undermined by the fact that the 'but for the race of the victim' test is itself conduct-orientated, since a prerequisite is a criminal offence.

Possibly one additional justification for the government's approach, might lie in the relative simplicity of the 'but for the race of the victim' test, with no requirement being evident for determining a *mens rea*. It is submitted that this argument is again seriously undermined by the government's promotion of a racial hostility approach that concentrates on the act of demonstrating racial hostility and excludes consideration of any *mens rea* or intent. No doubt this approach can be considered as acceptable because the jury should have determined the *mens rea* for the basic offence before they went on to determine whether the offence involved a racial element. This surely indicates that any objection to the racial discrimination 'but for' test approach should not lie with the simplicity of a test that excludes *mens rea*. If anything, a simple test that relates to any racial element associated with a crime should be welcomed, since it provides for a greater opportunity for consistency in the application of legal decisions.

Plea-bargaining? One disadvantage of the government's racial motivation/ hostility approach, is that the additional verdict method inevitably opens up the prospect of plea-bargaining – i.e. the defence seeking to plead guilty to one offence on the understanding that the prosecution will not present evidence in relation to other more serious charges. This possibility is enhanced by a desire on behalf of the government to reduce the expense of the justice system.[56]

Normally any lesser charge cases, such as common assault and harassment, would be heard summarily in a Magistrates Court. However, given that the government proposes to introduce up to two-year prison sentences for the racial aspect of certain crimes, it is clear these cases will need to be dealt with by the Crown Court.[57]

It is not just the trial by jury that would need to be referred to the Crown Court – but also the sentencing of defendants who plead guilty to the relevant racial offence.[58] This must logically apply, since magistrates' powers are limited to cases where the sentence is one of six months' imprisonment or less.

At a time of financial restrictions being imposed on the judicial system, these changes could result in legal costs escalating in these types of cases. For example, racial common assault and harassment cases could involve an appearance at the Magistrates Court, with subsequent referral to the Crown Court. Even if as a matter of policy all racial cases were to be referred to the Crown Court, the costs are greater for Crown Court hearings – with jury hearings lasting longer and often involving more senior counsel. Further, while costs may escalate, it is also worth recalling that the number of convictions could marginally drop due to conviction rates being lower in the Crown Court (90.8 per cent) than in the Magistrates Courts (98 per cent).[59]

These figures, however, combine guilty and not guilty pleas. If we exclude those pleading guilty, it seems the conviction figures reach 75 per cent in the Magistrates Court – compared to 59.9 per cent in the Crown Court. What is more, for reasons that are not apparent, a smaller percentage of convictions are found in cases involving racial motivation than in cases for crime in general.

For example, the CPS Racial Incident Monitoring Scheme for 1996–97 indicates that 79.25 per cent of cases result in a guilty finding. This signifies a drop in conviction rates compared to crime in general.

It follows that one logical outcome that may develop, due to the new method of additional verdicts, is that of plea-bargaining. Indeed, it would make both economic and judicial sense for a prosecutor to accept a guilty plea for say, common assault, with a sentence of up to six months' imprisonment, than to risk an expensive 'lose all' racial common assault trial in the Crown Court (where chances of acquittal are greater). A Home Office research project confirmed the existence of plea-bargaining by lawyers with the following words:

> The two most frequent reasons given for a change in advice on pleas on the day scheduled for trial were 'a bargain with the prosecution' and 'information about probable sentence'. The most frequent forms of concession were that, in consideration of one or more pleas of guilty, the prosecution should offer no evidence, or agree to the defendant being bound over, on other charges.[60]

Further, one of the recommendations of the Royal Commission on Criminal Justice[61] would, if adopted, increase the amount of plea-bargaining by introducing the possibility of a 'sentence canvass' before the judge in all cases.

Certainly the existence of plea-bargaining has the potential of undermining the intent of establishing symbolic sentencing for racist crime.[62] It would do this because defendants, on advice from lawyers, may opt for pleading guilty to the lesser basic offence in the full knowledge that a judge would impose the lesser penalty. Indeed, it should not be possible[63] for a judge in sentencing for a basic offence – that falls within the parameters of sections 29 to 32 of the Crime and Disorder Act 1998[64] – to take into account aggravating features such as racial motive/hostility unless the defendant is charged with a racial offence and he is found guilty of that offence.

The 'but for the race of the victim' test could prevent plea-bargaining problems. It is submitted that the 'but for the race of the victim' approach also has the advantage of enabling the judiciary to prevent plea-bargaining. That is because in cases involving racial hostility there is an obvious requirement for evidence to be presented. Whereas in any inter-racial case, considered under the 'but for' principles, the jury have the evidence from the basic offence and could then simply be required to determine if that offence would have been committed 'but for the race of the victim'. Accordingly, this approach could be applied in all cases – thereby undermining any prospect of plea-bargaining.

Conclusion

Within this chapter I have examined a number of approaches to penalising a racial element associated with a crime. These can be loosely summarised as consisting of:

1   the traditional or *Ribbans* approach, with the judge treating any racial motive as an aggravating feature when sentencing;

2   the jury determining a racial motive, with a longer sentence applying if proven;

3   the jury determining racial hostility, with a longer sentence applying if proven;

4   the penalising of crime that occurs because of the race of the victim – this being established by utilising a 'but for the race of the victim' approach, with a longer sentence applying if proven.

In effect the government – due to concerns that option 1 was not working effectively – have taken a form of compromise, by combining options 1, 2 and 3. The combined model – found in the Crime and Disorder Act 1998 – places a Court under a statutory duty to treat as an aggravating feature crime that involves racial hostility, or there is evidence of such motivation. What is more, the legislation introduces a new concept of additional racial hostility offences with regards to assault and/or harassment, with enhanced sentencing where guilt is proven beyond reasonable doubt.

This new legislation appears to show tremendous potential for tackling militant racism, with the enhanced sentencing policy likely to demonstrate that racist crime is unacceptable and that those who commit such acts can expect to be dealt with harshly by the courts.

However, this combination does present a worrying feature. Indeed, as welcome as this toughening up on racist crime may be, it is important to reflect that the anti-racist net may be cast too wide. This applies because a demonstration of racial hostility is likely to catch a person who may not possess a racial motive, but – possibly instinctively – have used racist language to hurt their victim even further. Whatever the value of enhanced sentencing for those who commit racist crimes, it seems harsh to send someone to prison as a racist criminal, when they may not have possessed a racial motive. For example, if we assume no racial motive exists, and D argues with V (who happens to be black) over support for a football team, punching and abusing him. It seems unfair that D could serve a much longer period in prison if he used the words 'You black pig' than he would if he used the words 'You fat pig'.

Another problem, with the UK/British legislative approach, is that plea-bargaining seems an inevitable outcome as defendants may play the system by opting to plead guilty to the basic offence in the expectation that the racial hostility element will be dropped. This could be overcome by the Crown Prosecution Service refusing to enter into plea-bargains, but this seems a little like resisting an incoming tide. To this end, it seems disappointing that the tried and tested 'but for the race of the victim approach' was not adopted, since a court could decide this issue, in all inter-racial cases, thereby preventing plea-bargaining.

This 'but for' approach also has the advantage that it can be applied without the complexities of determining a motive. It has been tried and tested, operating with simplicity in direct discrimination cases. Further, it is not quite so restrictive as the racial hostility approach, since it enables a jury to consider the wider circumstances of the case when deciding if the offence would have occurred but for the race of the victim. After all this is the very definition of a racial offence – if the offence would have happened irrespective of the race of the victim then it cannot be a racial offence.

Notes

1   William Wilson, *Criminal Law*, Longman, 1998, concluding comments to the chapter 'Punishment', p. 57. In this chapter Wilson examines retributive and utilitarian theories of punishment.
2   The term 'rules' here is referring to laws. But it is also synonymous with the term 'norm'. See the reference to 'norm' in the *Oxford Thesaurus*, Oxford University Press, 1991. This usage also seems consistent with that applied by Wilson.
3   The example which Clarkson and Keating give is that a desire (motive) to help the poor might cause me to steal in order to feed them: this motive would be ignored by the law: I would clearly have an intent to steal and would be convicted of theft.
4   Wilson (op. cit., p. 63) argues: 'Criminal liability typically hangs upon the establishment of some prohibited conduct, usually an act but exceptionally an omission, together with an accompanying, and concurrent, mental attitude. The former is known as *actus reus*, the latter as *mens rea*'.
5   Smith and Hogan, *Criminal Law*, 6th edn, Butterworths, 1988, pp. 78–9.
6   Example: it could amount to blackmail if I threatened to expose A to the authorities unless he makes a charitable donation. I may not be liable if my motive was simply to compensate

the charity for say some improper business practices conducted by A. Thus, in cases of blackmail, much depends upon the facts – with both fact and motive relevant issues to be taken into account.

7   *Racial Attacks and Harassment*, Third Report, Vol. 1, Session 1993–94, para. 80.

8   *Chaplinsky v New Hampshire* (1942) 313 US 568 at 572, per Murphy J.

9   *The Times Law Reports*, 25 November 1994.

10 Pursuant to section 36 of the Criminal Justice Act 1988.

11 When asked by Mr Harris 'What is the problem?', the defendants replied ''Cause you're black'. There is also no other explanation for the crime – no theft, no previous contact etc.

12 Richard Ford, *The Times*, 11 April 1995. Also, case report as supplied by the Office of the Lord Chief Justice.

13 Pre-trial publicity suggested a racially motivated attack, though the prosecution did not make such claims.

14 In a case involving an admission of guilt it is generally the case that the accused is sentenced on the basis of the defence presentation – that is unless there are significant differences between defence and prosecution, at which point a Newton Hearing will take place.

15 In the year ending 1997–98 the police recorded 13,878 racial incidents (Source: *Statistics on Race and the Criminal Justice System*, Home Office, December 1998).

16 Paragraphs 6 and 7 of the Home Affairs Select Committee Report, *Racial Attacks and Harassment*, HMSO, 1994. See also Peter Jepson, 'The Definition of a Racial Incident', [1998] *NLJ* 1838. In this article, I argue that the ACPO definition needs to be changed so that the police look for racial hostility rather than racial motivation – i.e. so as to comply with the requirements of the Crime and Disorder Act 1998. The MacPherson Report (published 15 February 1999) recommended that a racial incident should be redefined to be 'a racist incident is any incident which is perceived to be racist by the victim or any other person'. This recommendation has been accepted by the Home Secretary who has undertaken to ensure that the new definition is universally adopted by the police, local government and other relevant agencies (see *Stephen Lawrence Inquiry: Home Secretary's Action Plan*, Home Office, March 1999).

17 This is alarming, given that the police and CPS are working to the same ACPO definition and working with essentially the same facts. It seems strange that the police files should not indicate a racial element in such a large number of cases. One explanation given is that the police simply fail to tick an appropriate box on a referral form! Whatever the merit, or otherwise, of this explanation it is clear such differences give ammunition to the chorus of claims that the police are unsympathetic to racist crime.

18 Of the 182 defendants, 26 had proceedings dropped or discontinued on public interest grounds.

19 In the year 1996–97 there were 13,151 racial incidents recorded by the police.

20 It is important to recognise that the interpretation put on the CPS statistics is not precise and is prone to difficulties in terms of accuracy of data. For example, some of the 2.3 per cent of increased penalty cases may not come from the pool of 13,151 police-reported racial incidents – this being due to the CPS disagreeing with the police on what constitutes a racial incident in 66 per cent of cases?

21 *Racial Violence and Harassment – A Consultation Document*, Home Office, September 1997.

22 Section 82(2).

23 That is the basic offences without the racial motivation or hostility.

24 As per Section 28 of the Crime and Disorder Act 1998.
25 Racial group is determined, as per Section 28(2), by reference to race, colour, nationality (including citizenship) or ethnic or national origins.
26 Section 28(3).
27 Which provides the irony that the government has sought to ensure that racial hostility displayed in relation to any crime can result in an enhanced sentence. The only exception to this being the crime of stirring up racial hatred, which remains at a fine and/or imprisonment of up to a maximum of two years. On the 5 January 1999 the Home Office confirmed that the government were reviewing the level of sentencing associated with these Part III Public Order offences so as to rectify this situation. The Home Office indicated that the comments of Judge George Bathurst Norman, expressed while sentencing Atkinson in the case concerning 'The Stormer' (see 'Nazi Cowards Terrorised Frank Bruno's Mother', *Searchlight*, October 1997), that 'Parliament has fixed the maximum penalty for this type of offence as two years. It may be that Parliament should look again at the activities such as yours and reconsider whether the maximum sentence is sufficient – because in my opinion it is not' has resulted in a review of the maximum sentence.
28 For a discussion on the difference between racial motivation and hostility see below in this chapter. See also Peter Jepson, 'The Definition of a Racial Incident', [1998] *NLJ* 1838.
29 Not all cases that go to the Crown Court involve a jury. For example, if the defendant pleads guilty there is no need for a jury, but the case may still need to be heard in the Crown Court due to the level of sentencing.
30 'Racial harassment alarm or distress' under Section 31(1)(c) of the Crime and Disorder Act 1998 can be determined in the Magistrates Court due to a maximum sentence of a Level 4 fine maximum of £5,000.
31 This should apply even in cases where the minimal criminal damage threshold of £5,000 means that the case can be held in the Magistrates Court. This is because Section 82(2(a) of the Crime and Disorder Act 1998 places the Court under a statutory duty to treat crime that displays racial motive and/or hostility as 'aggravating' and a factor that increases the seriousness of the offence. See Peter Jepson, *Tackling Militant Racism* (15 August 1998), http://www.peterjepson.com
32 This does not mean that there will fewer appeals – it certainly seems likely, at least for the first few years after introduction, that there could be an influx of appeals from defendants who believe that the judge has used his discretion harshly in determining an appropriate sentence.
33 There was also an important issue that the defendant had not been cross-examined over the racist motive. This is of fundamental importance since it goes to the root of the principles of natural justice. Therefore it is reasonable to accept that the *Leaney* appeal may well have been successful on these grounds alone.
34 Section 28(1)(b).
35 Something Lord Taylor argued existed in *Ribbans* but he did not consider existed in *Leaney*.
36 Section 28(1a).
37 [1993] Crim LR 300.
38 Indeed a simple illustration of this point is that should Tom (an indigenous white man) punching Muhammad and say – 'take that you black bastard' he would be clearly guilty of demonstrating racial hostility. This would apply even if the motive for the attack were not racial – but jealousy, with Muhammad being sexually friendly with Tom's wife. For a

more detailed analysis of this point see Peter Jepson, 'The Definition of a Racial Incident', [1998] *NLJ* 1838.

39   Ivan Hare (1997), 'Legislating Against Hate – The Legal Response to Bias Crimes', *Oxford Journal of Legal Studies*, Vol. 17, p. 430. Ivan Hare is a Fellow of Trinity College, Cambridge.

40   Under Section 28(1b) of the Crime and Disorder Bill.

41   Under Section 28(1a).

42   Under the legislation this is defined as race, colour, nationality (including citizenship) or ethnic or national origins.

43   The may deal with race, gender, religion, gays and lesbians etc. See Ivan Hare, *op. cit.*, p. 414.

44   Ian Loveland, 'Hate Crimes and the First Amendment', *Public Law* [1994] 174.

45   See generally Marc L. Fleischauer, comment, 'Teeth for a Paper Tiger: A Proposal to Add Enforceability to Florida's Hate Crimes Act', 17 *Fla St. U.L. Rev* 697 [1990]. Also, see Note, 'Combating Racial Violence A Legislative Proposal', 101 *Harv L. Rev* 1270 (1990).

46   James Morsch, 'The Problem of Motive in Hate Crimes: The argument against presumptions of racial motivation', *The Journal of Criminal Law and Criminology* [1992] Vol. 82, p. 659.

47   485 NW 2nd 807 (Wis 1992), cert granted, 61 USLW 3435 (US 14 December 1992) (No. 92–415). For a resume on this case see Malik, 'Wisconsin Burning: Sentence Enhancement and the Freedom to Express Hate', *KCLJ* 6 (1995-6) 139.

48   The intended victim is useful in cases such as criminal damage, where the victim may be the landlord whose property is damages, but the intended victim is the tenant who may be attacked because of his/her race.

49   [1990] IRLR 288.

50   [1991] IRLR 513.

51   [1947] 2 All ER 372.

52   [1955] 2 QB 600.

53   [1955] 39 Cr App Rep 72.

54   [1951] P35 at p36-7. [1950] 2 All ER 458. This passage has frequently met with judicial approval. For example see *Blyth v Blyth* [1966] AC 643 at 673.

55   *R v Wood* (1911) 7 Cr. App Rep 56.

56   It seems that consideration was given to including a proviso in the legislation that places the Crown Prosecution Service under a statutory duty to pursue racial charges where the evidence so justifies. This would have had the effect of ensuring that plea-bargaining is not driven by financial matters, but this approach was abandoned after the CPS gave to the Minister an assurance that they were fully committed to pursuing racial charges. For a discussion of this area see Peter Jepson, *Tackling Militant Racism* (15 August 1998), http://homepages.nationwiseisp.net/~jepson/militant.htm. See also David Wolchover and Anthony Heaton Armstrong, 'New Labour's Attack on Trial by Jury', [1998] *NLJ* 1613, who argue that financial pressures have led to a government consultation paper – 'Determining Mode of Trial in Either-Way Cases' – on reducing the number of trials by jury.

57   In October 1997, at a joint meeting organised by the Society of Labour Lawyers and the Society of Black Lawyers, Mike O'Brien MP – Home Office Minister – accepted that these racial crime cases will likely be heard in Crown Courts. He defended this decision on the basis that enhanced penalties are an important symbol that society will not tolerate racial violence.

58 Part 1 of the Criminal Justice Act 1991 indicates that having heard the evidence in a case the magistrates may commit the case to the Crown Court if they take the view that the offence is so serious that a greater punishment should be inflicted than they have the power to impose.

59 See CPS Annual Report for 1996–97.

60 Riley and Vennard, *Triable-Either-Way Crown Court or Magistrates' Court*, Home Office Research Study No. 98, HMSO, 1988, p. 20. To same effect see Hedderman and Moxon, *Magistrates' Court or Crown Courts? Mode of trial decision and sentencing*, Home Office Research Study No. 125, HMSO, 1992, pp. 22–4.

61 Report Cm 2263 HMSO.

62 This was recognised in the MacPherson Report, which recommended that the CPS and Counsel should ensure that no-plea-bargaining should ever be allowed to exclude evidence of racial motivation. Note, however that this recommendation does not rule out plea-bargaining.

63 Possibly, if a judge were to be made part of the plea-bargaining process he could ensure that he used his discretion to impose a harsh sentence for crimes that display a racial element within the basic offence parameters. However, not only are judges excluded from any plea-bargaining process in the UK/Britain, this seems incompatible with the intent behind the Crime and Disorder Act 1998 since any racial hostility/motive will not have been established by a jury or a guilty plea.

64 Section 29 assault (consisting of GBH, ABH and common assault); Section 30, criminal damage; Section 31, public order offences; Section 32, harassment.

8   Conclusion

During the period I have been researching and writing this book there have been significant changes to British laws that are capable of tackling racist crime. Indeed, such has been the pace of change, since the General Election of 1997, it has been impossible to quantify and fully assess the value of the legislative change.

Significant and Radical Reform

For example, the Crime and Disorder Act 1998 seems capable of having a significant impact with regards to tackling militant racism.[1] As I display in chapter 7, those committing racially aggravated offences can now expect a long prison sentence should they be found guilty of racist crime. Indeed, the changes are not minimal but significant. By way of illustration, a person found guilty of committing a common assault could face up to six months imprisonment. By comparison, if additional racial charges are brought, and the court determines that at the time of committing the basic offence racial hostility was demonstrated, then a sentence of up to two years could be applicable for racial common assault. What is more, these radical changes do not apply to just common assault, but to a whole range of offences associated with violence.[2] Section 82 of the Crime and Disorder Act 1998 requires a Judge in determining sentence in relation to *any* offence, to treat racial hostility – demonstrated at the time of committing the basic offence, as an aggravating feature that increases the seriousness of the offence and therefore the sentence. Further, as a result of Section 82 (2)(b) of the Crime and Disorder Act 1998, a judge is now under a statutory duty to state in open court that the offence was so aggravated.

While the Crime and Disorder Act 1998 will inevitably make it more difficult for militant racists, its success is dependent upon the police identifying a racial incident, arresting and charging suspects and passing appropriate racial details to the Crown Prosecution Service. As the case of Stephen Lawrence has shown, there does exist a lack of confidence in the ability of the police to identify racial incidents and it certainly does not help that they are currently working to a 1986 ACPO guideline definition of a racial incident which is inconsistent with the law as it now stands. As I argued within chapter 7, in order to fulfil the potential of the Crime and Disorder Act 1998, it is important that the police move away from this procedural requirement to look for racial motivation and start looking instead for racial hostility. There is a distinction between racial motivation and racial hostility, with the law now requiring evidence of racial hostility in order to determine racial aggravation. It, therefore, makes little sense for the police to be looking for racial motivation – especially since it is much more difficult to identify than the more objective criteria available in relation to racial hostility.[3] However, the means of rectifying this anomaly is procedural rather than legislative, and it does seem that following an assessment of the findings of the Stephen Lawrence Public Inquiry the police will be required to make changes to the ACPO guidelines.[4]

As the Crime and Disorder Act 1998 demonstrates, almost every criminal offence can now result in a longer sentence where racial hostility is associated with the basic offence. Despite such dramatic legal changes, there have recently been calls for yet more legislation to tackle racist crime. For example, in the alternative Christmas Day message of 1998 the Stephen Lawrence Family called for more crimes to tackle racism, in particular they called for a new offence of 'racist murder'. This plea was made, presumably on the basis that to murder on the grounds of racial malice should be considered as more serious than to murder on the grounds of malice? The justification for such an approach seems to be based upon that which exists for tackling racially-aggravated crime. It is a desire to send out a symbolic message that says: 'any crime motivated by racial hostility is unacceptable'. Indeed, in the words of the Home Office consultative document,[5] it is to 'send a strong message to society at large that such racist crime is unacceptable and that it will be dealt with very seriously by the police and the courts'. Despite such an argument, there is a danger that to introduce laws to establish a new offence of 'racist murder' could lead to a political backlash, with militant racists likely to make political capital by arguing that this new law is evidence of a government that values a black person's life more than that of a white person. While in reality this would be untrue, since a black person could also face prosecution for a racist murder of a white victim, it seems inevitable that such legislative change would be a hot political potato. Possibly, the strongest argument against establishing a new offence of 'racist murder' comes from the fact that there appears to be no logical level of sentencing that would justify such a change. In the case of common assault and racial common assault the deterrent difference in sentencing level is six months to two years.[6] Murder already carries a life sentence and the only practical means of increasing such a sentence would be to require a life sentence that expresses a specific minimum served.[7] This approach can already be taken under the Crime and Disorder Act 1998, with a judge being statutorily bound to treat racial hostility as an aggravating feature which increases the seriousness of the basic offence. Accordingly a judge, in passing sentence in relation to a murder that displays racial hostility, already has powers to make a recommendation that determines a minimum that should be served. For such minimal sentence recommendations to become practice, a guideline or direction from the Lord Chief Justice is all that is necessary.

Do we Need More Laws to Tackle Racist Crime?

This call for new laws to tackle racist crime clearly relates to the first questions I asked in this book – 'Do we need any more laws to tackle racist crime?' The answer from my book is that in Britain we do not need more laws, but we would benefit from amending existing laws so that they can be more effective in tackling militant racism. Indeed, throughout this book I have examined a whole range of existing laws that can tackle militant racism, such is the diversity of these laws that they range from the Criminal Damage Act 1971 to offences under the Malicious Communications Act 1988. Despite such variety, the proposals in this book for legislative change relate almost exclusively to Part III of the Public Order Act 1986. For example, there are strong grounds for amending the Public Order Act 1998 so that person(s)[8] can become criminally liable for not just stirring up racial hatred, but also for stirring up racial discrimination. As I argued in chapter 4, incitement to racial discrimination can lay the foundations for racial hatred, thus a decision to tackle the stirring up of racial discrimination can be justified on the basis of tackling not just crime, but the causes of crime. Indeed, so long as along with these changes there are the necessary prerequisites of 'threat, abuse and insult' this should not be a controversial or problematic legislative reform. Certainly, such legislative change would be entirely consistent with the international obligations of the UK, in relation to the International Convention on the Elimination of All Forms of Racial Discrimination (CERD Convention) and the International Covenant on Civil and Political Rights (ICCPR).[9]

   A number of other changes are also needed to the Public Order Act 1986. A small but illustrative example comes from the reforms of the Crime and

Disorder Act 1998. As I have already shown in this chapter, Section 82(1) requires a court to treat racial aggravation as an aggravating factor that increases the seriousness of any offence. This expressly applies to all forms of criminal offence, with the exception of that referred to under sections 29 and 32 of the Crime and Disorder Act 1998 and also (indirectly) sections 18–23 of the Public Order Act 1986. This indirect reference applies because these public order offences are themselves racial offences and the double jeopardy principle means that it would be unjust for a judge to increase sentence due to racial aggravation – when race is already a key element of the basic offence. Although the Home Office may well accept that in light of the increased tariff for racial offences there is a need to increase the level of sentence from the current maximum of two years imprisonment.

One classic example of another necessary change to the Public Order Act 1986 relates to religious terminology that may stir up racial hatred (discrimination). As I show in chapter 4, under current public order laws a militant racist can stir up racial hatred through the use of 'threatening, abusive or insulting words', while avoiding prosecution because he applies religious terminology rather than racial. Indeed, although it is legally explicable, it seems almost nonsensical that I could produce a leaflet that said 'Attack a Muslim for Christmas' and it could not amount to the offence of stirring up of racial hatred, but if I said 'Attack a Sikh for Christmas' it would. Such loopholes that derive from legislative boundaries only serve to undermine the value of British race law, and it is clear that change in this area is long overdue.[10]

Tackling Racial Offence

While these limited changes would certainly tidy up the law, they are not significant in the sense of widening the scope of laws that tackle militant racism. They would, as is the aim of this book, make it more difficult for a militant racist to carry out his activities, but they still make no attempt to deal with the distribution of material that may be 'racially offensive' and stir up racial discrimination or hatred.

Indeed, while I acknowledged from the outset that such 'racially offensive' materials may not be directly responsible for any increase of racist crime in localities, I have accepted the community representative arguments that indirectly such material raises racial tensions which at times results in an increase in racial conflict. Accordingly, I have assessed a variety of racist materials that have been circulated[11] and reached the conclusion that a great deal of the material (that displays a person who can be identified as a publisher) is generally designed to avoid prosecution because it is neither 'threatening, abusive and/or insulting', despite the fact that an intent or likelihood exists that it would stir up racial hatred. Even changing that law, so that the stirring up of racial discrimination is an offence, would not dramatically adjust matters since the material is generally not clearly 'threatening, abusive or insulting'. Thus, I came to the conclusion that, adding the term 'racial offence' to the prerequisites would have the potential for making it almost impossible for militant racists to produce material that stirs up racial discrimination/hatred. While such a result may on face value seem desirable – since it would help fulfil my aim of tackling not just the crime, but the causes of racist crime – the problem with this approach is that it may undermine the concept of freedom of expression and could therefore be in danger of being found to be incompatible with the Convention on Human Rights.

Compatibility with the Convention on Human Rights

Despite this, the proposal to add the term 'racial offence' to the prerequisites for a Part III Public Order Act 1986 prosecution is a central feature of this book. However, as I explain in chapter 5, I do not lose sight of the fact that incompatibility with the 'Convention on Human Rights' should be avoided at all costs. This derives from both a desire to respect human rights and because, as per the Human Rights Act 1998, a minister is now statutorily bound to inform the House of Commons, in writing, if his Bill is incompatible with the Convention on Human Rights. The probable consequences of which being, that any Bill that is openly declared as being incompatible may still become law, but it can be expected to have an exceedingly troublesome passage through Parliament. To this extent, I have sought to ensure that the proposals to tackle 'racially offensive' material are reasonably compatible with the Convention on Human Rights, or at least are not incompatible.

The approach I have taken is to cushion the 'incompatibility' impact the proposals would have on tackling 'racially offensive' material. I have done this by recognising the conflict between freedom of expression and the need to tackle 'racially offensive' material and proposing a form of legislative compromise. This consisting of 'counter-message legislation' which will allow publication of words that are 'racially offensive', so long as associated with the offending words is a counter-message that warns of the possible racial content and displays a message consistent with the government's anti-racist policy of saying 'No to Racism'.[12] Logically, any person who produces material that is 'racially offensive', and which does not display a counter-message, could face prosecution. The idea being that they would, if found guilty, be penalised on the same basis as applies to material that is 'threatening, abusive or insulting' and may stir up racial hatred (discrimination).[13]

Naturally, as in determining the issue of whether material is 'threatening, abusive or insulting', there will always be a question of fact as to whether any words used can be considered to be 'racially offensive'. Obviously, the courts must be the final arbitrators of such issues, with my proposals arguing that this should be a question of a combination of statutory interpretation with regards to 'race' and applying a 'ordinary usage – natural meaning – methodology' with regards to 'offence'.[14] However, in order to help ameliorate any interpretative difficulties, I have indicated that there should be a *bona fide* defence – in relation to the *mens rea* – if any defendant could show that he sought advice from a body like the Commission for Racial Equality and it advised that a counter-message was not necessary due to the innocuous nature of the material.

The counter-message principle can equally be applied to speech, though of course the factual evidence may be more problematic in relation to proof – both in terms of the 'racial offence' of the material and of the nature of any counter-message expressed. As in all such situations, the necessary proof required must be that of proof beyond reasonable doubt, though once that the prosecution have established a *prima facie* case of 'racial offence' – the onus will inevitably fall upon the defendant to show that a *bona fide* counter-message was displayed or given.

While in practice these proposals can work, the big question about these counter-message proposals is – Are they incompatible with the Convention on Human Rights? As I argued in chapter 5, Article 10 of the Convention on Human Rights provides for freedom of expression, which includes not just the right of the expresser, but also of the receiver of the expression. It is thereby argued that the counter-message proposals enhance freedom of expression since they do not deny the right of the expresser to articulate 'racially offensive' views, while enhancing the rights of the receiver by effectively alerting him to the fact that the material may be 'racially offensive'.

The expresser may feel aggrieved that the counter-message may contradict some of his words, but all that it does is give an alternative view for the reader to consider. Possibly more importantly, the proposals give the receiver a choice. He can tell from the counter-message that the material may be 'racially offensive', so he is able to choose whether to read, and risk offence, or ignore the material. In effect, the counter-message acts as a form of government health warning, without denying the freedom of expression.

To this extent, it must be considered that the proposals are not incompatible with the Convention on Human Rights. However, any such doubt may be removed by the decisions of the ECHR Commission who have generally declined to facilitate applicants who seek to utilise Article 10 to develop racist expression. Indeed, they have interpreted the ECHR in a way consistent with Article 14, so that a person can only secure his/her right of freedom of expression, under the ECHR, if s/he displays no discrimination on grounds of sex, race, colour, national origin etc. This *Glimmerveen* approach[15] of the Commission was approved by the European Court of Human Rights in the case of *Jersild v Denmark*.[16] Though, as I pointed out in chapter 5, it is important to reflect when considering the contradiction between Article 10 and 14 (and any other Article), that the issue of proportionality is always a criterion that weighs in the mind of the Court of Human Rights.

The Twofold Advantage of the Counter-Message Proposals

Possibly, the counter-message proposals can be criticised for giving legislative form and authority to 'racially offensive' material. However, the facts are that such material is already lawful under existing legislation and the changes would still outlaw existing racist material that is 'threatening, abusive and/or insulting' and which stirs up racial hatred. In fact, I am proposing no similar counter-message defence in relation to this kind of material, understanding that this should remain a criminal offence. Rather, the idea is to extend the parameters of the Public Order Act 1986 so as to punish those who produce 'racially offensive' material that stirs up racial discrimination/hatred unless they display a counter-message. The specific advantage of the counter-message is twofold, with a possible third dimension. First it is educational, in that it educates both the author and the reader that material which is 'racially offensive' is undesirable and that society does not approve of such terminology. Secondly, it provides the receiver with a choice. He can read and risk being offended, or turn his back on material which may be inconsistent with a 'general will' of our civilised society – which now accepts, through the ratio of international covenants, that people should be treated equally irrespective of their race. The possible third dimension is that the very existence of the counter-message may undermine support for politically organised racist activity, with volunteer activists likely to be reluctant to walk the streets to deliver material which displays a message rejecting racism.

A Catholic priest[17] once expressed to me that, in his view, racism exists in all of us – 'the key is how that racism is managed'. The proposals in this book are not, and could never be, a magical solution in relation to the problems of racial intolerance that exists within society. Indeed, the proposals simply improve the anti-racist laws of the Britain and therefore make management of militant racist activity more effective. They do this, by making it more difficult for militant racist to stir up racial discrimination and or hatred.

Equally importantly, through a form of educational process, the counter-message proposals aim to alert our inner consciousness into recognising that we all need to manage any particular inner feelings of racism that we may possess. Indeed, the proposals seek to help us all to recognise a 'general will' of society that says 'No to racism'.

Notes

1   'Militant racism' was defined in chapter 1 as 'combative and aggressive action, or activity, in support of a cause which signifies and promotes antagonism/hostility towards people of other races'.

2   See chapter 7. Also see Peter Jepson, 'The Definition of a Racial Incident', [1998] *NLJ* 1838.

3   *Ibid.*

4   The then Home Secretary accepted a recommendation of the MacPherson Report that the definition of a racial incident should be changed to 'a racist incident is any incident which is perceived to be racist by the victim or any other person'. See *Stephen Lawrence Inquiry: Home Secretary's Action Plan*, Home Office, March 1999. There is a danger that the proposed definition is too subjective and will result in many more incidents being classed as racial. There is a danger this could undermine confidence in the judicial process, since only a small percentage of these racial incidents will result in a prosecution for racial hostility. An alternative, and narrower approach, is to establish a racial incident which is based upon 'racial hostility' – this is more objectively determined and would provide consistency with the racially aggravated offences established in the Crime and Disorder Act 1998. For a discussion on this area and issues associated with a racial motive in the Stephen Lawrence case, see Peter Jepson, 'Was Stephen Lawrence's Murder Racially Motivated', http://www.peterjepson.com, 10 June 1999.

5   *Racial Violence and Harassment – A Consultative Document*, Home Office, September 1997.

6   This was discussed in chapter 7.

7   In *Sentencing and Criminal Justice* (p. 49) Andrew Ashworth advises that a judge makes a recommendation as to a minimum life sentence served in fewer than 10 per cent of cases. In such cases the judge notes down the detention 'necessary to meet the requirements of retribution and deterrence'.

8   The term 'persons' can be interpreted to include individuals and organisations (see chapter 5).

9   See chapter 4.
10   See discussion in chapter 4. Also, see Peter Jepson, *Tackling Religious Terminology that Stirs up Racial Hatred*, http://www.peterjepson.com, 13 January 1999.
11   See chapter 3.
12   The exact nature of the counter-message in terms of its size, positioning etc. has not been considered, but a simple clause that requires that a counter-message must be prominently displayed on the face of any racially offensive material, or preceding any racially offensive speech may suffice.
13   See chapter 5.
14   See chapter 5 for consideration of this matter.
15   Case numbers 8348 and 8406/78 – see also the section entitled 'European Convention for the Protection of Human Rights' in chapter 5 and the section 'Compatibility with the Convention on Human Rights'.
16   19 ECHR 1, at p. 28 – the *Jersild* case involves the freedom of the press and media to report racist issues and will be discussed in more detail later in this chapter under 'Press Freedom'.
17   Canon Gerry Burke, Parish Priest of St Lawrence of Feltham.

Bibliography

Cases

Re HK [1967] 1 All ER 226.

R v Bow Street Stipendiary Magistrate ex pa South Coast Shipping Co. Ltd [1993] 1 All ER 219.

R v Chief Metropolitan Stipendiary Magistrate, ex parte Choudhary [1991] 1 All ER 306, [1990] 3 WLR 986 Queen's Bench Divisional Court.

R v Clarke (No. 2) [1964] 2 QB 315.

R v Clarke [1992] 13 Cr.App.R.(S).640.

R v Cole (and others) [1993] Crim L.R. 300.

R v Courts [1987] 1 All ER 120 CA; [1988] 2 All ER 120 HL.

R v DPP ex parte London Borough of Merton – Divisional Court case number: CPS [CO/3019/1998.

R v East Sussex County Council ex parte Tandy – case report [1998] *NLJ* 781.

R v Edwards [1983] 5 Cr App R (S) 145.

R v Gloucestershire CC and the Secretary of State ex parte Barry (H of L) [1997] 2 All ER 1.

R v Harrow LBC ex parte D [1989] 3 WLR 1239.

R v Hepworth and Fearnley [1955] 2 QB 600.

R v Home Office ex pa Ruddock and others [1987] 2 All ER 518.

R v Leaney (*The Times*, 11 April 1995). Case report supplied by the office of the Lord Chief Justice.

R v Maloney [1985] 1 All ER 1025.

R v Martagh and Kennedy [1955] 39 Cr. App Rep 56.

R v Miller [1954] 2 QB 282.

R v Minister of Defence ex parte Smith [1995] IRLR 585.

R v MOD ex parte Smith and Grady [1996] IRLR 100.

R v Norfolk CC ex parte M [1989] 2 All ER 359.

R v Phillips – Newcastle Magistrates Court (*The Times*, 12 December 1991).

R v Rankin and Irvine [1993] 14 Cr.App.R.(S).636.

R v Ribbans, Duggan and Ridley (*Times Law Reports*, 25 November 1994).

R v Secretary of State for the Home Department (ex parte Sandhu) [1983] 3 CMLR 131 (*The Times*, 10 May 1995).

R v Secretary of State for the Home Department (ex parte Brind) [1991] 1 All ER 720

R v Spratt (*The Times*, 14 May 1990).

R v Stamford [1972] 2 All ER 727.

R v Venna [1976] QB 421 CA. Criminal Division [1975] 3 All ER 788.

R v Wood (1911) 7 Cr. App Rep 56.

A-G ex rel. Tilley v Wandsworth LBC [1981] 1 WLR 854.

Lodge v DPP (*The Times*, 26 October 1988).

London and Blackwell Railway Co. v Cross [1886] 31 ChD 354.

London Borough of Camden v McIntyre (see *Making the Law Work Against Racial Harassment*, Report of the Legal Action Group Research Project, 1990).

London Borough of Merton v Edmonds and Tyndall, case no. CO/1711/92, Divisional Court 28 June 1993.

Lowdens v Keaney [1903] 2 IR 82.

Malik v Bertram Personnel Group [1990] Case No: 4343/90.

Mandla v Dowell Lee [1983] IRLR 209 HL.

Marleasing SA v La Comercial Internacional de Alimentacion [1990] SA 106/89.

Marshall v Southampton and West Hampshire Health Authority [1986] 152/84.

Meade v Haringey LBC [1979] ICR 494.

Merkur Island Shipping Corp v Laughton [1982] IRLR 218 HL.

Middlebrook Mushrooms v TGWU [1993] IRLR 232 CA.

Miller v Jackson [1977] QB 966 CA.

Miller v Minister of State of Pensions [1947] 2 All ER 372.

Morson v Netherlands (case nos 35 and 36/82).

Muller v Switzerland [1988] A 133.

Nold v Commission Case 4/73 [1974] ECR 491.

Otto-Preminger-Institut v Austria [1994] A 295–A.

P & S v Cornwall County Council C–13/94.

Padfield v Minister of Agriculture, Fisheries and Food [1988] AC 997, HL.

Proctor v Bailey (1889) 42 ChD 390.

Seaward v Patterson [1897] 1 Ch 545.

Secretary of State for Education v MB Tameside [1976] 3 All ER 665 HL.

Seide v Gillette Industrial Ltd [1980] IRLR 427.

Stevens v UK [1986] 11674/85, 46 DR 245.

T v Belgium – ECHR Case 9777/82.

The Sunday Times Case [1979] 2 EHRR 245.

Thomas v NUM (South Wales) [1985] 2 All ER 1.

Tod-Heatley v Benham [1888] 40 ChD 80.

Variola Spa v Amministrazione Italiano delle Finanze [1973] 34/73.

Vogt v Germany – Case No 7/1994/454/535.

Wandsworth LBC v Winder [1985] AC 461.

Webb v EMO Air Cargo (UK) Ltd [1993] IRLR 27. HL.

Webster v Southwark London Borough Council [1983] QB 698.

West Midlands Passenger Transport Executive v Singh [1988] ICR 614, IRLR 186.

Wheeler v Leicester City Council [1985] 2 All ER 1106, HL.

Wilson v Pringle [1986] 2 All ER 440 CA. Civil Division.

Wisconsin v Mitchell 485 NW 2nd 807 (Wis 1991), cert granted, 61 USLW 3435 (US Dec 14 1992) (No 92–415).

X v Federal Republic of Germany – ECHR Case 92351/81.

X v Italy – ECHR Case 6741/74.

Yates v Morris [1950] 2 All ER 577.

Z Ltd A–Z and AA–LL [1982] QB 558 (Court of Appeal).

Statutes

Accessories and Abettors Act 1861.
Broadcasting Act 1981.
Children Act 1989.
Chronically Sick and Disabled Persons Act 1970.
Contempt of Court Act 1981.
Crime and Disorder Act 1998.
Criminal Damage Act 1971.
Criminal Justice Act 1988.
Criminal Justice and Public Act 1994.
Disability Discrimination Act 1995.
Education Act 1944.
European Communities Act 1972.
European Communities (Amendment) Act 1993.
Football (Offences) Act 1991.
Highways Act 1980.
Housing Act 1985.
Human Rights Act 1998.
Interpretation Act 1978.
Local Government Act 1972.
Malicious Communications Act 1988.
Offences Against the Persons Act 1861.
Post Office Act 1953.
Prevention from Eviction Act 1977.
Prevention to Religious Hatred (Northern Ireland) Act 1970.
Protection from Harassment Act 1997.
Protection of Children Act 1978.
Prosecution of Offences Act 1985.
Public Order Act 1936.
Public Order Act 1986.
Public Order (Northern Ireland) Act 1987.
Race Relations Act 1976.
Representation of the Peoples Act 1983.
Sex Discrimination Act 1975.
The Tobacco Products Labelling (Safety) Regulations 1991.
Trade Union and Labour Relations (Consolidation) Act 1992.

Equal Treatment Directive 76/207.
European Convention on Human Rights.
International Covenant on Civil and Political Rights.
Proposal for a European Parliament and Council Directive on Certain Legal Aspects of Electronic Commerce in the Internal Market (unofficial text presented by the Commission 18-11-1998).
Rules of the Supreme Court – Order 52.
The International Covenant on the Elimination of All Forms of Religious Intolerance.
The International Convention on the Elimination of All Forms of Discrimination (CERD).

The Treaty on European Union 1993 (Maastricht Treaty).
The Universal Declaration on Human Rights.
Treaty of Rome.

Books

Abel, Richard, *Speech and Respect*, Sweet & Maxwell, 1994.
Ashjorn Eide et al., *The Universal Declaration of Human Rights: A commentary*, Scandinavian University Press, 1992.
Ashworth, Andrew, *Sentencing and Criminal Justice*, Butterworths, 1995.
Aye Maung, N. and Mirlees-Black, C., *Racially Motivated Crime: a British Crime Survey Analysis*, Home Office Research and Planning Paper 82, 1994.
Bailey, S.H., Harris, D.J. and Jones, B.L., *Civil Liberties Cases and Materials*, Butterworths, 1995.
Benewick, Robert, *The Fascist Movement in Britain*, Penguin Press, 1992.
Berlin, Isaiah, *Four Essays on Liberty*, Oxford University Press, 1975.
Bradley, A.W. and Ewing, K.D., *Constitutional and Administrative Law*, Longman, 1993.
Butler, D. and Kavanagh, D., *The British General Election of February 1974*, Macmillan Press, 1974.
Cathcart, Brian, *The Case of Stephen Lawrence*, Viking (Penguin Group), 1999.
Clarkson, C.M.V. and Keating, H.D., *Criminal Law: Text and Materials*, Sweet & Maxwell, 1990.
Coliver, Sandra (ed.), *Striking a Balance: Hate Speech, Freedom of Expression and Non-Discrimination*, Article 19 of the Human Rights Centre of the University of Essex, 1992.
Collini, Stefan, *J.S. Mill 'On Liberty' and Other Writings*, Cambridge University Press, 1989.
Cotterell, R., *The Sociology of Law*, Butterworths, 1992.
Deakin, S. and Morris, G.S., *Labour Law*, Butterworths, 1995.
Devlin, Patrick, *The Enforcement of Morals*, Oxford University Press, 1965.
Dicey, A.V., *The Law of the Constitution*, Macmillan, London 1959.
Dinwiddy, John, *Bentham*, Oxford University Press, 1989.
Dworkin, R.M., *Taking Rights Seriously*, Duckworth, London, 1977.
Dworkin, R.M., *The Philosophy of Law*, Oxford University Press, 1991.
Edwards and Waelde, *Law and The Internet*, Hart Publishing, 1997.
Feldman, D., *Civil Rights and Civil Liberties in England and Wales*, Clarendon Press, 1993.
Ford, Glyn, *Fascist Europe: The Rise of Racism and Xenophobia*, Pluto Press, 1992.
Ford, Glyn, *The Evolution of a European*, Russell Press, 1993.
Gray, John, *Liberalism*, University of Minnesota Press, 1986.
Griffin, Roger, *Fascism*, Oxford University Press, 1995.
Harlow, C. and Rawlings, R., *Law and Administration*, Weidenfeld and Nicolson, 1988.
Harris, D., O'Boyle, M. and Warbrick, C., *Law of the European Convention on Human Rights*, Butterworths, 1995.
Harrison, Ross, *Bentham: A fragment of government*, Cambridge University Press, 1988.
Horspool, Margot, *European Union Law*, Butterworths, 1998.
Jacobs, J.B. and Potter, K., *Hate Crimes: Criminal Law and Identity Politics*, Oxford University Press, 1998.

Kymlicka, Will, *An Introduction to Contemporary Political Philosophy*, Oxford University Press, 1997.

Lawrence, Frederick M., *Punishing Hate-Bias Crime under American Law*, Harvard University Press, 1999.

Lawson-Cruttenden, Timothy and Addison, Neil, *Blackstone's Guide to the Protection from Harassment Act 1997*, Blackstone Press, 1997.

Leng, M., Taylor, R. and Wasik, M., *Blackstone's Guide to the Crime and Disorder Act 1998*, Blackstone Press, 1998.

Lester, A. and Bindman, G., *Race and Law*, Penguin Books, 1972.

Livingstone and Morison, *Law, Society and Social Change*, Dartmouth Publishing Co., 1990.

Lowe, N. and Surfin, B., *Borrie and Lowe – The Law of Contempt*, Butterworths, 1996.

Loveland, Ian, *Constitutional Law: A critical introduction*, Butterworths, 1996.

McLellan, David, *Karl Marx: The Legacy*, BBC, 1983.

Oliver, Dawn, *Government in the United Kingdom*, Open University Press, 1991.

Plamentz, J., *Hobbes: Leviathan*, Fontana Paperbacks, 1963.

Rawlings, H.F., *Law and the Electoral Process*, Sweet & Maxwell, 1988.

Rawls, J., *A Theory of Justice*, Oxford University Press, 1971.

Robertson, Geoffrey, *Freedom, the Individual and the Law*, Penguin Books, 1989.

Rousseau, Jean-Jacques, *The Social Contract and Discourses*, trans. G.D.H. Cole, Everyman's Library, 1913.

Satnam, Virdee, *Racial Violence and Harassment*, Policy Studies Institute, London, 1995.

Shepherd, Robert, *Enoch Powell*, Pimlico, 1997.

Sibbitt, Rae, *The Perpetrators of Racial Harassment and Racial Violence*, Home Office Research Study 176, 1997.

Smith, A.T.H., *The Offences Against Public Order (1986)*, Sweet & Maxwell, 1987.

Smith, J. and Wood, J., *Industrial Law*, Butterworths, 1993.

Smith, J.C. and Hogan, B., *Criminal Law*, Butterworths, 1988.

Stone, R., *Textbook on Civil Liberties*, Blackstones, 1994.

Strauss, L. and Cropsey, J., *History of Political Philosophy*, University of Chicago Press, 1987.

Sumner, W.G., *Folkways*, The Athenaeum Press, 1907.

Tapper, Colin, *Cross on Evidence*, Butterworths, 1990.

Thompson, D., *Political Ideas*, Penguin Press, 1986.

Thornton, Peter, *Public Order Law*, Blackstone Press Ltd, 1997.

Van Dijk and Van Hoof, *Theory and Practice of the European Convention on Human Rights*, Deventer (Netherlands), 1990.

Wade, E.C.S. and Bradley, A.W., *Constitutional and Administrative Law*, Longman, 1993.

Wade, H.W.R., *Constitutional Law*, Oxford University Press, 1988.

Wade, H.W.R., *Administrative Law*, Clarendon Press, Oxford, 1988.

Wadham, J. and Mountfield, H., *Blackstone's Guide to the Human Rights Act 1998*, Blackstone Press, 1999.

Wallace, J. and Mangan, M., *Sex, Laws and Cyber-space*, Henry Holt & Co., 1997.

Wilson, William, *Criminal Law*, Longman Press, 1998.

Articles

'A World of Difference: The International Distribution of Information. The Media and Developing Countries', Garbo, G., UNESCO, 1985.

'Action promised over Internet Racism', *The Times*, 16 September 1998.

'An Organisation's Liability for Racial Harassment', Peter Jepson, http://www.peterjepson.com, 29 September 1998.

'Anti-mosque Campaign Provokes Violence', *Searchlight*, August 1996.

'Anti-racist Groups Defend Rights of the BNP', *The Times*, 29 September 1995.

'Attempt to Block Zundal Fails', *Searchlight*, March 1996.

'Banning Organisations like Combat 18 and the White Wolves', Peter Jepson, http://www.peterjepson.com.

'Black Police Join Forces on Racism', *The Guardian*, 4 April 1995.

'BNP Booklet Calls for Murder of "Race-mixers" ', *Searchlight*, October 1995.

'BNP Keeps Links with Violent Neo-Nazis', *The Guardian*, 26 October 1994.

'BNP "Party Day" Descends into Farce', *Searchlight*, December 1995.

'Bomb Charge Man in Court', *The Guardian*, 4 May 1999.

'Bottling it out in Blackpool, *Searchlight*, September 1995.

'Britain Lags in Battle to Beat Racism says the UN', *Daily Telegraph*, 21 August 1993.

'Britain to take 1000 Refugees a Week', *The Times*, 5 May 1999.

'Britannia Rules the Game?', *Searchlight*, April 1995.

'British American Links', Nick Lowles, *Searchlight*, May 1999.

'By-election Prompts New Call to Ban BNP Candidates', *Hounslow, Feltham and Hanworth Times*, 11 August 1995.

'C18 Terror Spreads', *Searchlight*, April 1995.

'Cafe Society? It's a piece of cake', Adam Barnard, *The Times*, 7 October 1998.

'Call to Tackle Police Prejudice', *Searchlight*, April 1996.

'College Blames Extremists for Religious Riot', *Hounslow, Feltham and Hanworth Times*, 3 January 1995.

'Condon's Apology is not enough, say Lawrences', *The Independent*, 2 October 1998.

'Coroners' Inquests and the Stephen Lawrence Inquiry', [1999] *NLJ* 418.

'Councils Evict Racist Tenants', *Searchlight*, April 1995.

'Councillors Appeal Against Expulsion', *Feltham Chronicle*, 17 October 1996.

'Crawley Mosque Vandalised', *Searchlight*, April 1995.

'CRE Attacks Anti-black Rule for Asylum Seekers', *The Guardian*, 24 November 1995.

'Crime and Disorder ASBOs', Micheal Rowan, [1999] *NLJ* 1051.

Cybersitter: Where do we want you to go today?, Cyber-rights and Cyber-Liberties (UK), http://www.cyber-rights.org.

'Doing the enemy's work', BNP Leader John Tyndall, http://ngwwmall.co/frontier/bnp/, March 1996.

'EC Targets Racism on the Internet', Glyn Ford MEP, *Searchlight*, March 1996.

'Equal Rights for All', Peter Tatchell, [1997] *NLJ* 233.

'Equality, Democracy and the Constitution', Ronald Dworkin (1990), *Albert L. Rev*, 324.

'Fanning the Flames of Hatred', *Searchlight*, September 1998.

'Far-right Football Thugs Engineered Riot over Ulster', *The Times*, 17 February 1998.

'Fast Track Justice', Sein Enright, [1996] *NLJ* 487.

'Fears of Huge Caseload Delay Human Rights Law', *The Times*, 5 May 1999.

'Free Speech Anger over Nurembourg Files Ban', *Practical Internet*, Issue 26, 1999.

'Freedom of Speech in Britain, A Brief Legal Primer', BNP web site, http://www.bnp.net/, 20 September 1997.

'Growing Concern as Nazis Focus on Denmark', *Searchlight*, September 1995.

'Growing up in London's Deep South', *Searchlight*, September 1998.

'Hate Crimes and the First Amendment', Ian Loveland, [1994] *Public Law* 174.

'Hate on the Internet', Louise Bernstein, *Searchlight*, March 1996.

'Homes of Neo-Nazi Members Raided', *The Times*, 11 November 1994.

'How Combat 18 is using Football', *Searchlight*, March 1995.

'Incorporating Human Rights, the Process Begins', Philip Leach, [1997] *NLJ* 1595.

'Internet Nazi quits lost cause', *Searchlight*, August 1996.

'Is Equality a Constitutional Principle?', Professor Jeffrey Jowell, *Current Legal Problems* [1994] 1.

'Israel Planning Ethnic Bomb as Saddam Caves in', *The Sunday Times*, 15 November 1998.

'IWF Says Porn is Increasing', *Practical Internet*, Issue 26, 1999.

'Kew Gardens Fights to block Terminal 5', *Evening Standard*, 11 June 1998.

'Law as an Instrument of Social Change', William E. Evan, *The Sociology of Law: A social-structured perspective*, New York Free Press, 1980.

'Lawrence Inquiry Disappoints', Gerry Gable, *Searchlight*, April 1999.

'Lawyers and Human Rights', John Wadham, [1998] *NLJ* 1667.

'Legislating against Hate. The legal response to bias crimes', Ivan Hare, *Oxford Journal of Legal Studies*, Vol. 17 [1997] 430.

'Love thy Neighbour', Philip Plowden, [1999] *NLJ* 479.

'Magistrates Court or Crown Courts? Mode of trial decision and sentencing', Hedderman and Moxon, Home Office Research Study No. 98, HMSO, 1992.

'Man Charged, Working Alone', *The Guardian*, 3 May 1999.

'McLibel Internet Site Hit by Thousand Worldwide', *Tribune*, 15 March 1996.

'Met Launches Units to Combat Victimisation', *Surrey Comet*, 11 June 1999.

'Millenium Plea for Libraries', *The Guardian*, 21 March 1996.

'Morally Unjust to Evict Families of Racist Children', Peter Jepson, *The Chronicle*, 26 September 1996.

'Natural Porn Killers', Mike McCormack, *.net*, April 1996.

'Nazi Cowards Terrorised Frank Bruno's Mother', *Searchlight*, October 1997.

'Neo-Nazi Group Claims Brixton Bomb', *Searchlight*, May 1999.

'Neo-Nazi Group Admits Bombing', *The Times*, May 1999.

'Net Tackles Racism in Schools', *Education Direct*, Ziff Davis, February, 1999.

'New Labour's Attack on Trial by Jury', David Wolchover and Anthony Heaton-Armstrong, [1998] *NLJ* 1613.

'NF (Nationalistische Front] Grows Stronger in Face of State Ban', *Searchlight*, October 1995.

'Noisy Neighbour Evicted by Council', *Hounslow, Feltham and Hanworth Times*, 19 April 1996.

'Parents Face Eviction over Race Attack by Children', *Feltham Chronicle*, 25 July 1996.

'Playing the Race Card', *Searchlight*, December 1995.

'Police Accused of Failing to Acknowledge Racial Crimes', *The Independent*, 20 October 1998.

'Police Accused of Racist Culture', *The Independent*, 3 August 1998.

'Police Chief Admits to Racism in Ranks', Kathy Morris, *The Independent*, 14 October 1998.

'Police Clear up Rate Falls Despite Budget Increase', *The Times*, 30 January 1997.

'Police Given Pocket Guides on Racial Attacks', *The Times*, 9 October 1998.

'Police Launch New Equality Policy', *Searchlight*, February 1995.

'Porn: the darker side of the Internet', Gervase Webb and Mark Hughes-Norman, *Evening Standard*, 12 April 1999.

'Protection from Discrimination', Geoffrey Bindman, [1988] *NLJ* 1617.

'Race Bombers Strike Again', *The Mail on Sunday*, 25 April 1999.

'Race Discrimination and the Importance of Asking the Right Question', J. Ross (1991), *ILJ*, Vol. 20, No. 3, p. 208.

'Race Unit Reopens Fire Death Inquiry', Jason Bennetto, *The Independent*, 4 November 1998.

'Racial Arrest Victim Wins Police Damages', *The Times*, 17 March 1995.

'Racial Violence and Harassment in Europe', Robin Oakley, Council of Europe, 1992.

'Racism in Football Alive and Kicking', *Searchlight*, November 1997.

'Racist Child Outlaws', *Hounslow, Feltham and Hanworth Times*, 12 January 1996.

'Racist Police Officer Suspended', *Searchlight*, November 1995.

'Right-wing Extremism, Racism or Youth Violence? Explaining violence against foreigners in Germany', W. Willems, *New Community*, 21(4), 1995.

'Roll out the Barrel', *Searchlight*, September 1998.

'Scott Clears Waldegrave of Intent to Mislead', http://www.hm-treasury.gov.uk, 16 March 1996.

'Sensible Censorship', *PC Advisor*, 26 June 1997.

'Skinhead Mob Storm Anti-Nazi League Protest', *Hounslow, Feltham and Hanworth Times*, 8 September 1995.

'Social Change and the Law of Industrial Accidents', Friedman and Ladinsky, 67 *Col L Rev*, 50.

'Software Stops Pupils Seeing Net Porn', *The Times*, 13 January 1999.

'Success and Failure: The new politics and the old', Tony Lecomber, *Spearhead*, March 1996.

'Tackling Militant Racism', Peter Jepson, http://www.peterjepson.com, 15 August 1998.

'Tackling Religious Terminology that Stirs up Racial Hatred', Peter Jepson [1999] *NLJ* 554.

'Targets Set in Drive to Combat Racism', *The Independent*, 19 October 1998.

'Teeth for a Paper Tiger: A Proposal To Add Enforceability to Florida's Hate Crimes Act', Marce L Fleischaur, [1990] 17 *Fla St UL Rev* 697.

'The BNP in East London, Stepping Stone to Race War', *Searchlight*, September 1998.

'The Definition of a Racial Incident', Peter Jepson, [1998] *NLJ* 1838.

'The International Convention on the Elimination of All Forms of Racial Discrimination', Schewelb, *International and Comparative Law Quarterly Review* 996 [1966] 997.

'The McLibel Case', [1996] *NLJ* 363.

'The Problems of Motive in Hate Crimes', James Mosch, *The Journal of Criminal Law and Criminology*, Vol 82, 1992, p. 659.

'The Racist Thugs will Never Stop me Teaching', Hugh Muir, *Daily Telegraph*, 23 March 1998.

'The Starting Point', Geoffrey Bindman, [1995] *NLJ* 62.

'Through Patterns Not Our Own: A study of the regulation of racial violence on the council estates of east London', Cooper and Qureshi, New Ethnicities Research and Education Group of the University of East London, 1993.

'To Ban or Not to Ban?', Nick Lowes and Steve Silver, *Searchlight*, June 1999.

'Triable-Either-Way Crown Court or Magistrates Court', Riley and Vennard, Home Office Research Study No. 98, HMSO, 1988.

'Tyndall at the Last Chance Saloon', *Searchlight*, September 1995.

'Veteran racists behind anti-mosque campaign', *Searchlight*, November 1996.

'Violence as BNP and Anti-Nazi League Clash', *Hounslow Chronicle*, 7 September 1995.

'Was Stephen Lawrence's Murder Racially Motivated', Peter Jepson, http://www.peterjepson. com, 10 June 1999.

'We Won't let Them Pull our Society Apart', Jack Straw (Home Secretary), *The Mail on Sunday*, 2 May 1999.

'When the Tiber Failed to Foam', *Searchlight*, June 1997, http://www.s-light.demon.co.uk/stories/powell.htm.

'Who Watches the Watchmen Part II', Yaman Akdeniz, http://cyber-right.org/watchmen-ii.htm.

'Wipe out Racism in the Borough – Evicted after 3 years of hate', *Hounslow, Feltham and Hanworth Times*, 17 May 1996.

'Wisconsin Burning: Sentence Enhancement and the Freedom to Express Hate', [1995–6] *KCLJ* 6 139.

Reference and Miscellaneous Materials

'15ᵗʰ UK Periodic Report to the UN Committee on the Elimination of All Forms of Racial Discrimination relating to the period up to 31 March 1999', draft report of Home Office Race Equality Unit, 1999.

'Action on Racial Harassment: Legal Remedies and Local Authorities', Report of the London Legal Aid Action Group and London Housing Unit, 1988.

'Action Plan on Promoting Safer Use of the Internet', *EC Official Journal*, http://www2.echo.lu/iap/pressrel.html.

Black's Law Dictionary, 6th edn, St Paul, Minn. West Publishing Co., 1991.

Collin, P.H., *Dictionary of Government and Politics*, Peter Collin Publishing, 1988.

Concise Oxford Dictionary, 8th edn, ed. by R.E. Allen, Clarendon Press, Oxford.

'Decision No/98/EC of the European Parliament and of the Council', http://www2.echo.lu/iap/position/en.html.

'Hidden from View: A study of racial harassment in Preston', Preston Borough Council, 1992.

'Information on the Criminal Justice System in England and Wales', Home Office Research and Statistical Department, 1995.

'Jack Straw Announces Implementation Date For The Human Rights Act', Home Office Press Release 153/99, 18 May 1999.

Khan, Jean, 'Consultative Commission on Racism and Xenophobia', European Union, The Council, 1995.

'Kahn Report – European Union The Council – Consultative Commission on Racism and Xenophobia', Brussels, 23 May 1995.

'Legislating Against Terrorism', Command Paper 3178, HMSO, December 1998.

'Multilateral Treaties Deposited with the Secretary-General', United Nations, 1998.

'Offences Against Religion and Public Worship (1985)', Law Commission Report No. 145.

Parekh, Bhikhu, 'Racial Violence: A Separate Offence?', report of the All-Party Parliamentary Group on Race and Community (Houses of Parliament Session 1993/4).

Percy, Andrew, 'Ethnicity and Victimisation: Findings from the 1996 British Crime Survey', Home Office Statistical Bulletin, Issue 6/98, 3 April 1998.

'Project Trawler: Crime of the Information Highway', National Criminal Intelligence Service, http://www.ncis.co.uk/newpage1.htm, 26 June 1999.

'Race and Equal Opportunities in the Police Service', CRE, 1996.

'Race and the Criminal Justice System', Home Office, December 1997.

'Race Discrimination', Cmnd 6234, HMSO 1976.

'Racial Attacks and Harassment', Home Affairs Select Committee, HMSO, 1994.

'Racial Violence and Harassment', consultation document, Home Office, September 1997.

Report on the seminar 'Law, Blasphemy and the Multi-Faith Society', organised and published by Commission for Racial Equality, September 1989.

'Royal Commission on Criminal Justice', Command paper 2263, HMSO.

Scruton, Roger, *A Dictionary of Political Thought*, Pan Books 1982.

'Statistics on Race and the Criminal Justice System', Home Office, 1998.

'Stephen Lawrence Inquiry' Comments of the Home Secretary, *Hansard*, 24 February 1999.

'Stephen Lawrence Inquiry: Home Secretary's Action Plan', Home Office, March 1999.

'Street Report 1967' produced by H.Street, G. Lowe and G. Bindman.

'The 1998 British Crime Survey', Mirrlees-Black, Budd, Partridge, Mayhew, Home Office Statistical Bulletin Issue 21/98.

'The Frank's Committee Report', Command Paper 218, 1957.

'The Stephen Lawrence Inquiry', report of Sir William MacPherson of Cluny, HMSO 1999.

'The Work of the Department of Social Security and its Agencies', HMSO, 1995.

'Violence and the Viewer' , Report of the Joint Working Party on Violence on Television, 1998.

'When Hate Comes to Town: Community Responses to Racism and Fascism', *Searchlight* Community Handbook, *Searchlight* Education Trust, 1995.

'Working Together under the Children Act 1989', Department of Health Guidelines, HMSO, 1991.

Index